Autodesk®
Architectural Desktop 2005

A Comprehensive Tutorial

Autodesk®
Architectural Desktop 2005
A Comprehensive Tutorial

H. Edward Goldberg, AIA
Registered Architect

PEARSON

Prentice
Hall

Upper Saddle River, New Jersey
Columbus, Ohio

Library of Congress Cataloging-in-Publication Data

Goldberg, H. Edward.
  Autodesk Architectural desktop 2005 : a comprehensive tutorial / H. Edward Goldberg, AIA.
    p. cm.
  Includes index.
  ISBN 0-13-170124-X
  1. Architectural drawing--Computer-aided design. 2. Autodesk Architectural desktop. I. Title.
  NA2728.G672 2005
  720'.28'40285536--dc22

                 2004022426

Executive Editor: Debbie Yarnell
Managing Editor: Judith Casillo
Editorial Assistant: ReeAnne Davies
Production Editor: Louise N. Sette
Production Coordination: Robert Kern, TIPS Technical Publishing, Inc.
Design Coordinator: Diane Ernsberger
Cover Designer: Thomas Mack
Production Manager: Deidra M. Schwartz
Marketing Manager: Jimmy Stephens

This book was set in Janson by TIPS Technical Publishing, Inc. It was printed and bound by Courier Kendallville, Inc. The cover was printed by Phoenix Color Corp.

Disclaimer:
The publication is designed to provide tutorial information about AutoCAD® and/or other Autodesk computer programs. Every effort has been made to make this publication complete and as accurate as possible. The reader is expressly cautioned to use any and all precautions necessary, and to take appropriate steps to avoid hazards, when engaging in the activities described herein.

Neither the author nor the publisher makes any representations or warranties of any kind, with respect to the materials set forth in this publication, express or implied, including without limitation any warranties of fitness for a particular purpose or merchantability. Nor shall the author or the publisher be liable for any special, consequential or exemplary damages resulting, in whole or in part, directly or indirectly, from the reader's use of, or reliance upon, this material or subsequent revisions of this material.

Pearson Prentice Hall™ is a trademark of Pearson Education, Inc.
Pearson® is a registered trademark of Pearson plc
Prentice Hall® is a registered trademark of Pearson Education, Inc.

Pearson Education Ltd.
Pearson Education Singapore Pte. Ltd.
Pearson Education Canada, Ltd.
Pearson Education Japan

Pearson Education Australia Pty. Ltd.
Pearson Education North Asia Ltd.
Pearson Educacion de Mexico, S.A. de C.V.
Pearson Education Malaysia Pte. Ltd.

10 9 8 7 6 5 4 3 2
ISBN: 0-13-170124-X

I dedicate this book to the women I love,
my mother Lillian,
my wife Judith Ellen,
and my daughter Allison Julia.

Acknowledgments

I want to thank all the wonderful and dedicated people at the Building Systems division of Autodesk in New Hampshire for their professional assistance and for their friendship. Special thanks go to Julian Gonzalez, Bill Glennie, and Dennis McNeal on the ADT 2005 team.

I want to acknowledge Sara Ferris and Lara Sheridan at CADALYST magazine for being so wonderful to work with.

I want to acknowledge Art Liddle, past editor of CADALYST, who introduced me to this excellent program.

How to Use This Book

This book has been organized into two main parts: "Sections," typically made of several tutorial exercises that illustrate commands, and "Putting it all together," which uses the knowledge gleaned from the sections to create a building.

The exercises in this book have been designed as tutorials for most of the major commands and routines used in operating Autodesk Architectural Desktop 2005. Rather than require the student to read a great deal of verbiage and theory, this book was designed to use the "hands-on" method of learning, with each exercise guiding the student through the typical use of the commands for a subject. It is intended that the student perform the exercises first before attempting to use the program to design a building. It is also intended that the student perform the sections in the order presented, as they often add information for later exercises. Even if a student understands a particular command, it might still be helpful to complete that exercise either to gain new insight or to compare operator strategy. This book assumes a general knowledge of standard AutoCAD or AutoCAD LT up to Release 2004. Students without knowledge of Paperspace and Modelspace will be at a very great disadvantage. It is also important that the student have a good understanding of the Windows operating system and be able to quickly navigate the various navigation trees in that system.

Because buildings are so complex, and the variations are so numerous, 3D Computer Aided Architectural Design (CAAD) programs such as Autodesk Architectural Desktop are not inherently easy to use. In my opinion, Autodesk Architectural Desktop has never been a program for the computer or CAD novice. Because of its complexity, one can become very frustrated when first approaching its multitude of commands, even though the programmers have gone to great effort to make this software user friendly.

This author believes that the sign of a good operator depends on several fundamental working values.

■ Use the least number of keystrokes for a particular operation. Do not use the full typed name of a command if the command can be performed with a letter alias.

■ Use the Space bar on the keyboard while operating the program instead of the Enter key, except when inserting text.

■ Use a strategy of operating this program as one would play a game of chess, thinking several moves ahead, and never moving backwards unless absolutely necessary.

Walk-through

Autodesk® Architectural Desktop 2005

A Comprehensive Tutorial

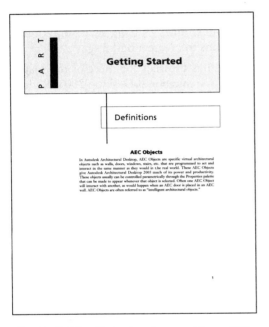

Part I—Getting Started sections provide essential information, preparing users for the guided tutorial on Autodesk Architectural Desktop 2005, including Definitions, Concepts, Abbreviations, and more.

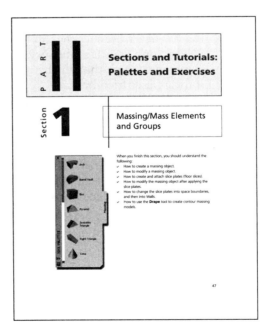

Part II—Sections and Tutorials presents Tool Palettes in the order in which they are commonly used.

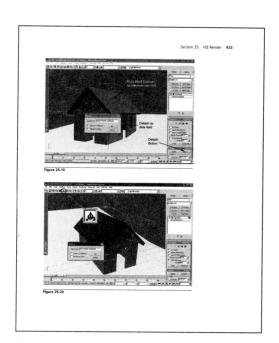

Numerous walk-throughs and hands-on activities teach commands and routines in relation to the production of architectural drawings.

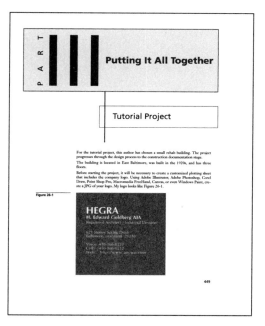

Part III—Putting It All Together uses the knowledge gleaned from the Sections and Tutorials to create a building.

Contents

PART II   Sections and Tutorials: Palettes and Exercises   47

Section 9

Section 10

Section 11

Section 12

Section 13

Section 14

Section 15

Section 16

Section 17

Section 18

Detail Components and the Detail Component Manager   343

Section 19

Property Set Definitions and Property Sets   355

Section 20

Schedules and Schedule Tags   367

Autodesk®
Architectural Desktop 2005

A Comprehensive Tutorial

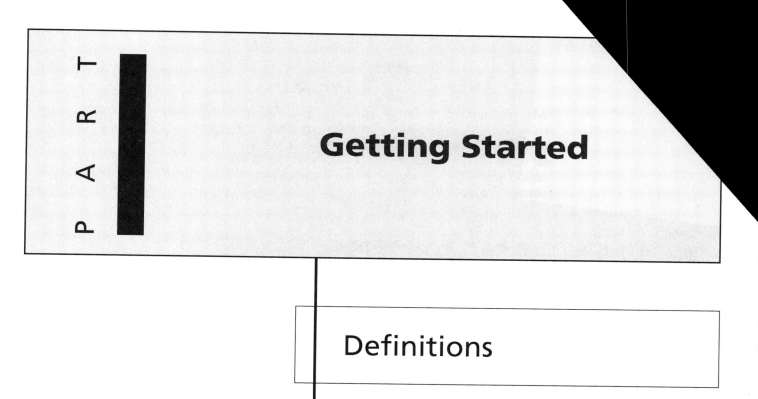

Definitions

AEC Objects

In Autodesk Architectural Desktop, AEC Objects are specific virtual architectural objects such as walls, doors, windows, stairs, etc. that are programmed to act and interact in the same manner as they would in the real world. These AEC Objects give Autodesk Architectural Desktop 2005 much of its power and productivity. These objects usually can be controlled parametrically through the Properties palette that can be made to appear whenever that object is selected. Often one AEC Object will interact with another, as would happen when an AEC door is placed in an AEC wall. AEC Objects are often referred to as "intelligent architectural objects."

Styles

…es are information contained in drawings (DWG), and they control the parame-
…of AEC Objects. Because of the software programming, this information directly
…ols Autodesk Architectural Desktop 2005's basic drawing entities, such as lines
…circles. Since styles do not contain any entities, they provide a very efficient
…od for controlling content within the program and a very quick transfer of that
…t over the Internet.

Multi-view Blocks

Although there is a plethora of AEC or programmed content, there is always need
for specialized content. Here, Architectural Desktop provides a variation on its standard "Block" system known to users of AutoCAD and AutoCAD LT. Multi-view
blocks allow the user to place content in one view and have the appropriate view of
that content appear in other views at the same time. Although Multi-view blocks
don't have the intelligence, they can increase productivity greatly. Architectural
Desktop 2005 includes many routines that depend on Multi-view blocks. An exercise
in the creation of Multi-view blocks is given in this book.

Tool Palettes

New to Autodesk Architectural Desktop 2004 and continuing in Architectural Desktop 2005 are tool palettes. These palettes can be sized, renamed, modified, and moved. Most of the major architectural routines are represented as icons or pictures, and they can be implemented by either dragging into or clicking in the Drawing Editor from these palettes. The developers of the program have replaced most of the standard toolbars and icons with this method in order to optimize the drawing environment for maximum productivity.

Check Boxes

Check boxes indicate the on or off state of available options. If they are in a group, several check boxes can be selected at the same time.

Radio Buttons

Radio buttons (the name comes from the button selectors on car radios) indicate the on or off state of available options. Only one button in a group of buttons can be chosen.

Contextual Menus

Contextual (Context – Sensitive) menus became popular when Microsoft introduced Windows 95. Autodesk Architectural Desktop 2005 makes extensive use of these menus to control options and subcommands of various components. Contextual menus typically are summoned by clicking the right mouse button on a specific object, entity, or spot in the interface. Through programming, the appropriate menu or "context" will appear for that object at that point in its command structure. As an example, clicking the right mouse button on a door within a wall will provide all the commands available for the door and its relationship to the wall.

Concepts

As with previous versions of Autodesk Architectural Desktop, this new release uses three different concepts for eventually creating documentation. These concepts are the mass model concept, the space planning concept, and the virtual building concept. Of course, you can always operate Autodesk Architectural Desktop 2005 as a typical 2D electronic CAD drafting program, but that really negates the benefits of the virtual building features, and eliminates much of the intrinsic volumetric information endemic to the virtual building.

The Mass Model

The mass model concept is unique to Architectural Desktop and is based on a modeling tradition called "massing model" used by many architects. In that system, the architect or designer makes a cardboard, wood, or clay "study model" of the building. These small models often show the relationship between parts of the structure while also indicating scale and the effect of light and shadow on the facades. Typically the architect would create more sophisticated models later while creating the construction documents.

In Architectural Desktop 2005, you can make very sophisticated virtual massing models. These massing models can then be sliced into "floorplates" or horizontal sections from which walls can be generated automatically. These walls are the connection point between the massing model and the construction documentation in Architectural Desktop 2005.

Space Planning

The space planning concept is one that has been used by architects and designers for years. In this concept, rectangles and circles represent building program areas. The designer then places these forms in relationship to each other to create "flow diagrams." After the relationships have been established, they are then used to help create the form of the structure. In Autodesk Architectural Desktop 2004, the developers took this one step farther by combining a 3-D component to the relationships. Every space planning object also contains information about floor-to-ceiling heights, and floor-to-floor heights. After the space planning has been completed, the space plan can be converted automatically into three-dimensional walls into which doors, windows, and so on can be added. These three-dimensional walls, etc. can then form the basis for construction documents. Besides being the basis for construction documents, the space plan can be culled for space information that can be transferred to data base programs.

The Virtual Building Model

The virtual or 3D model differs from standard electronic drafting with the concept of placing components of a building much as one would place objects in the real world. Instead of drawing lines and circles, one places doors, windows, walls, roofs, and so on, which can be controlled or modified parametrically and relate to each other as they would in the real world. To this end Architectural Desktop 2004 has a myriad of parametric tools. The virtual building concept has been greatly discussed by architects and designers and is generally accepted as the direction that CAAD is progressing. Autodesk Architectural Desktop 2005 and its previous releases have always been considered leaders in this trend.

Questions and Answers about Autodesk Architectural Desktop 2005

The following information was gleaned from Autodesk Press releases. The author has selected this information to answer questions that might be in readers' minds.

What are the key areas of improvement in Autodesk Architectural Desktop 2004 and Architectural Desktop 2005?

Autodesk Architectural Desktop 2004 and 2005 have more than 300 enhancements that address

- Ease of use
- Drafting and design
- Construction documentation
- Drawing and level management
- Design visualization
- File sharing and collaboration

Key features include

- A streamlined user interface
- Customizable tool palettes
- Direct object manipulation
- Automated file, level, and sheet management
- Easier, fully coordinated annotation
- Construction detailing
- Integrated photorealistic rendering and animation with VIZ Render

These enhancements to Autodesk Architectural Desktop software offer more productivity, more efficiency, more flexibility, and smoother collaboration and data exchange than ever before.

Has the user interface changed for Autodesk Architectural Desktop?

Yes. The user interface for Architectural Desktop 2005 continues the improvements seen in Architectural Desktop 2004 and will be quite familiar to users of that product. The streamlined user interface introduced with Autodesk Architectural Desktop 2004 improves on traditional CAD design software and earlier versions of Architectural Desktop in terms of look and feel and overall functionality. Highly visual, simpler, and more intuitive, the interface helps you increase productivity using process-focused tools that make the software easier to use. With less focus on dialog boxes and more emphasis on designing directly in the workspace, the design tools in the software are easily accessible. Furthermore, enhanced tool palettes, the Properties palette, and the new Content Browser complement this redesigned workspace to help you work more efficiently.

? **Are Autodesk Architectural Desktop and Autodesk® Revit® files interoperable?**

Yes. You can exchange drawing information (2D DWG files) between Autodesk Architectural Desktop and the Autodesk Revit software through their respective Export to AutoCAD features.

? **Which versions of AutoCAD do Autodesk Architectural Desktop software's Export to AutoCAD feature support?**

This release supports Export to AutoCAD 2004, AutoCAD 2005, and AutoCAD 2000 DWG and DXF™ formats, as well as Release 12 DXF. This makes it possible for users of AutoCAD 2000, AutoCAD 2000i, AutoCAD 2002, and AutoCAD 2004 to open Autodesk Architectural Desktop 2005 files without using object enablers.

? **Can I export more than one Architectural Desktop file at a time?**

Yes. With Architectural Desktop 2005, you can export multiple Architectural Desktop files.

Enhanced e-transmit functionality allows users to transmit multiple entire projects, sheet sets, and specific DWGs.

? **What is the Autodesk AEC Object Enabler?**

The Autodesk AEC Object Enabler is a free downloadable and distributable utility that gives AutoCAD user functionality and design flexibility through the power of Autodesk Architectural Desktop objects. With the proper version of the AEC Object Enabler, any AutoCAD 2000, AutoCAD 2000i, AutoCAD 2002, AutoCAD 2004, or AutoCAD 2005 user can have full compatibility with Autodesk Architectural Desktop objects. The AEC Object Enabler is included with AutoCAD 2005. For more information and to download the AEC Object Enabler, go to

http://www.autodesk.com/aecobjecten.

? **Will Autodesk continue to develop Autodesk Architectural Desktop?**

Yes. With well over 300,000 Autodesk Architectural Desktop licenses worldwide, Architectural Desktop clearly continues to be a powerful AutoCAD-based solution for Autodesk architectural customers.

? **What does Drawing Management do for me?**

Earlier (pre-2004) releases of Autodesk Architectural Desktop simply enabled you to continue to manage projects using existing standards for manually organizing file structure and xref relationships. While continuing to respect your practices and standards, Autodesk Architectural Desktop has now introduced the drawing management feature for users who want to take advantage of automated project, drawing, and level management. For those familiar with AutoCAD 2005, the Sheet Set Manager feature of that product has been integrated seamlessly into the Architectural Desktop 2005 Drawing Management's Project Navigator.

? **Besides the Drawing Management feature, how has project coordination improved?**

Coordination has been improved through the addition of Materials, a new feature that provides both graphic and non-graphic detail to your drawings for design, documentation, and visualization purposes. In addition, extended scheduling functionality enables you to tag through xref and schedule external drawings. Also, interoperability with Autodesk Building Systems improves coordination between disciplines. New sheet management and callout functionality have been integrated into Architectural Desktop. Now, sheet numbers, callouts, sections, and elevations are coordinated with one another, making it easy to manage, plot, and archive your sheets.

? **How does VIZ Render differ from Autodesk VIZ?**

VIZ Render, Autodesk Architectural Desktop's native visualization tool, uses some of the core technology developed in Autodesk VIZ. Much of the photometric lighting and rendering technology from (Discreet®) 3ds max® software has been included in VIZ Render. However, VIZ Render has been optimized to accept the data organization from Autodesk Architectural Desktop in a much more efficient way, and the entire user interface has been revised and simplified to make the process of creating high-quality visualization more accessible to Architectural Desktop users. The guiding principle in using VIZ Render is that Architectural Desktop is the model authoring application. You organize and build the model exclusively in Architectural Desktop and then seamlessly link to VIZ Render for rendering.

? **Can I export VIZ Render files to Autodesk VIZ?**

Yes. VIZ Render files (DRF) can be exported to Autodesk VIZ or 3ds max software, and VIZ Render can also import files (MAX) from both Autodesk VIZ and 3ds max.

? **Is a network version of Autodesk Architectural Desktop available?**

Yes. Autodesk Architectural Desktop software uses standard Autodesk network license management. For more information, see "Platforms, System Requirements, and Network" later in this section.

? **Have there been any improvements to the Network Installation Wizard?**

Yes. The Network Installation Wizard (NIW) now gives you the flexibility of pointing content and support files to various locations, including a central location to allow everyone access and to free up valued hard-disk space on local machines. It also gives you the option of installing any or all of the content/support files to a central location, various locations, or directly on the computer where the product is being installed. Install according to your best practices.

? **What is building information modeling, and how does it apply to Autodesk Architectural Desktop?**

Building Information Modeling (BIM) is an innovative approach to building design, construction, and management introduced by Autodesk in 2002. BIM delivers high-quality information about project design scope, schedule, and cost when you need it and how you need it, dramatically helping reduce inefficiencies and risk throughout the building process. The ability to keep this information up to date and accessible in an integrated digital environment gives architects, engineers, builders, and owners a clear overall vision of their projects. It also contributes to the ability to make better decisions faster, helping raise the quality and increase the profitability of projects.

Although building information modeling is not itself a technology, it does require suitable technology to be implemented effectively. Examples of some of these technologies, in increasing order of effectiveness, include

• CAD

• Object CAD

• Parametric Building Modeling

With a high level of effort, CAD-based software can be used to achieve some of the benefits of BIM. With some effort, so can object CAD-based software. Parametric Building Modeling (PBM) software offers the highest level of effectiveness with the least effort, but it also requires a full commitment to building information modeling (a new way of working). There is no other way to use PBM to support a traditional drafting workflow.

Autodesk Architectural Desktop is built on object CAD technology, adding intelligent architectural and engineering objects to the familiar AutoCAD platform. It can be used to deliver BIM benefits with significantly less effort than CAD technology. Since it is built on AutoCAD, however, it can also be used very productively for design and documentation in a traditional drafting or CAD-based workflow unrelated to BIM. For more information about BIM and Autodesk's strategy for the application of information technology to the building industry, please see Autodesk's white paper on the subject at http://www.autodesk.com/bim.

What are intelligent architectural objects?

The ObjectARX® technology used in Autodesk Architectural Desktop enables you to create intelligent architectural objects that know their form, fit, and function and behave according to their real-world properties. This technology improves software performance, ease of use, and flexibility in design. Intelligent architectural objects respond directly to standard AutoCAD editing commands in the same way that common AutoCAD drawing objects (such as lines, arcs, and circles) do. Yet they also have the ability to display according to context and to interact with other architectural objects. Object-based technology transforms ordinary geometry into intelligent architectural objects whose behavior models that of physical objects.

What is the significance of door, wall, window, and other architectural objects?

These intelligent objects improve design productivity and efficiency because they behave according to the specific properties or rules that pertain to them in the real world.

Architectural objects thus have a relationship to one another and interact with each other intelligently. For example, a window has a relationship to the wall that contains it. If you move or delete the wall, the window reacts appropriately. In addition, intelligent architectural objects maintain dynamic links with construction documents and specifications, resulting in more accurate and valuable project deliverables that can be used to manage a building throughout its lifecycle. When someone deletes or modifies a door, for example, the door schedule is updated automatically.

Will Autodesk Architectural Desktop and Autodesk Revit be combined into a single product in the future?

No. Autodesk Architectural Desktop is based on the AutoCAD platform. Autodesk Revit is based on an entirely different technology and principle of operation. Thus, the products cannot be combined, and Autodesk has no plans to do so.

? **What is the significance of 3D in Autodesk Architectural Desktop?**

Because the objects in Autodesk Architectural Desktop describe real-world building components, both 2D and 3D representations can be created automatically, and either one can be used to view or edit the model. This conveniently and smoothly integrates 2D and 3D functionality and allows exploration of design ideas within CAD in a fashion similar to the way architects and designers envision their designs. For example, you can quickly and easily create 3D massing studies in the initial phases of the design process to explore multiple design scenarios. Or you can develop a floor plan in 2D and then immediately see a perspective view of it in 3D. You can even use 3D to visually check for any type of interference in your design.

Additionally, Autodesk Architectural Desktop 2005 has introduced many features that allow you to work in 3D easily. 3D also provides you with exportable geometric information that can be used for other applications to perform functions like energy analysis.

? **Has 2D functionality been enhanced in Autodesk Architectural Desktop 2005?**

Yes. Although recent releases of Autodesk Architectural Desktop offer many new 3D features, the software's intelligent objects and architectural tools provide important benefits for 2D design development and construction documentation. You have all the functionality of AutoCAD plus powerful architectural design and drafting tools, including a significant new detailing toolkit that vastly accelerates the production of construction details. Therefore, you can create key project deliverables more efficiently and accurately.

? **Is Autodesk Architectural Desktop interoperable with other Autodesk products?**

Yes. AutoCAD is the foundation for an interoperable family of Autodesk products, including Autodesk Architectural Desktop. Sharing the same database framework component—ObjectDBX™ for reading and writing drawing files—helps to ensure that each generation of Autodesk products is interoperable with Autodesk Architectural Desktop. These include industry-specific products such as Autodesk Building Systems, Autodesk Revit, Autodesk Map™, AutoCAD® Mechanical, Autodesk Mechanical Desktop®, and Autodesk Land Desktop®, as well as software that addresses many industries such as Volo® View, Autodesk Express Viewer, Autodesk Raster Design, and Autodesk OnSite View. Because there has been no file format change between the Autodesk 2004 and 2005 generations of products, Architectural Desktop is interoperable with the majority of applications in both of these release cycles.

? **Is Autodesk Architectural Desktop 2005 compatible with earlier releases of Autodesk Architectural Desktop?**

Earlier versions of Architectural Desktop are forwards-compatible with the current release; i.e., designs created in earlier versions of Autodesk Architectural Desktop easily migrate to the current release of Architectural Desktop. Autodesk Architectural Desktop 2005 is backwards compatible with Architectural Desktop 2004 at the object level (AEC objects used in Architectural Desktop). Architectural Desktop 2005 and Architectural Desktop 2004 are *not* backwards compatible at the object level with earlier releases of Architectural Desktop, but files created in these versions of the software can be saved as DWG files to be read by versions of Autodesk Architectural Desktop based on AutoCAD 2000, AutoCAD 2000i, and 2002 platforms.

? **Will my third-party applications work with the current release of Autodesk Architectural Desktop software?**

Your existing third-party applications may or may not be compatible with the current release of Autodesk Architectural Desktop. Contact your independent software supplier for details. For more information about the availability of third-party applications compatible with the current release of AutoCAD and Architectural Desktop, visit http://www.autodesk.com/partnerproducts.

? **Is Architectural Desktop compatible with Industry Foundation Classes (IFCs)?**

Yes. IAI-certified support for IFCs is currently provided in Autodesk Architectural Desktop through G.E.M. Team Solutions GbR. A trial version of the IFC-Utility2x for Architectural Desktop can be downloaded at http://www.inopso.com, the web site of Inopso GmbH, a partner of G.E.M. Team Solutions which distributes the plug-in.

? **Autodesk Architectural Desktop 2005 has AutoCAD 2005 as its foundation. Has the AutoCAD 2005 drawing file format (DWG) changed from the AutoCAD 2004 products, as it did between AutoCAD 2000 and AutoCAD 2004?**

No. The AutoCAD 2005 DWG file format is the same as the AutoCAD 2004 format. The AutoCAD 2004 file format was updated and is different from the AutoCAD 2000, AutoCAD 2000i, and AutoCAD 2002 DWG file format. This new format was necessary to provide performance enhancements, smaller file sizes, presentation graphics, and drawing security.

? **Can I run Autodesk Architectural Desktop side by side with other AutoCAD platform–based applications?**

Yes. You can install the current release of Autodesk Architectural Desktop side by side with any other AutoCAD 2000i–, AutoCAD 2002–, AutoCAD 2004–, or AutoCAD 2005–based product. These products include Autodesk Architectural Desktop, Autodesk Building Systems, Autodesk Mechanical Desktop, AutoCAD Mechanical, Autodesk Land Desktop, Autodesk Map, and AutoCAD LT® software.

? **How can I find technical support information for Autodesk Architectural Desktop 2005?**

You can learn about all support options from your local Autodesk Authorized Reseller or Distributor. Visit http://www.autodesk.com/archdesktop-support and find a knowledge base of commonly asked support questions. Also, you can ask questions and read information about the use of Autodesk products in the peer-to-peer discussion groups on http://www.autodesk.com/discussion. Autodesk hosts topical discussion groups about specific products, including Autodesk Architectural Desktop, and about general topics, such as drafting techniques and customization. Alternatively, Autodesk software manuals and documentation are a great source of answers to your support questions.

? **How do I obtain direct technical support?**

Autodesk® Subscription is the best way to keep your design tools and learning up to date. In the United States and Canada, for an annual fee you get the latest versions of your licensed Autodesk software, web support direct from Autodesk, self-paced training options, and a broad range of other technology and business benefits. You must purchase a subscription at the time you purchase or upgrade an Autodesk product. For more information, contact your Autodesk Authorized Reseller or visit http://www.autodesk.com/subscription.

Autodesk Systems Centers (ASCs) and Autodesk Authorized Resellers also provide support services for Autodesk Architectural Desktop software and all other Autodesk products. In the United States and Canada, call 800-964-6432 to locate an ASC or reseller near you, or visit http://www.autodesk.com/reseller. You can find a complete list of support options from Autodesk at http://www.autodesk.com/archdesktop-support.

? **Can I rely on my AutoCAD knowledge to use Autodesk Architectural Desktop? How quickly can I learn the new features in Autodesk Architectural Desktop?**

Autodesk Architectural Desktop builds on the speed, performance, and familiarity of AutoCAD, so AutoCAD users have a strong foundation from which to learn Autodesk Architectural Desktop.

? **Where do I find training courses for Autodesk Architectural Desktop 2005?**

Training courses are available from Autodesk Professional Services as well as at Autodesk Authorized Training Center (ATC®) locations and Autodesk Authorized Resellers. Training courses are available through Autodesk Professional Services, and include Autodesk Virtual Classroom Training (online, instructor-led), custom training to match your organization's specific needs, as well as Autodesk Classroom Training. To obtain more information about Autodesk's training services, visit

http://www.autodesk.com/archdesktop-training.

Other helpful training resources include the online discussion groups you can access through the Autodesk Architectural Desktop Communication Center. The Communication Center also features industry specific news, tips and tricks, product updates, and Autodesk Architectural Desktop software manuals and online documentation.

? **Should I get training with this release?**

Although Autodesk Architectural Desktop takes advantage of your existing knowledge of AutoCAD software, some training is recommended. Training improves productivity, increases return on investment, and enhances your Autodesk Architectural Desktop knowledge.

? **What consulting services are available for Autodesk Architectural Desktop 2005?**

Autodesk Professional Services provides customer consulting offerings for project assessments, process audits, implementation services, networking setup, application porting, and other custom services to help you get the best possible return on your investment in Autodesk technology. For more information on Autodesk Professional Services, contact your Autodesk Account Executive or your local Autodesk Authorized Reseller; or visit http://www.autodesk.com/professionalservices.

Platforms, System Requirements, and Network

Do I need to buy new hardware to run Autodesk Architectural Desktop 2005?

Following are the minimum hardware and operating system requirements for running Autodesk Architectural Desktop.

Description Minimum Requirement

Operating system
- Microsoft® Windows 2000 Professional, SP3, or later
- Windows XP Professional, SP1, or later
- Windows XP Home Edition, SP1, or later
- Windows XP, Tablet PC Edition

Windows 95, 98, and NT are no longer supported.

CPU
Intel® Pentium® 4 or AMD K7 with 1.4 GHz processor

RAM
512 MB (1 GB recommended)

Hard Disk Space
650 MB free and 75 MB swap space

Display Resolution
1024×768 with True Color

Why was the hardware requirement raised from pre-2004 releases of Architectural Desktop?

The hardware requirements are defined in order to ensure that customers have expected performance when fully using the product. With Autodesk Architectural Desktop 2004, these requirements were raised accordingly. Not only did Autodesk Architectural Desktop 2004 contain a new and robust visualization tool, VIZ Render, that really benefits from robust systems, but this release also supports the Materials feature which provide, surface and section hatching as well as texture mapping in shaded views.

I'm upgrading from Autodesk Architectural Desktop 3.3, but my hardware does not meet the minimum requirements for this release; can I still use the current release of Autodesk Architectural Desktop effectively?

Yes—if you are using Architectural Desktop strictly for drafting and design. On hardware that does not meet the minimum system requirements however, you should avoid using certain features that may cause below optimal performance. These features include VIZ Render and Materials with surface hatching enabled.

Is Autodesk Architectural Desktop software available on CD only?

Yes. Autodesk Architectural Desktop is available only on CD.

? **Have there been any improvements to software deployment through network licensing?**

Yes. Enhanced Autodesk standard licensing software helps you get the full benefit from your Autodesk Architectural Desktop licenses. For example, with the new license-borrowing feature you can install a time-limited license on your computer while disabling the license on the server for that same period. You can then run Autodesk Architectural Desktop without having a connection to the license server.

? **Are there any changes to the licensing for stand-alone seats?**

Yes. SafeCast is now the stand-alone licensing technology used in Autodesk products worldwide. For customers in the United States and Canada, this is a change in the stand-alone licensing.

Why change SafeCast? CD-Secure and SafeCast store licensing information on the user's hard drive, typically on the hard disk. Examining re-authorization statistics, it became clear that a number of technical issues with storing information on the hard drive could be resolved by implementing a new feature of SafeCast.

What will this feature do instead? This feature will store a duplicate set of licensing information in the computers registry. For the types of errors that render the hard-drive storage ineffective, there will now be a fallback location in the registry, which will allow the licensing system to continue without error.

? **Where can I purchase Autodesk Architectural Desktop?**

Autodesk Architectural Desktop is available worldwide. Contact your local Autodesk Authorized Reseller or Distributor for more information. To locate one near you, visit http://www.autodesk.com/reseller.

Autodesk Architectural Desktop is also available through the Autodesk online store at http://www.autodesk.com/estore.

? **Is Autodesk Architectural Desktop being released as an English-only product?**

No. This product will be released worldwide. Versions of this product will be available in a wide range of languages and with localized content in many countries. For information on product availability contact your local Autodesk Authorized Reseller or Autodesk Systems Center (ASC).

? **Is subscription available for Autodesk Architectural Desktop?**

Yes. Subscription is available in most countries around the world for many of Autodesk's products including Autodesk Architectural Desktop. Autodesk Subscription is the best way to keep your design tools and learning up to date. In the United States and Canada, for an annual fee you get the latest versions of your licensed Autodesk software, web support direct from Autodesk, self-paced training options, and a broad range of other technology and business benefits. You must purchase a subscription at the time you purchase or upgrade an Autodesk product. For more information, contact your Autodesk Authorized Reseller or visit

http://www.autodesk.com/subscription.

Installing Autodesk Architectural Desktop 2005

Autodesk Architectural Desktop 2005 ships with 3 CDs labeled 1 of 3, 2 of 3, and 3 of 3.

Installing Autodesk Architectural Desktop 2005 is relatively easy; follow the following directions.

1. Insert the disk labeled 1 of 3 in your CD drive and close the CD tray.
2. If your Windows Operating system is set for **Autorun**, the CD will begin to self load.
3. If the CD does not self load, go to the next step.
4. In the Microsoft Windows Desktop, select the **Start** button, and pick the Run icon to bring up the Windows **Run** dialog box.
5. In the Windows **Run** dialog box, press the **Browse** button, and select the CD drive letter (labeled ADT 2005-1).
6. In the ADT 2005-1 directory on the CD drive, select **Setup**, and press the **OK** open button to return to the **Run** dialog box.
7. In the **Run** dialog box, press the **OK** button to start the installation process.

Be prepared to wait for several seconds until the main Autodesk Architectural Desktop 2005 screen appears (see the figure below).

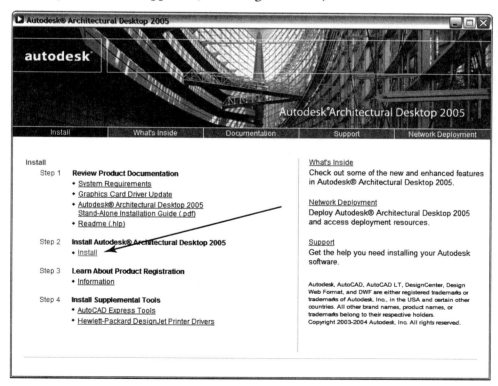

In the main Autodesk Architectural Desktop 2005 installation screen, you can choose from several sources of information. It is a good idea to select each of these sources in order to make sure that you have met the correct hardware and operating system requirements for the program. If everything is OK, do the following.

8. Select the underlined word **Install** in **Step 2**, and wait several seconds until the **Autodesk Architectural Desktop 2005 Setup** dialog box appears (see the figure below).

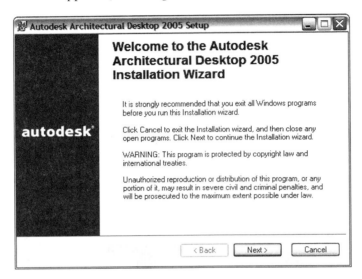

9. In the **Autodesk Architectural Desktop 2005 Setup** dialog box select the **Next** button to bring up the Autodesk Software License Agreement.

10. If you accept the agreement, select the **I accept** radio button, and press the **Next** button to bring up the **Serial Number** data field (see the figure below).

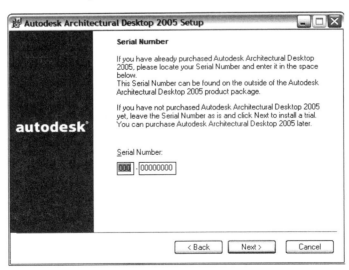

11. In the **Serial Number** data field, enter the serial number that comes with your copy of the program, and press the **Next** button to bring up the **User Information** data field (see the figure below).

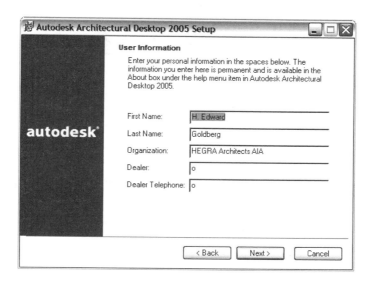

12. After entering your personal information, press the **Next** button to bring up the **Remote Content Installation** screen (see the figure below).

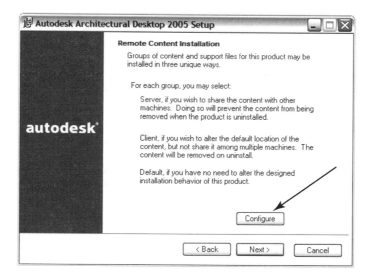

13. Press the **Configure** button to bring up the **Remote Content and Support File Settings**. Unless you want to put the content on a Client or server for others to access, press the **Default** radio button, and then press the **OK** button to return to the **Remote Content Installation** screen (see the figure below).

14. In the **Remote Content Installation** screen, press the **Next** button to bring up the **Select Installation Type** screen. This author prefers the **Custom** radio button. The following information illustrates that use; if you prefer, you can select the **Typical**, **Compact** or **Full** installation options.

15. In the **Select Installation** type screen, select the **Custom** radio button, and press the **Next** button.

16. After selecting the **Custom** radio button and pressing the **Next** button, the **Feature** dialog box will appear (see the figure below). For each feature that you want to install, activate the **Will be installed on local hard drive** field. Activate to install on the local hard drive the **Imperial** content, **VIZ render**, and **Program Files**. When finished selecting, press the **Next** button to bring up the **Destination Folder** dialog box.

17. In the **Destination Folder** dialog box, accept the destination location (**c:\ program files\Autodesk Architectural Desktop 2005** by default) or change the location to suit your computer (see the figure belolw).

Note: Regardless of where you place the Autodesk Architectural Desktop 2005 program, it will always create a folder for keeping your project files on the **C** drive in the **My Documents** folder.

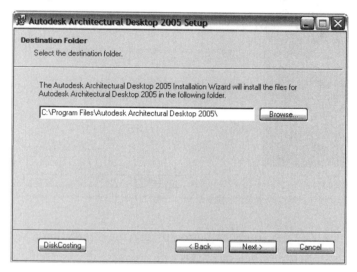

18. Press the **Next** button to bring up the **Choose a default text editor for editing text files** dialog box—accept the default text editor location or browse to the location in which it exists, and check the **Display the Autodesk Architectural desktop 2005 shortcut on my desktop** check-box (see the figure below).

19. Press the **Next** button to bring up the **Are you ready to begin installation?** (just a last check) dialog box (see the figure below).

20. Press the **Next** button to start the installation.

21. Insert the other CDs when requested on screen.

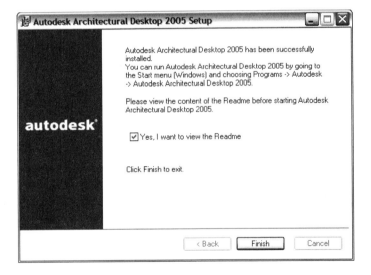

Tip After you have saved an Autodesk Architectural Desktop drawing, you can also start the program by dragging and dropping that drawing icon onto the Architectural Desktop icon. This will automatically start Architectural Desktop 2005, and bring up that drawing.

Abbreviations

In order to make this book easier to understand, shortcut abbreviations are often used. The following list codifies those abbreviations.

Please Read Before Proceeding

Activate a field   Refers to selecting a selection made up of a sentence.

Activate a viewport   Refers to clicking in a viewport to make it the active viewport.

ADT or ADT 2005   Refers to Autodesk Architectural Desktop 2005

AEC Objects   Refers to any Autodesk Architectural Desktop 2005 intelligent object such as walls, stairs, schedules, etc.

Ancillary   Refers to space between the ceiling and the floor above.

Browse   Refers to searching through the file folders and files.

Contextual menu   Refers to any menu that appears when an object or entity is selected with a **Right Mouse Button (RMB)**.

Dialog box   Refers to any menu containing parameters or input fields.

Display tree   Refers to Microsoft Windows folder listing consisting of + and – signs. If a + sign appears, then the listing is compressed with more folders available.

Drawing editor   Refers to the drawing area where drawings are created.

Drop-down list   Refers to the typical Windows operating system list with arrow. When selected, a series of options appear in a vertical list.

DWG   Refers to an Architectural Desktop Drawing.

Elevation View   Refers to **Front**, **Back**, **Right** or **Left Views**, perpendicular to the ground plane.

Layouts   Refers to drawing areas. All layouts except the **Model Layout** can be broken down into **Paper Space** viewports. More layouts can be added.

Plan View   Refers to looking at a building from the **Top View**.

Press the Enter button   Refers to any **Enter** button in any dialog box on the screen.

Press the Enter key   Refers to the keyboard **Enter** key (the **space bar** will usually act as the **Enter** key, except when entering dimensions, text, or numerals).

Press the OK button   Refers to any **OK** button in any dialog box on the screen.

RMB   Refers to clicking using the **Right Mouse Button**. This is most often used to bring up contextual menus.

Tooltips   Refers to the information that appears when the cursor is held momentarily over an icon.

Viewports   Refers to **Paper Space** viewports.

The Autodesk Architectural Desktop 2005 Interface

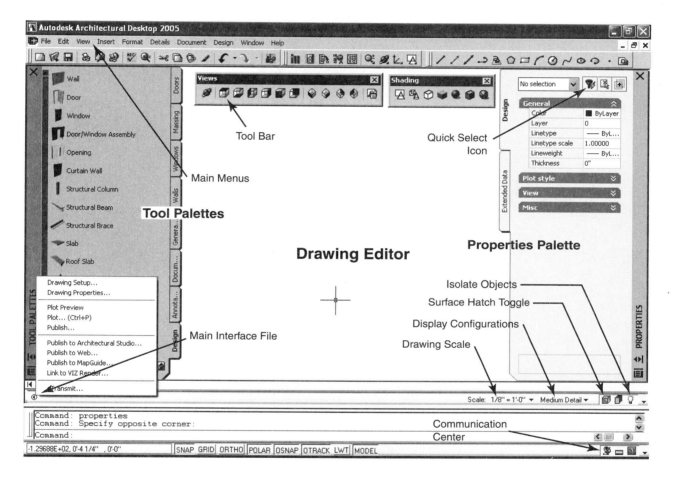

Autodesk Architectural Desktop 2005's interface is based on AutoCAD 2004.

Tool Palettes

Tool palettes are brand new to Autodesk Architectural Desktop 2005. You use them to organize and make available all your desired tools and assets such as doors, windows, and walls.

Autodesk Architectural Desktop 2005 ships with seven default tool palettes and the **Properties** palette in place. These can be easily modified or deleted, or new palettes can be added.

Bringing Up the Tool Palettes

The tool palettes can be brought up by three methods:

a. Typing **toolpalettes** in the **Command line**.

b. By pressing **Ctrl + 3** on the keyboard.

c. By selecting the **Tool Palettes** icon.

Resizing the Palette

You can resize the tool palettes by moving your cursor to the cut corner at the bottom of the palettes. Your cursor will change to a "double arrow." Click, hold, and drag vertically and horizontally to resize, as shown in the figure below.

If you have more tool palettes than are showing, a "stair step" icon will appear at the bottom of the last tab name. (See the figure below.)

If you click on the "stair step" icon, a menu will appear that you can use to select all the tool palettes, as shown in the figure below.

Auto-hide

Because the palettes cover some of the Drawing Editor, there is a control called **Auto-hide** that opens and closes the palette when the cursor is moved over its surface. The following figures show the icon used to turn **Auto-hide** on or off.

Tool Palettes Properties

The **Tool Palettes Properties** give access to options necessary to control the size, location, and appearance of the palettes. **Tool Palettes Properties** also allow for creation and renaming of palettes. (See the figures below.)

Allow Docking

Allows the palette to attach to the sides of the Drawing Editor.

Transparency

Makes the palette transparent, allowing entities on the Drawing Editor to be seen.

View Options

Changes the sizes of the **Tool Palette** icons, as shown in the figure below.

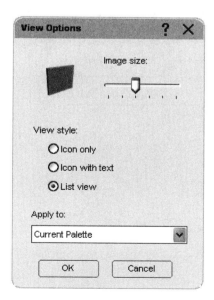

New Palette

Creates new palettes.

Rename Palette Set

Renames the entire set of palettes.

Customize

Groups, adds, deletes and renames tool palettes.

1. Select the **Customize** option from the **Tool Palette** contextual menu to bring up the **Customize** dialog box.

2. In the **Customize** dialog box, select the **Tool Palettes** tab.

3. **RMB** in the **Tool Palettes** list to bring up the contextual menu for creating, renaming, and deleting tool palettes.

4. **RMB** in the **Palette Groups** list to bring up the contextual menu for creating or deleting tool palette groups.

5. Select a palette group, **RMB** to bring up the contextual menu for creating, renaming, deleting, and making a tool palette group current.

6. Drag and drop selections from **Tool Palettes** into **Palette Groups**.

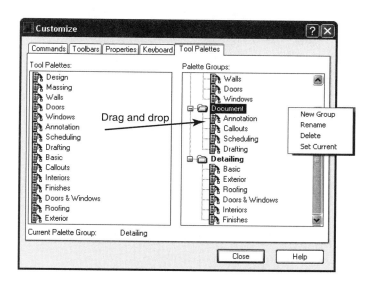

The Properties Palette

The **Properties** palette changes depending on the AEC Object or entity that is selected. All the properties of the selected object can be changed in this palette. The palette also contains the **Quick Select Icon**; this is very useful in selecting objects, especially when several objects are located together.

Bringing Up the Properties Palettes

The Properties palettes can be brought up by three methods:

    a. Typing properties in the **Command line**.

    b. By pressing **Ctrl + 1** on the keyboard.

    c. By double-clicking any AEC Object or entity (see the figure below).

Quick Select

To use Quick Select, select the **Quick Select** icon at the top of the **Properties** palette (see the figure below, top) to bring up the **Quick Select** dialog box (see the figure below, bottom).

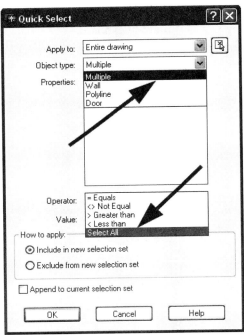

As you add content into the drawing, more object types will be available in the **Object Type** drop-down list.

The Content Browser

The Content Browser locates all your AEC tools such as walls, windows, and doors. You drag your tools into your tool palettes using AutoDesk's idrop technology. You can also drag AEC content back into your tool palettes to create new tools. After creating a new tool palette, it is a good idea to drag a copy of the tool palette back into the **My Tool Catalog** folder in the Content Browser to save a copy of the palette.

Bringing Up the Content Browser

The Content Browser can be brought up by three methods:

a. Typing **aeccontentbrowser** in the **Command line**.

b. By pressing **Ctrl + 4** on the keyboard.

c. By selecting the **Content Browser** icon (see the figure below).

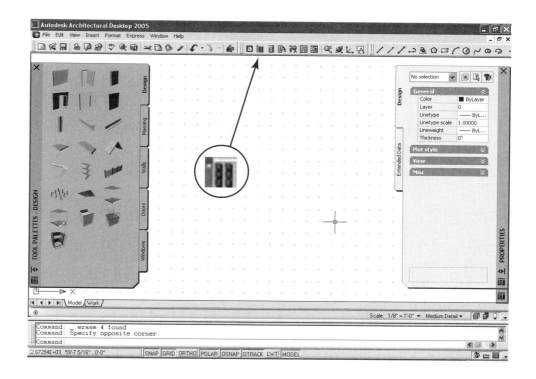

The Content Browser starts off with the Catalog Library, which contains several catalogs (see the figure below).

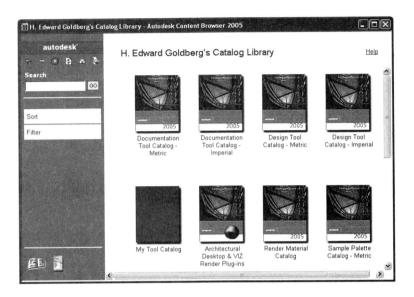

Click the **Modify Library View Options** icon to open the **Content Browser Preferences** dialog box. Here you can set the number of Catalog rows and new Catalog types.

Click the **Add or Create a Catalog** icon to open the **Add Catalog** dialog box. Here you can create a new **Catalog** or add an existing **Catalog** from a location such as a **website**.

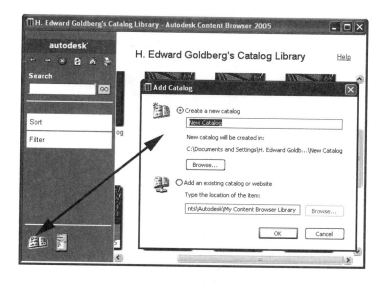

You drag content from the Catalog folders into your tool palettes, as shown in the figure below. (Make sure **Auto-hide** is turned off when you do this.)

You can also create a tool by just by dropping an ADT Object from the drawing to a tool palette, a style from **Style Manager** to a tool palette, or a piece of AEC Content from the **Custom** tab in the **DesignCenter**.

Note: Some objects use fixed images like the Schedule Tool, AEC Dimension Tool, and the Layout Object Tools.

The following tool catalogs are supplied with the program:

Catalog Name	Contents
Autodesk® Architectural Desktop Stock Tool Catalog	A catalog that contains the standard, stock tools in Autodesk Architectural Desktop
Autodesk® Architectural Desktop Sample Palette Catalog - Imperial	A sampling of tools in imperial units for objects such as doors, walls, and windows
Autodesk® Architectural Desktop Sample Palette Catalog - Metric	A sampling of tools in metric units for objects such as doors, walls, and windows
Architectural Desktop Design Tool Catalog - Imperial	Content tools in imperial units for design and documentation of multiview blocks and symbols
Architectural Desktop Design Tool Catalog - Metric	Content tools in metric units for design and documentation of multiview blocks and symbols
Architectural Desktop Documentation Tool Catalog - Imperial	Content tools in imperial units for annotation and documentation
Architectural Desktop Documentation Tool Catalog - Metric	Content tools in metric units for annotation and documentation
Autodesk® Sample Render Material Catalog	Architectural render materials for use with Autodesk Architectural Desktop and Autodesk VIZ Render
My Tool Catalog	An empty tool catalog provided so that you can create your own tool set
Autodesk® Architectural Desktop Tutorial Palette Catalog	A catalog of the tools used in the metric-based Autodesk Architectural Desktop tutorial
Autodesk® Architectural Desktop Tutorial Tool Catalog	A catalog of the tools used in the imperial-based Autodesk Architectural Desktop tutorial
Architectural Desktop VIZ Render Plug-ins	Links to third-party plug-ins for Autodesk Architectural Desktop

You cannot add or remove items from the Autodesk-supplied tool catalogs, but you can create your own tool catalogs. You can also copy other tool catalogs and website links into your catalog library.

The Open Drawing Menu

The **Open Drawing Menu** icon is located at the bottom left of the Autodesk Architectural Desktop 2005 interface (see the figure below).

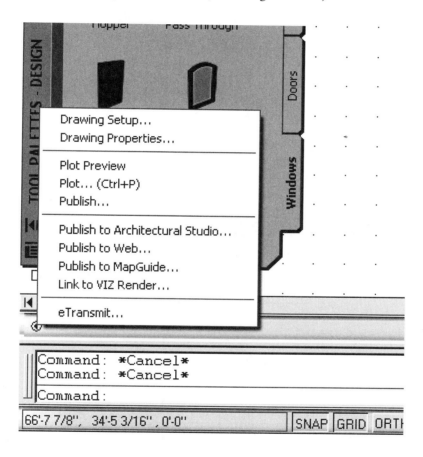

Drawing Setup

Selecting **Drawing Setup** brings up the **Drawing Setup** dialog box with tabs to set drawing units, scale, layers, and display. The **Drawing Setup** dialog box can also be accessed from the **Format** menu in the **Main** toolbar (see the figures below).

Publish – DWF Publisher

Selecting **Publish** brings up the **Publish** dialog box (see figure below). In this dialog box, press the **Publish Options** button to select the publish options for the DWFs (see figure below).

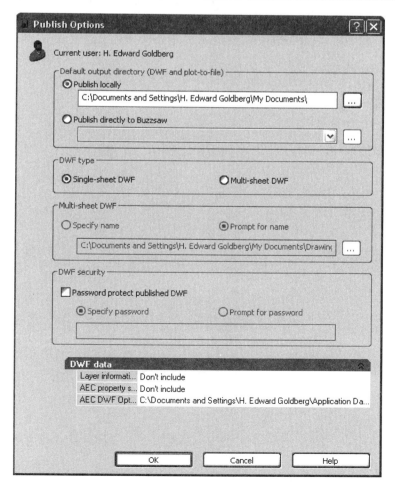

Publish to Architectural Studio

If you have Autodesk Architectural Studio, and it is running, you can send your 2D and 3D information to that program.

Publish to Web

Selecting **Publish to Web** opens an easy-to-use wizard to create a Web page with idrop capability (see the figure below).

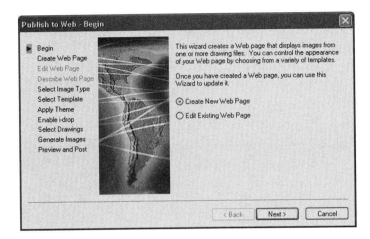

Publish to MapGuide

If you have MapGuide installed, you can deploy MapGuide GIS and digital design data applications on the Internet, on your intranet, or in the field.

Link to Autodesk VIZ Render

The VIZ Render will give you access to photorealistic rendering plus animation. The process is described in the Viz Render section of this book.

eTransmit

Selecting **eTransit** creates a compressed email package of your drawings with all necessary files. It also includes a transmittal (see the figure below).

P A R T

II

Sections and Tutorials: Palettes and Exercises

Section

1

Massing/Mass Elements and Groups

When you finish this section, you should understand the following:

✔ How to create a massing object.
✔ How to modify a massing object.
✔ How to create and attach slice plates (floor slices).
✔ How to modify the massing object after applying the slice plates.
✔ How to change the slice plates into space boundaries, and then into Walls.
✔ How to use the **Drape** tool to create contour massing models.

Massing objects can be dragged or inserted either from the **Design Tool** palette, or by typing **MassElementAdd** on the **Command line**.

Massing and Mass Modeling

Mass modeling is unique to Autodesk Architectural Desktop 2005. It replicates the system frequently used by architects on large buildings. The initial design studies for large buildings are often modeled in clay or wood first. These small models generally show the relationship between parts of the building while indicating scale as well as how light and shadow react with the facades. Mass modeling is meant to be a quick process, akin to the building blocks we all played with as children.

With massing, Autodesk Architectural Desktop 2005 takes the concept of mass modeling one step farther. Not only can you model the concept, but also within the program, you can take that model through to the document creation stage automatically.

The **Massing** tool palette comes with 16 preconfigured primitives (3D shapes). The primitives can be dragged or inserted into your drawing from the tool palette. The size of the primitive can be preset or can be modified when inserting. This can be determined by selecting yes or no from the **Specify on Screen** drop-down list in the **Properties** tool palette when inserting the primitive. Selecting and pulling on grips or changing parameters in the **Properties** tool palette associated with massing can easily modify each primitive's size and shape.

After a massing model has been created, floor slices can be created from the model. These floor slices can be used as a basis for area and space studies, or for eventually generating walls. It is this method that allows you to quickly model a building and electronically convert that model into construction documents.

The following exercises are designed to give you a hands-on feel for using the **Massing** feature of the program. After doing these exercises, I recommend that you explore all the primitives, and try making new ones using the **Extrusion and Revolution** feature as well as the **Convert to Mass Element** tool that converts solid models and AEC Objects into mass elements.

Hands-On

Creating a Massing Object

1. Start a new drawing using the Architectural Building Model and View (Imperial - ctb) template.

2. Change to the Work Layout.

3. Change to the NE Isometric View.

4. Select the **Massing** tool palette.

5. Drag the **Box Primitive** massing icon to the drawing area or click once on the Box icon and move your cursor to the drawing area. *Don't click in the drawing area yet!* Move your cursor to the closed **Properties** toolbar to open it (see Figure 1-1).

6. When the **Properties** toolbar opens, notice a blue asterisk icon (settable option upon insertion) next to the **Specify on screen** option. Select No from the drop-down list (this will allow you to preset the

Figure 1-1

Width, **Depth**, and **Height** of the box). Set the Width to **60**′, Depth to **260′**, and Height to **60′** (see Figure 1-2).

7. Once the size properties have been set, click to locate the **BOX** primitive, and then press **Enter** twice to accept the default rotation and close the command. Save this file.

Hands-On

Modifying a Massing Object

1. Select the primitive to activate its grips, and then select **Free Form** from the **Shape** drop-down list to make the massing box editable (see Figure 1-3).

  Note: Before the massing primitive has been changed to a free form, it can be adjusted in the standard ADT 2005 manner by activating grips and entering dimensions, or pulling on the grips.

Figure 1-2

Figure 1-3

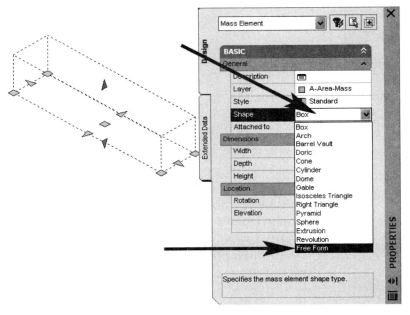

2. Select the free form, and move your cursor over the "dot," right-mouse-click, and select **Split Face** from the contextual menu (see Figure 1-4).

You can recognize an editable free form shape because its grips will be changed to dots. Selecting the dots will select the faces of the free form massing object (see Figure 1-5).

3. Set your **OSNAP** settings to **Endpoint** and **Perpendicular**.

4. Enter **fro** in the **Command line** and click on the upper right corner of the face.

5. Move the cursor to the left along the top of the face, and then enter **80'** in the **Command line** and press **Enter**.

Figure 1-4

Figure 1-5

6. Finally, move your cursor down to the lower edge of the face until the **Perpendicular Osnap** icon appears, and then click to split the face. Press the **Esc** key to complete the command (see Figure 1-6).

Select the dot on the new face, to see your options when "pulling" thru by grabbing the control dot on the face and dragging the face away, then pressing the **Ctrl** key on the keyboard to cycle thru the options.

There are six adjustments that can be made to the faces. These are cycled thru by grabbing the control dot on the face and dragging the face away, then pressing the **Ctrl** key on the keyboard to cycle thru the options. Figure 1-8 shows illustrations of different variations. It also illustrates moving

Figure 1-6

Figure 1-7

edges. Pushing or pulling on the vertical tabs that appear at the edges can move these edges.

By using various primitives and adjusting them by splitting, pushing, pulling, and moving their faces, you can quickly create a mass model of your proposed building.

Now continue on to the next step in the hands-on tutorial.

7. Pull on the dot and press the **Ctrl** key on your keyboard until the face pulls forward.

8. Enter **60'** in the **Command line** and press **Enter** (see Figure 1-9).

9. Drag another box massing object into the drawing area.

10. This time, similar to Step 6, select **YES** from the drop-down list next to the **Specify on screen** option on the **Properties** tool palette. (This will now allow you to adjust your massing object while placing it.

11. Make sure your **End Point Osnap** is active.

12. Place a box massing object on top of the massing object that has been modified previously.

Figure 1-8

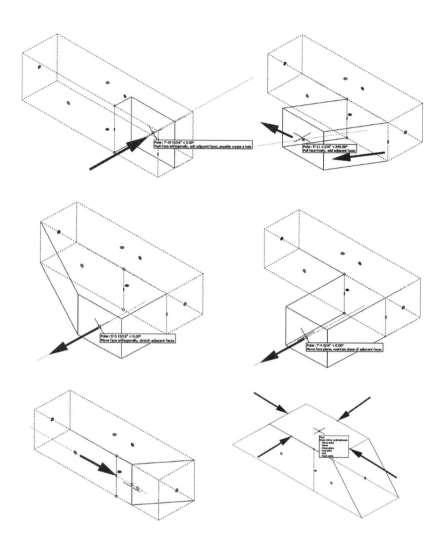

13. With the new box massing object selected, right-mouse-click and
select **Boolean > Union** from the contextual menu (see Figure 1-10).

You have now created a modified massing object made from two massing
objects (see Figure 1-11).

Figure 1-9

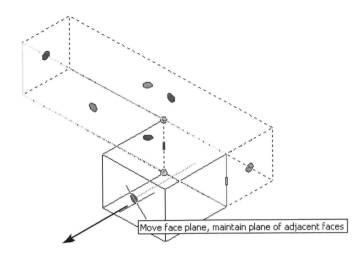

Move face plane, maintain plane of adjacent faces

Figure 1-10

Figure 1-11

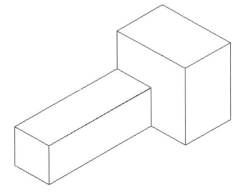

Hands-On

Creating and Attaching Slice Plates (Floor Slices)

1. Select the **Massing** tool palette, and select the **Slice** icon (see Figure 1-12).

2. Click in the Top viewport.

3. Enter 11 in the **Command line** and press **Enter**.

4. Select a spot near the massing model, and then place a second to create a rectangle. (**Note:** This rectangle is just a marker; make it big enough to be comfortable for you to see.)

5. Accept the default **Rotation (0.00)**, accept **Starting height (0")**, and set the distance between slices to 10'–0" then press the enter key to complete the comman.

6. Select all the markers with a window crossing, **RMB**, and select **Attach Objects** from the contextual menu that appears.

7. Select the massing object that you created in the previous section and press **Enter**.

You have now created 11 slice plates (floor slices) in your massing object (see Figure 1-13).

Slice Plates

Slice Markers

Figure 1-12

Figure 1-13

8. Change to the **NW Isometric View** and select the topmost slice marker.

9. **RMB** and select **Set Elevation** from the contextual menu.

10. Enter **115'** in the **Command line** and press **Enter** (note that the topmost slice plate moves downward). Save this file.

! **Note:** Slice plates can also be adjusted by selecting the Front View, and moving the slice markers in the Y direction.

Hiding the Slice Markers

1. Select one of the slice markers, **RMB**, and select **Edit Object Display** from the contextual menu that appears to bring up the **Object Display** dialog box.

2. Double-click on the word **General** to bring up the **Display Properties** dialog box.

3. Turn the **Cut Plane** and **Outline** visibility off, and then press the **OK** buttons on the dialog boxes to complete the command and return to the Drawing Editor.

Hands-On

Modifying the Massing Object After Applying the Slice Plates

1. Select another box massing object from the **Massing** tool palette, and give it a 30′ width, 60′ depth, and 60′ height.

2. Place the new object as shown in Figure 1-14.

3. Select the original massing object, **RMB**, select **Boolean > Subtraction** from the contextual menu, and select the new massing object.

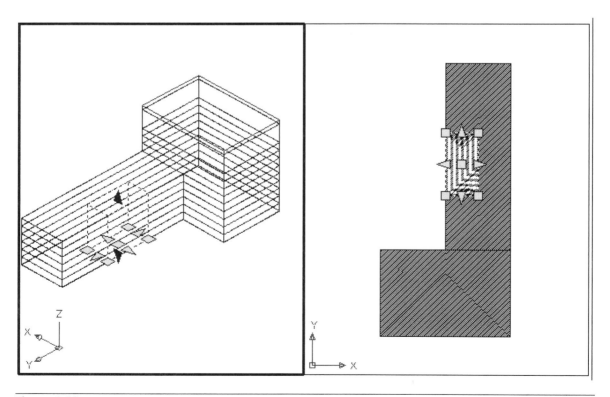

Figure 1-14

Note: If you have trouble selecting the massing objects because you keep selecting the slice plates instead, you can temporarily turn off the visibility of their layer.

   4. Enter **Y** (Yes) in the **Command line** to erase the layout geometry.

Notice that the slice plates follow the new outline created by the Boolean subtraction (see Figure 1-15).

   5. Using the massing object modification techniques, modify the massing object.

Figure 1-15

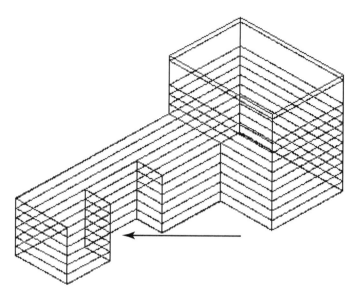

   6. Create new massing objects and Boolean them to the original object.

The slice plates will always follow the modified massing object (massing model) (see Figure 1-16).

   7. **RMB** in an empty space in the Drawing Editor, select Object Viewer from the contextual menu, and select the massing object.

   8. Turn on **Perspective** and **Flat Shaded** to see the model (see Figures 1-17 and 1-18). Save the file.

Figure 1-16

Figure 1-17

Figure 1-18

Hands-On

Changing the Slice Plates into Space Boundaries and Walls

1. Use the previous exercise's file.
2. Change to the **Model Layout**.
3. Change to SW **Isometric View**.
4. Select the **Content Browser** icon from the **Main** toolbar to bring up the Content Browser.
5. Select the **Autodesk Architectural Desktop Stock Tool Catalog > Architectural Object Tools > Page 2**, and drag the **Space Boundary** tool into your tool palette.
6. **RMB** on the **Space Boundary** tool and select **Apply Tool Properties > Slice** from the contextual menu that appears.
7. Select all the slices and press **Enter**.
8. Select the **Quick Select** icon from the **Properties** palette, select **Space Boundary** from the **Object Type**, **Select All** from the **Operator**, and press **OK**.
9. While the space boundaries are selected, open the Properties palette, and change the **Base Height** to **10'-0"**.
10. Select any other slice and change its particular height to match your needs.
11. Select each space boundary, **RMB**, and select **Convert to Walls** from the contextual menu that appears.

The slices have now been converted to wall objects.

Using the Drape Tool to Create Contour Massing Models

1. Start a new drawing using the Architectural Building Model and View (Imperial - ctb) template.
2. Change to the **Model Layout**.
3. Change to the **Top View**.
4. Using the **Rectangle** tool from the **Draw** menu, draw and modify until you get a drawing similar to that in Figure 1-19.

Figure 1-19

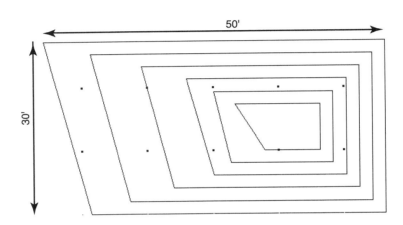

5. Select each modify rectangle, **RMB**, and change the elevation of each to 2'-0" increments with the smallest rectangle having an elevation of 12'-0".
6. Change to **SW Isometric View** (see Figure 1-20).
7. Select the **Drape Tool** from the **Massing** tool palette, select all the contours, and press **Enter**.
8. Select two opposite corners of the bottommost modified rectangle, and press **Enter**.

Figure 1-20

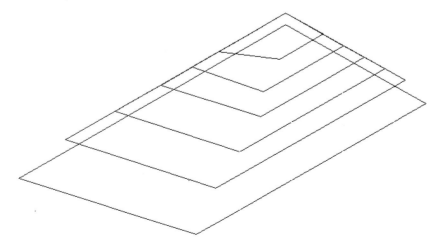

9. Accept the mesh size of 30, and press **Enter**.

10. Enter **2'-0"** in the **Command line** for the base thickness and press Enter to complete the command.

11. Erase the modified rectangles.

12. Press the **Gouraud** icon in the **Shading** toolbar to shade the contour massing model (see Figure 1-21).

Figure 1-21

Space and Space Boundary Objects

When you finish this section, you should understand the following:

✔ How to create a spaces tool palette.
✔ How to create a space object.
✔ How to create a simple space plan with space objects.
✔ How to apply space boundaries.
✔ How to use the **Space Auto Generate** tool.
✔ How to use the **AEC Modify Trim** option.
✔ How to use the **AEC Modify Divide** option.
✔ How to use the **AEC Modify Merge** option.
✔ How to use the **AEC Modify Crop** option.
✔ How to use the new ADT 2005 space object grip features.

Space objects and space boundary objects create a sophisticated but easy-to-use space-planning system.

Space objects can contain Property Set Data that can be retrieved automatically and read in AEC schedules. They can also represent ceilings and floors in cut sections.

The space object represents contained 3D space. It includes floor and ceiling thickness, floor-to-ceiling heights, elevation, and ancillary space heights. All the aforementioned attributes can be modified easily. The space object does not contain wall information.

The space boundary object represents the area that contains space. It includes wall thickness and height, which can be modified through the **Properties** tool palette. The space object does not contain floor or ceiling information.

Space boundary objects can Manage the space objects that they contain.

Space Objects Properties Tool Palette

Number	Name	Purpose
1	Style	Select from available space styles
2	Space height	Floor-to-ceiling height
3	Floor boundary thickness	Floor thickness
4	Ceiling boundary thickness	Ceiling thickness
5	Height above ceiling	Distance above top of ceiling to top of wall (when space boundary or wall is generated)
6	Specify On Screen	Change length and width by dragging on screen
7	Constrain	Constrain dragging of object to only **Area, Length, Width,** or **None**
8	Area	Preset area value of space object
9	Length	Preset length value of space object
10	Width	Preset width value of space object
11	Target Dimensions	Preset space object style values
12	Rotation	Preset rotation angle of space object
13	Elevation	Preset elevation of space object

Hands-On

Creating a Spaces Tool Palette

1. Click on the tool palettes **Properties** icon at the bottom left of the tool palette to pop up the **Tool Palette** contextual menu.

2. Select **New Palette** and name it **Spaces** (see Figure 2-1).

3. Select the **Contact Browser** icon from the **Main** toolbar to bring up the Content Browser.

4. Select the **Autodesk Architectural Desktop Stock Tool Catalog** to open the next page.

5. At the next page, select **Architectural Object Tools** to open the next page.

6. Click on **Next** in the bottom right corner of the page to bring up **Page 2**.

7. Click on the **iDrop** icon and drag space, space boundary, and **Space Auto Generate** tool onto your new **Spaces** tool palette.

8. Repeat this process selecting the **Architectural Desktop Documentation Tool Catalog - Imperial > Schedule Tags > Room & Finish Tags** and dragging the **Space Tag** into the **Spaces** tool palette (see Figure 2-2).

You have now created and populated your own **Spaces** tool palette.

Figure 2-1

Figure 2-2

Hands-On

Creating a Space Object and Labeling It with a Space Tag

1. Start a new drawing using the Architectural Building Model and View (Imperial - ctb) template.
2. Change to the **Model Layout**.
3. Change to the **Top View**.
4. From the **Main menu**, select **Format > Style Manager** to bring up the **Style Manager** dialog box.
5. Select the **Architectural Objects** folder and double-click on **Space Styles**. RMB and Select New from the contextual menu.
6. Create several new space styles and call them **Hall**, **Small Office**, **Large Office**, **Men's Toilet Room**, **Women's Toilet Room**, and **Entrance**. Press the OK button to close this dialog box.
7. Click on the **Space** icon on the **Spaces** tool palette, and move your cursor over the **Properties** tool palette to open it.
8. Set the following:
    a.   Style = **Hall**
    b.   Space height = **7'-0"**
    c.   Ceiling boundary thickness = **2"**
    d.   Floor boundary thickness = **4"**
    e.   Height above ceiling = **1'-6"**
    f.   Specify on screen = **Yes**
    g.   Constrain = ***NONE***
9. Click in the Drawing Editor and press **Enter** three times to complete the command.

You have now placed a space object called Hall.

10. Click on the **Space Tag** icon on the **Spaces** tool palette and select the space object you just placed.
11. Press **Enter** to center the tag on the object and bring up the **Edit Property Set Data** dialog box.
12. Select the **Add Property Sets** icon (Figure 2-3) to bring up the **Add Property Sets** dialog box (Figure 2-4).

! **Note:** The **Edit Property Set Data** dialog box is where you enter information to be stored in the space object.

The **Add Property Sets** dialog box contains check boxes to determine if you wish to include room finish and/or room object information in the space object.

13. In the **Add Property Sets** dialog box check the **RoomFinishObjects** and **RoomObjects** check boxes and press **Enter** to return to the **Edit Property Set Data** dialog box.
14. Stretch the **Edit Property Set Data** dialog box to its full extent.
15. In the **Edit Property Set Data** dialog box enter the data shown in Figure 2-5.

Figure 2-3

Figure 2-4

 Note: The yellow lightning bolts in the **Edit Property Set Data** dialog box signify information that already exists in the space object (see Figure 2-5).

16. Press **OK** to complete the command and return to the Drawing Editor.

You now have a tagged space object (see Figure 2-6). Save this drawing.

Figure 2-5

Figure 2-6

Hands-On

Creating a Simple Space Plan with Space Objects

1. Use the previous exercise.
2. Change to the **Model Layout**.
3. Change to the **Top View**.
4. Select the **Space** icon from the **Spaces** tool palette you created.
5. Move your cursor over the **Properties** palette to open it.
6. Set the following:
   a.   Style = **Hall**
   b.   Space height = **9'-0"**
   c.   Floor boundary thickness = **12"**
   d.   Ceiling boundary thickness = **2"**
   e.   Height above ceiling = **0"**
   f.   Specify on screen = **No**
   g.   Constrain = ***NONE***
   h.   Length = **10'-0"**
   i.   Width = **10'-0"**
7. Click in the **Drawing Editor** and press **Enter** twice.
8. Select the **Space Tag** icon from the **Spaces** tool palette you created, select the space object you placed in Step 7, and press **Enter** twice.
9. Turn **POLAR** on.
10. Select the Hall to activate its grips.
11. Select the right center grip, drag to the right (0°), enter **30'-0"** in the **Command line**, and press **Enter** (see Figure 2-7).

Figure 2-7

12. Select the top center grip, and drag in the 270° direction 3'-0".

Your Hall should now be 40' × 7' wide. Press **ESC** to exit the command.

13. Again select the **Space** icon from the **Spaces** tool palette you created.

14. In the **Properties** palette set the following:
    a.   Style = **Entrance**
    b.   Space height = **12'-0"**
    c.   Floor boundary thickness = **12"**
    d.   Ceiling boundary thickness = **2"**
    e.   Height above ceiling = **0"**
    f.   Specify on screen = **No**
    g.   Constrain = ***NONE***
    h.   Length = **10'-0"**
    i.   Width = **30'-0"**

15. Place the **Entrance** space as shown in Figure 2-8.

Figure 2-8

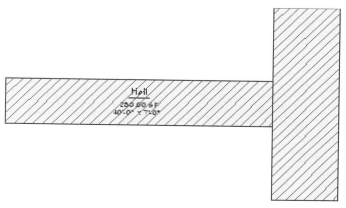

16. Select the **Entrance** space, **RMB**, and select **AEC Modify Tools**, then select **Divide** from the contextual menu that appears.

17. Drag a line across the Entrance space to create two spaces as shown in Figure 2-9.

Figure 2-9

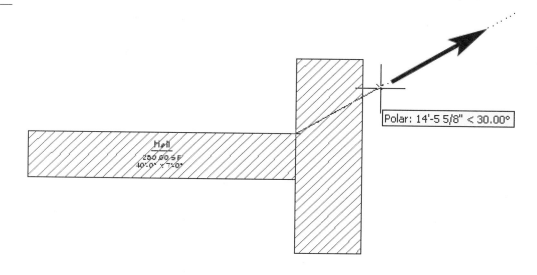

18. Again select the **Space** icon from the **Spaces** tool palette you created.

19. In the **Properties** palette set the following:

    a.   Style = **Large Office**

    b.   Space height = **7'-0"**

    c.   Floor boundary thickness = **12"**

    d.   Ceiling boundary thickness = **2"**

    e.   Height above ceiling = **0"**

    f.   Specify on screen = **No**

    g.   Constrain = ***NONE***

    h.   Length = **10'-0"**

    i.   Width = **15'-0"**

20. Enter **D** in the **Command line** and press **Enter** until the insertion point of the Large Office space object is at the upper left of the object.

21. Snap the Large Office space object, the Hall, as shown in Figure 2-10.

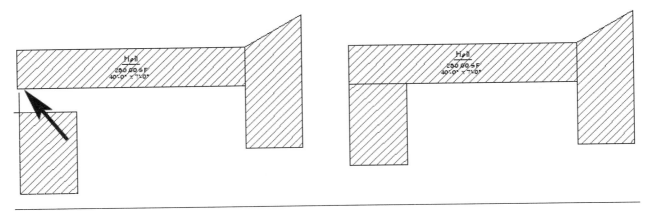

Figure 2-10

22. Array the Large Office four columns to the right, and mirror it as shown in Figure 2-11.

23. Complete the space plan by adding the toilet rooms.

24. Select the **Space Tag** icon from the **Spaces** tool palette, select each space, and press **Enter** to continue placing each tag until all the space are labeled (Figure 2-12).

Figure 2-11

Figure 2-12

Hands-On

Applying Space Boundaries

1. Use the previous exercise.

2. RMB on the **Space Boundary** icon and select **Apply tool properties to > Space** from the contextual menu that appears.

3. Move your cursor over the **Properties** palette to open it.

4. Select the **Quick Select** icon; select **Space Boundary** from the **Object Type** drop-down list.

5. Choose **Select All** from the **Operator** drop-down list, and press the **OK** button.

6. Again move your cursor over the **Properties** palette to open it.

7. Select **Solid** from the **Boundary** type drop-down list.

8. Press the **Esc** key twice to complete the command.

Space boundaries have been placed around the spaces (see Figure 2-13).

Figure 2-13

Hands-On

Modifying Space Boundaries

1. Start a new drawing using the Architectural Building Model and View (Imperial - ctb) template.

2. Change to the **Model Layout**.

3. Change to the **Top View**.

4. Select the **Space** icon from the **Spaces** tool palette you created.

5. Insert a space in the Drawing Editor with the following properties:

   a. Style = **Standard**
   b. Space height = **8'-0"**
   c. Floor boundary thickness = **12"**
   d. Ceiling boundary thickness = **2"**
   e. Height above ceiling = **2"**
   f. Specify on screen = **No**
   g. Constrain = ***NONE***
   h. Length = **30'**
   i. Width = **30'**

6. From the **Design** Palette, **Pick** the **Space Boundary** icon. **RMB**, select **Apply Tool Properties to > Spaces**, and select the space.

7. Using **Quick Select**, find and change the space boundary to Solid boundary type, with a width of 12".

8. Change to the **SW Isometric View**.

9. Double-click the space boundary to open its **Properties** palette.

10. Select **Ceiling stops at boundary** from the **Ceiling condition** drop-down list the upper wall will appear in a boundary condition.

11. Enter **3'-0"** in the **Upper extension** data field and press **Enter**.

12. Press the **Esc** key twice to clear the space boundary's grips (see Figure 2-14).

Figure 2-14

13. Select the space boundary again, and **RMB** anywhere in the Drawing Editor to bring up the contextual menu.

14. Select **Edit Edges** from the contextual menu.

Note: **Edit Edges** and **Add Edges** are the options Architectural Desktop uses to edit any segment of a space boundary.

15. Select the space boundary again, and **RMB** anywhere in the Drawing Editor to bring up the contextual menu.

16. Select **Edit Edges** from the contextual menu.

17. Select the edge shown in Figure 2-15, and press **Enter** to bring up the **Boundary Edge Properties** dialog box.

18. Select the **Dimensions** tab.

This tab contains controls for the type, width, and justification of space boundaries.

19. Select the **Design Rules** tab.

This tab contains controls for the space boundary conditions at the ceiling and floors in relation to spaces.

20. Uncheck the **Automatically Determine from Spaces** check box.

Figure 2-15

This will disconnect the relationship of the chosen space boundary segment from the adjacent space.

21. In the B-Upper Extension data box, enter **8'-0"**.

22. Select the **Ceiling Stops at Wall** radio button, and press **Enter**.

The top of the space boundary segment is now **8'-0"** above the ceiling of the adjacent space (Figure 2-16).

Figure 2-16

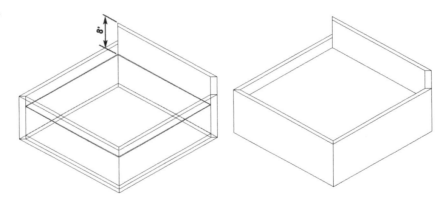

23. Change to the **Top View**.

24. Select the space boundary, **RMB**, and select **Insert Joint** from the contextual menu that appears.

25. Select the midpoint of the leftmost space boundary segment.

Nothing will appear to happen, but a joint has been added. (If you change to **SW Isometric View**, you can see the joint.)

26. Select the space boundary again and notice that two more grips appear on the leftmost segment.

27. Click and drag one of the new grips to the left (180°) **10'-0"** and press **Enter**.

Notice that the Space Object fills the space. This is because the **Manage spaces** check box is checked (Figure 2-17).

28. Undo the command, and return to Step 27 of this exercise.

29. Repeat Step 27, but hold down the **Ctrl** button while dragging the grip.

Figure 2-17

30. Again enter **10'-0"** in the **Command line** and press **Enter**.

31. Double-click the space boundary again to open its **Properties** palette.

Notice that the space boundary drags a rectangular space out from the segment (Figure 2-18).

 Repeat this process inserting joints and pulling on different grips (see Figure 2-19).

Figure 2-18

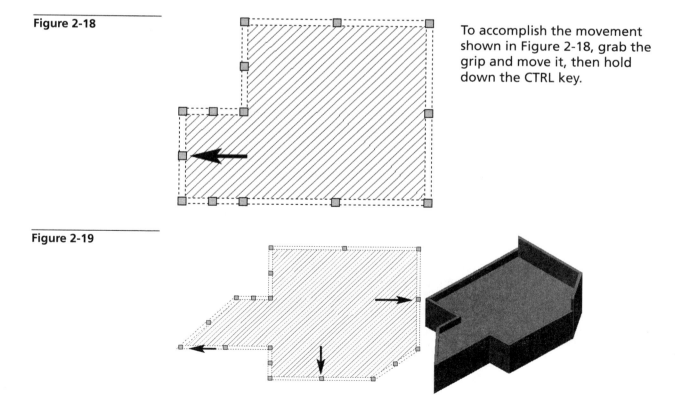

To accomplish the movement shown in Figure 2-18, grab the grip and move it, then hold down the CTRL key.

Figure 2-19

32. Double-click on the space boundary again to bring up its **Properties** palette.

33. Change the selection in the **Manage contained spaces** drop-down list to **No**.

This disconnects the intelligent linkage between the space boundary and the adjacent space object.

34. **RMB** anywhere in the Drawing Editor to bring up the contextual menu.

35. Select **Remove Edges** from the contextual menu.

36. Select the segment shown in Figure 2-20, and press **Enter** to complete the command.

37. Change to the **Top View**.

Figure 2-20

38. Double-click on the space boundary again to bring up its **Properties** palette.

39. Change the **Manage contained spaces** drop-down list back to **Yes** to reconnect electronically the space boundary and the space object.

40. Again **RMB** anywhere in the Drawing Editor to bring up the contextual menu.

41. Select **Add Edges** from the contextual menu.

42. Move your cursor over the **Properties** palette to open it.

43. Set **Width** to **18"**.

44. Turn the **Near** and **Perpendicular** snaps on.

45. Near snap to the right-hand space boundary segment, and add three 109-00 segments returning perpendicular to the starting segment as shown in Figure 2-21. These new segments are now part of the original space boundary.

To add a Space object to the **Added Edges**, use the **Space Auto Generate** tool, which is demonstrated in the following exercise.

Figure 2-21

Hands-On

Using the Space Auto Generate Tool

1. Start a new drawing using the Architectural Building Model and View (Imperial - ctb) template.

2. Change to the **Model Layout**.

3. Change to the **Top View**.

4. Select **Format > Style Manager** from the **Main** toolbar to bring up the **Style Manager** dialog box.

5. Create five new space styles and call them **A**, **B**, **C**, **D**, and **E**, respectively, and then press the **OK** button.

6. Using lines, polylines, and a circle, create the 2D drawing shown in Figure 2-22.

7. Select the **Space Auto Generate** tool from the **Spaces** tool palette to bring up the **Generate Spaces** dialog box (see Figure 2-23).

Figure 2-22

Figure 2-23

Figure 2-23

8. In the **Generate Spaces** dialog box set the following
   a.   Style = **A**
   b.   Name = **Room A**
   c.   Increment = **1** (this will record how many spaces have been placed)
   d.   Select the **Automatic** radio button
   e.   Filter = **All Linework**

9. Press the **Tag Settings** button to bring up the **Tag Settings** dialog box.

10. Check the **Add Tag to New Spaces** check box to open the **Tag Settings** dialog box. Select **Aec3_Room_Tag** from the **Tag Definition** drop down list, check the **Auto-Increment Numerical Properties** check box. Check the **Add Properties Set to New Spaces** check box, check the **Auto-Increment Numerical Properties** check box and set **Increment** to **1** (this will set the tag to increment the space 1 number each time a space is placed).

11. Press the **OK** button to close the **Tag Settings** dialog box, and click inside the A enclosure.–Don't close the **Generate Spaces** dialog box.

12. In the **Generate Spaces** dialog box, change the **Style** to **B**, and **Name** to **Room B**, and then click in the B enclosure. Repeat this process changing the Style and Name until all the spaces have been created with all the space styles.

13. Apply a space boundary to the spaces. To do this, **RMB** on the **Space Boundary** palette icon, select the **Apply Tools Properties to Space**, and select all the spaces.

14. Change the space boundary to **Solid** boundary. To do this, double click on the space boundary to bring up the **Properties** palette. In the **Properties** palette, select **Solid** from the **Boundary Type** drop down list. (see Figure 2-24).

15. Enter space on the **Command line** and press **Enter**.

Figure 2-24

16. Enter **Q** (Query) on the **Command line** and press **Enter**.

17. The **Space Information** dialog box will appear.

18. Select the **Space Info Total** tab.

Here you will see the quantities and areas of each space (Figure 2-25).

19. Press the **Create MDB** button and save the file for use in a database program such as Microsoft Access.

Figure 2-26 shows a shaded perspective of the space plan created using the **Space Auto Generate** tool.

Figure 2-25

Figure 2-26

Hands-On

New Autodesk Architectural Desktop 2005 Feature
Using the AEC MODIFY Tool To Modify Spaces

Using the Trim Option

1. Start a new drawing using the Architectural Building Model and View (Imperial - ctb) template.

2. Change to the **Model Layout**

3. Change to the **Top View**.

4. Select the **Space** object icon from the **Design** tool palette, and place a 10' x 10' Standard-style space object in the Drawing Editor.

5. Select the space object you just placed to activate its grips.

6. Drag the space object to 30' x 30', and press the **Esc** key to deselect the grips.

7. **RMB** in the Drawing Editor and select **AEC Modify Tools > Trim** from the contextual menu that appears (see Figure 2-27).

8. Select the space object and press **Enter**.

Figure 2-27

Figure 2-28

9. Select a point to the left of the space object, drag your cursor as shown in Figure 2-28, and click your mouse button. This creates your **Trim** line.

10. Move your cursor in the direction that you wish to trim, left of the line, and click the mouse button to trim the space object (see Figure 2-29).

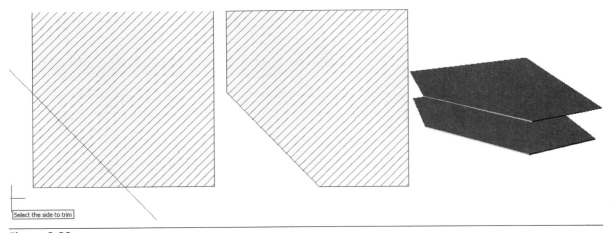

Figure 2-29

Using the Divide Option

11. With the space object *not selected,* **RMB** in the Drawing Editor and select **AEC Modify Tools > Divide** from the contextual menu that appears.

12. Select the space object and then press **Enter**.

13. Select two points in a similar manner as in the **Trim** exercise.

14. Move one division to the right (see Figure 2-30).

Figure 2-30

Using the Subtract Option

15. From the **Draw** toolbar, place two rectangles and a circle as shown in Figure 2-31.

16. With the space object *not selected,* **RMB** in the Drawing Editor and select **AEC Modify Tools > Subtract** from the contextual menu that appears.

17. Select the right object division and press **Enter**.

18. Select the rectangles and the circle and then press **Enter**.

19. Enter **Y** (Yes) in the **Command line** and press **Enter** (see Figure 2-32).

Figure 2-31

Figure 2-32

Using the Merge Option

20. From the **Draw** toolbar, place two rectangles and a circle as shown in Figure 2-33.

21. With the space object *not selected,* **RMB** in the Drawing Editor and select **AEC Modify Tools > Merge** from the contextual menu that appears.

22. Select the right object division and press **Enter**.

23. Select the rectangles and the circle and then press **Enter**.

24. Enter **Y** (Yes) in the **Command line** and press **Enter** (see Figure 2-34).

Figure 2-33

Figure 2-34

Using the Crop Option

25. From the Draw toolbar, place a rectangle and circle as shown in Figure 2-35.

26. With the space object *not selected*, **RMB** in the Drawing Editor and select **AEC Modify Tools > Crop** from the contextual menu that appears.

27. Select the space object division and press **Enter**.

28. Select the rectangle and the circle and then press **Enter**.

29. Enter **Y** (Yes) in the **Command line** and press **Enter** (see Figure 2-36).

Figure 2-35

Figure 2-36

Hands-On

New Autodesk Architectural Desktop 2005 Feature
Using the New ADT 2005 Space Object Grip Features

Adding and Removing a Vertex

1. Start a new drawing using the Architectural Building Model and View (Imperial - ctb) template.

2. Change to the **Model Layout**.

3. Change to the **Top View**.

4. Select the **Space** object icon from the **Design** tool palette, and place a 10' x 10' Standard-style space object in the Drawing editor.

5. Select the space object to activate its grips.

6. Move your cursor over the right **Edge** grip to show the grip's "tool tip" (see Figure 2-37).

Figure 2-37

7. Select the right **Edge** grip, and drag to the right (see Figure 2-38).

8. While dragging, press the **Ctrl** key on your keyboard to place the grips in **Add vertex** mode (see Figures 2-39 and 2-40).

9. Move your cursor over the new vertex to show the vertex's tool tip (see Figure 41).

Figure 2-38

Figure 2-39

Figure 2-40

Figure 2-41

10. Select the new vertex, press the **Ctrl** key on your keyboard, and click the mouse button to remove or move the vertex.

11. Remove the vertex.

12. Click the right **Edge** grip again and drag it to the right. While dragging, press the **Ctrl** key on your keyboard twice and then click to create an arc (see Figure 2-42).

Figure 2-42

Walls

When you finish this section, you should understand the following:

✔ How to place a wall object.

✔ How to change walls by dynamically pulling on grips.

✔ How to create wall sweeps.

✔ How to create wall endcaps using **Calculate Automatically**.

✔ How to use plan modifiers.

✔ How to use body modifiers.

✔ How to use the **Roof/Floor** line option.

✔ How to use interference conditions.

✔ How to use **Cleanups – Applying 'T' Cleanup** and **Wall Merge**.

✔ How to edit wall styles.

Wall objects can be dragged or inserted either from the **Design** tool palette, or by typing **walladd** in the **Command line**.

Walls

Wall objects are the basis of all buildings; they enclose space and give the building its character. Because buildings require a vast variety of wall types and configurations, these objects have become very sophisticated in Autodesk Architectural Desktop 2005.

In order to understand how to use ADT 2005's wall objects, one must first understand some basic ADT 2005 wall object conventions. Among these conventions are **Base Height, Baseline, Roofline Offset from Base Height, Floor Line Offset from Baseline**, and **Justification** (see Figure 3-1).

Figure 3-1

Wall Objects Properties Tool Palette

ADT 2005 contains controls and routines for modifying the shape of the wall itself. These include **Wall Sweeps, Wall Endcaps and Opening Endcaps, Plan Modifiers, Body Modifiers, Modifications to the Roof / Floor lines**, and **Interference Conditions**.

Number	Name	Purpose
1	Layer	Change this to place the wall on another layer
2	Style	Change this to change to another style such as 12" brick and block, etc.
3	Cleanup automatically	Change to Yes or No if you want the wall to join with similar components of intersecting walls
4	Cleanup group definition	Change to Style allowing Wall Cleanup between host and XREF drawings and/or allowing objects anchored to walls in other cleanup groups to be moved or copied to walls in this cleanup group
5	Segment	Change to either Line or Arc to create linear or curved walls
6	Width	Set the width for nonpreset walls
7	Base Height	Set a new base height
8	Length	Set a new wall length
9	Justify	Change whether the wall is placed and references from the left, center, right, or baseline of the wall

Hands-On

Placing a Wall Object

1. Start a new drawing using the Architectural Building Model and View (Imperial - ctb) template.
2. Change to the **Model Layout**
3. Change to the **Top View**.
4. Select the **Wall** icon from the **Design** tool palette and drag your cursor over the **Properties** palette to open the palette.

 Note: The blue asterisks are called "Add" icons and they represent properties that are available only when adding an object.

Here you will find all the size parameters that you can change upon insertion of a wall.

5. Set the following in the **Properties** palette:
   a. Style = **Standard**
   b. Width = **6"**
   c. Base Height = **10'-0"**
   d. Justify = **Left**
   e. Roof line offset from base height = **4'-0"**
   f. Floor line offset from base line = **-3'-0"**
6. Click in the drawing area and drag a 10'-0" long wall, and click a second time to complete the command.
7. Change to **SW Isometric View** (see Figure 3-2).

Figure 3-2

Hands-On

Changing Walls by Dynamically Pulling on Grips

Example: Dynamically changing the roof offset

1. Select the wall to activate its grips
2. Move your cursor over the leftmost top grip, and notice the tool tip.
3. Select the grip and move your cursor upward.
4. Tab to change the magenta-colored dimension selection.
5. Enter **8'-0"** for the "overall dimension of the roof offset, and press the **Enter** key to complete the command (see Figure 3-3).

Figure 3-3

Hands-On

Creating Wall Sweeps

1. Change to **Top View**.
2. Select the **CMU-8 Furring** icon from the **Walls** tool palette, and drag your cursor over the **Properties** palette to open the palette.
3. Place a new wall with the following properties:
   a. Style = **CMU-8 Furring**
   b. Width = **9-1/2"**
   c. Base Height = **10'-0"**
   d. Justify = **Left**
   e. Roof line offset from base height = **0**
   f. Floor line offset from base line = **0**
4. Change to **NW Isometric View**.
5. Select the wall, **RMB**, and select **Sweeps > Add** from the contextual menu that appears to bring up the **Add Wall Sweep** dialog box.
6. In the **Add Wall Sweep** dialog box enter the following:
   a. Wall Component = **CMU**
   b. Profile Definition = **Start from scratch**
   c. New Profile Name = **TEST SWEEP PROFILE**
7. Press the **OK** button. Select a location on the wall for editing, and a blue field with grips will appear (see Figure 3-4).
8. Grab the lower grip of the blue field, drag it in the direction of 180 degrees, enter 2'-0" in the **Command line**, and press the **Enter** (see Figure 3-5).
9. Select the **Rectangle** icon from the **Draw** menu and place a rectangle as shown in Figure 3-6.
10. Select the blue field, **RMB**, and select **Add Ring** from the contextual menu that appears.

Blue field with grips

Figure 3-4

Figure 3-5

rectangle

Figure 3-6

11. Select the rectangle, enter **Y** (Yes) in the **Command line**, and press **Enter**.

12. Accept **Join** in the Command line and press Enter.

13. Press the **Save All Changes** icon in the **In-Place Edit** dialog box to complete the command and create the new wall sweep (see Figure 3-7).

New Autodesk Architectural Desktop 2005 Feature

14. Select the wall again, **RMB**, and again select **Sweeps > Edit Profile In Place** from the contextual menu that appears.

15. Select a place on the wall to bring up the blue **Edit Profile In Place** field.

16. Select the edge grip of the **Edit Profile In Place** field as shown in Figure 3-8.

17. Drag the grip to the right, and press the **Ctrl** key on your keyboard

Figure 3-7

Figure 3-8

twice to convert the edge to an arc.

18. Click the mouse button to complete the command.

19. **RMB** on the blue **Edit Profile In Place** field, and select **Save As New Profile** from the contextual menu that appears to bring up the **New Profile** dialog box.

20. Enter a new name for the new wall sweep profile, and press the **OK** button.

You have now created a new wall sweep (see Figure 3-9).

Figure 3-9

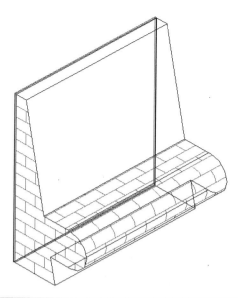

Hands-On

Creating Wall Endcaps Using Calculate Automatically

1. Create a new drawing.

2. Change to **Top View**.

3. Select the **CMU-8 Rigid-1.5 Air-2 brick 4 Furring 2** icon from the **Walls** tool palette and drag your cursor over the **Properties** palette to open the palette.

4. Place a new wall with the following properties:
   a. Style = **CMU-8 Rigid-1.5 Air-2 brick 4 Furring 2**
   b. Width = **1'-5"**
   c. Base Height = **10'-0"**
   d. Justify = **Left**
   e. Roof line offset from base height = **0**
   f. Floor line offset from base line = **0**

5. Zoom close to the left end of the wall (see Figure 3-10).

This will allow you to draw a new wall endcap on top of the existing wall.

6. Select **Format > Style Manager** from the **Main** menu to bring up the **Style Manager**.

7. In the **Style Manager**, left panel, expand the **Architectural Objects** folder.

8. In the **Architectural Objects** folder, expand the **Wall Endcap Styles**.

9. Click on the **CMU-8 Rigid-1.5 Air-2 brick 4 Furring 2** style to open it.

This endcap style will be in your **Style Manager** because you placed a CMU-8 Rigid-1.5 Air-2 brick 4 Furring 2 wall that uses this endcap style. For your own information, compare the endcap style in the **Style Manager** with the end of the wall you placed (see Figure 3-11), then close the **Style Manager** dialog box.

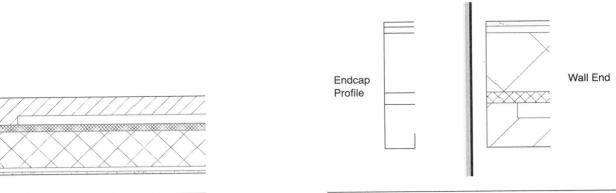

Figure 3-10

Figure 3-11

10. Select the **Polyline** icon from the **Draw** menu, and trace in a counterclockwise direction a new polyline for the end of each component in the wall.

This author has moved the wall away and moved each polyline to illustrate how they were created (see Figure 3-12).

11. Place a line that crosses all your new polylines as shown in Figure 3-13, and trim all ends of the polylines so that they are even.

Figure 3-12

Figure 3-13

 NOTE: If the ends are not even, the new endcap will be twisted!

12. Erase the trim line.

13. Move the original wall near the new polylines (see Figure 3-14).

14. Select the wall, **RMB**, and select **Endcaps > Calculate Automatically** from the contextual menu that appears.

15. Select all your new polylines with a window crossing and press **Enter**.

16. Enter **Y** (Yes) in the **Command line** to erase the polylines and press **Enter**.

Figure 3-14

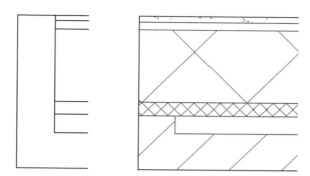

17. In response to **Modify Current Endcap Style**, enter **N** (No) in the **Command line** and press **Enter**.

18. In response to **Apply the new wall endcap style to this end as**, enter **O** (Override) in the **Command line** and press **Enter** to bring up the **New Endcap Style** dialog box.

19. In the **New Endcap Style** dialog box, enter **ENDCAP TEST** and press the **OK** button.

Your wall will now have your new endcap, and the new endcap style will appear in the **Style Manager** (see Figure 3-15).

To change your endcap back to the original, or to place your new endcap on the other end of the wall do the following:

20. Select the wall, **RMB**, and select **Endcaps > Override Endcap Style** from the contextual menu that appears.

21. Select a point on the end of the wall to bring up the **Select an Endcap Style** dialog box.

22. Select the endcap style you wish to replace and press the **OK** button.

Figure 3-15

Hands-On

Using Plan Modifiers

1. Clear the previous exercise.

2. Change to the **Work Layout**

3. Select the **CMU-8 Rigid-1.5 Air-2 brick 4** icon from the **Walls** tool palette, and drag your cursor over the **Properties** palette to open the palette.

4. Place a new 10'long wall in the **Top View** with the following properties:

   a. Style = **CMU-8 Furring**

   b. Width = **1'-3-1/2"**

   c. Base Height = **10'-0"**

   d. Justify = **Left**

   e. Roof line offset from base height = **0**

   f. Floor line offset from base line = **0**

5. Place an open polyline as shown in Figure 3-16.

Figure 3-16

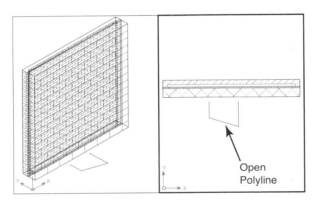

Open Polyline

6. Select the wall, **RMB**, and select **Plan Modifiers > Convert Polyline to wall Modifier** from the contextual menu that appears.

7. Select the polyline, enter **Y** (Yes) in the **Command line**, and enter **TEST WALL MODIFIER** in the **New Wall Modifier Style Name** dialog box that appears.

8. The **Add Wall Modifier** dialog box now appears. Press the **OK** button to end the command and add the wall modifier (see Figure 3-17).

9. To modify the modifier, double-click the wall to bring up the **Properties** palette.

10. Scroll down to the bottom of the **Properties** palette, and click on **Plan Modifiers** to bring up the **Wall Modifiers** dialog box. (Figure 3-18)

11. Place the dimensions shown in Figure 3-19.

12. Press **OK** and see the result (see Figure 3-20).

Figure 3-17

Figure 3-18

Figure 3-19

Figure 3-20

Hands-On

Using Body Modifiers

1. Clear the previous exercise.
2. Change to the **Work Layout**.
3. Select the **Wall** icon from the **Design** tool palette, and drag your cursor over the **Properties** palette to open the palette.
4. Place a new 10'-long wall in the **Top View** with the following properties:
   a. Style = **Standard**
   b. Width = **12**
   c. Base Height = **10'-0"**
   d. Justify = **Left**
   e. Roof line offset from base height = **0**
   f. Floor line offset from base line = **0**
5. Select the **Arch Massing** object from the **Massing** tool palette, and drag your cursor over the **Properties** palette to open the palette.
6. Place the **Massing** object with the following properties:
   a. Style = **Standard**
   b. Width = **5'-6"**

    c. Depth = **3'-0"**

    d. Height = **3'-0"**

    e. Radius = **2'-0"**

    f. elevation = **2'-0"**

7. Place it as shown in Figure 3-21.

8. Select the wall, **RMB**, and select **Body Modifiers > Add** from the contextual menu that appears.

9. Select the massing object and press **Enter** to bring up the **Add Body Modifier** dialog box.

10. Select **Subtractive** from the **Operation** drop-down list, and check the **Erase Selected Object(s)** check box (see Figure 3-22).

Figure 3-21

Figure 3-22

11. Finally, press the **OK** button to complete the command and add the body modifier (see Figure 3-23).

12. Insert a door in the wall and see how the body modifier affects the wall (see Figure 3-24).

Figure 3-23

Figure 3-24

Hands-On

Using Roof/Floor Line Option

1. Clear the previous exercise.
2. Select the **Wall** icon from the **Design** tool palette, and drag your cursor over the **Properties** palette to open the palette.
3. Place a new 10'-long wall in the **Top View** with the following properties:
   a. Style = **Standard**
   b. Width = **6**
   c. Base Height = **10'-0"**
   d. Justify = **Left**
   e. Roof line offset from base height = **0**
   f. Floor line offset from base line = **0**
4. Select the **NE Isometric** icon from the views toolbar to change to **NE Isometric View**.
5. Select the wall, **RMB**, and select **Roof/Floor Line > Edit in Place** from the contextual menu that appears to apply a blue editing field on the wall (see Figure 3-25).
6. Select the blue field, **RMB**, and select **Add Gable** from the contextual menu that appears.
7. Select the roof line—the wall adds a gable (see Figure 3-26).
8. Select the wall so the blue field reappears, **RMB**, and select **Add Step** from the contextual menu that appears. The wall adds a step (see Figure 3-27).

Figure 3-25

Figure 3-26

Figure 3-27

9. Select the wall so the blue field reappears, **RMB**, and select **Add Vertex** from the contextual menu that appears.
10. With the near Object Snap set, click on a point on the gable, and press **Enter**.
11. Select the wall again so the blue field reappears, and an additional vertex will appear where you clicked.

12. Drag on the vertex to change the wall and click to change the shape of the wall (see Figure 3-28).

13. Select the blue field, **RMB**, and select **Remove** from the contextual menu that appears.

14. Click on the gable to remove it.

15. Change to the **Front View**.

16. Place a polyline as shown in Figure 3-29. The polyline does not have to be on the same plane as the wall, only parallel to the plane of the wall.

17. **RMB** on the bluefield and select **Project to Polyline** from the contextual menu.

18. Select the top of the wall then select the polyline.

19. Enter **No** in the command line, and press the **Enter** key.

20. Press the **Save All Changes** icon in the **In-Place Edit** toolbar to complete the command.

21. Change to the **SW Isometric View**, and press the **Hidden** icon in the **Shading** toolbar (see Figure 3-30).

Figure 3-28

Figure 3-29

Figure 3-30

22. Double-click the wall you just edited to bring up its **Properties** palette.

23. Scroll down to the last field on the palette called **Roof/floor line**.

24. Click on the **Roof/floor line** field to bring up the **Roof and Floor Line** dialog box (see Figure 3-31).

25. Select the **Edit Floor Line** radio button, and select the vertex shown in Figure 3-32.

Figure 3-31

Figure 3-32

26. In the **Roof and Floor Line** dialog box, press the **Edit Vertex** button to bring up the **Wall Roof/Floor Line Vertex** dialog box (see Figure 3-33).

27. Enter **3'-0"** in the **Vertical Offset > Distance** data field.

28. Select the from **Baseline** radio button, and press **OK** to return to the **Roof and Floor Line** dialog box. Then press the **OK** to return to the Drawing editor.

You have now modified the wall floor line through the Roof/Floor dialog boxes (see Figure 3-34).

Figure 3-33

Figure 3-34

Hands-On

Using Interference Condition

1. Start a new drawing using the Architectural Building Model and View (Imperial - ctb) template.

2. Change to the **Model Layout**

3. Change to the **Top View**.

4. Place a Standard 6" wide 10'-0"-high, 10'-0"-long wall. Baseline = 0, Roofline = 0, Floorline = 0.

5. From the **Design** tool palette select the **Stair** icon, and place a Standard, Straight 3'-0" wide stair with a height of 10'-0" (see Figure 3-35).

If you don't understand how to place stairs, see the Section 8, Stairs, for exercises on placing and modifying stair objects.

6. Select the wall, **RMB**, and select **Interference Condition > Add** from the contextual menu that appears.

7. Select the stair you placed and press **Enter**.

8. Enter **S** (Subtractive) in the **Command line** and press **Enter**.

The interference area located above the stair and set in the stair **Properties** palette is removed from the wall (see Figure 3-36).

9. Double-click the stair to bring up its **Properties** palette.

10. Scroll down to **Interference > Headroom height**.

11. Change the headroom height to **4'**, and notice the change in the interference condition in the wall (see Figure 3-37).

Wall interference conditions will work in concert with any intelligent ADT AEC object.

Figure 3-35

Figure 3-36

Figure 3-37

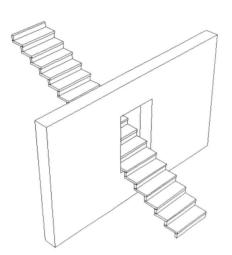

Hands-On

Cleanups – Apply 'T' Cleanup, and Wall Merge

1. Start a new drawing using the Architectural Building Model and View (Imperial - ctb) template.

2. Change to the **Model Layout**

3. Change to the **Top View**.

4. Place a Standard 6" wide 10'-0"-high, 10'-0"-long wall.

5. Select the walls, **RMB**, and select **Add Selected** from the contextual menu that appears.

6. Place another wall perpendicular to the first as shown in Figure 3-38.

7. Select the vertical wall segment, **RMB**, and select **Cleanups > Apply 'T' Cleanup** from the contextual menu that appears.

8. Select the horizontal wall to create the 'T' cleanup (see Figure 3-39).

9. Add another vertical wall adjacent to the vertical wall, make the adjacent wall 24" and overlapping it (see Figure 3-40).

10. Select the new wall segment, **RMB**, and select **Cleanups > Add Wall Merge Condition** from the contextual menu that appears.

11. Select the first walls and press **Enter**.

The wall is now merged into one wall, but the new segment can still be adjusted and moved separately (see Figure 3-41).

Figure 3-38

Figure 3-39

Figure 3-40

Figure 3-41

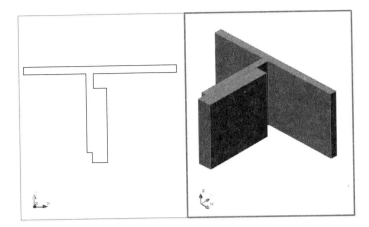

Hands-On

Editing Wall Styles

Base Height, Baseline, Edge, and **Floor** line concepts (see Figure 3-42)

In this exercise, you learn how to create a wall and foundation using the components shown in Figure 3-43.

Figure 3-42

Figure 3-43

Creating the wall style

1. Start a new drawing using the Architectural Building Model and View (Imperial - ctb) template.

2. Change to the **Model Layout**

3. Change to the **Top View**.

4. Select **Format > Style Manager** from the **Main** toolbar to bring up the **Style Manager** dialog box.

5. Open the **Architectural Objects** tree, select the **Wall Styles** icon, **RMB,** and select **New** from the contextual menu that appears.

6. In the right panel, rename the new style **TESTWALL** and deselect it.

7. Double-click on the icon next to the name **TESTWALL** to bring up the **Wall Styles Properties** dialog box.

8. Select the **Components** tab, and open the floating **Viewer** (see Figure 3-44).

Figure 3-44

Adding and Modifying Wall Components

On the **Component** tab, notice that the **Edge Offset** drop-down list reads BW* -1/2". This means that the edge offset is set to be half the width of the **Base Width** (BW). (BW refers to any wall having a parametric or user-enterable width.) I normally set the edge offset to the outer edge of the total wall (see Figure 3-45).

Figure 3-45

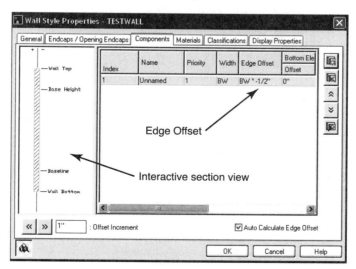

9. In the **Wall Style Properties** dialog box, click on the **Add Component** icon at the top right side of the **Components** tab, and add five components called **BRICK, CAVITY, BLOCK WALL, 14" BLOCK, FRAMING**, and **FOOTING**.

10. Set the settings for the components as shown in Figure 3-46.

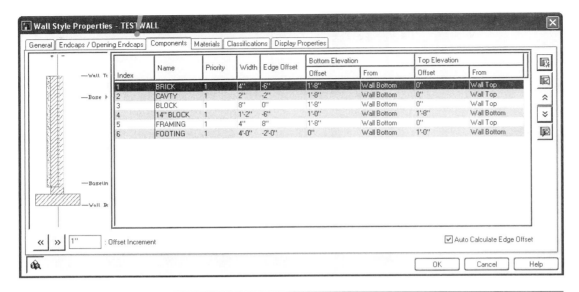

Figure 3-46

> **Note:** Set the settings one component at a time and observe the result in the inter-active viewer.

11. Change to the **Materials** tab.

12. Select the **Add New Material** icon to bring up the **New Material** dialog box.

13. Enter the name **BRICK SECTION**, and press the **OK** button to return to the **Materials** tab.

14. Activate the **BRICK** component, and select **BRICK SECTION** from the **Material Definition** drop-down list.

15. With the **BRICK** component still active, press the **Edit Material** icon to bring up the **Material Definition Properties** dialog box and activate its **Display Properties** tab (see Figure 3-47).

Figure 3-47

16. Activate the **General Medium Detail** display representation, check its **Style Override** check box, and press the **Edit Display Properties** icon to bring up the **Display Properties** dialog box.

17. Select the **Hatching** tab.

18. Activate the **Surface Hatch** display component, select the **Hatch** icon in the **Pattern** column, and select **AR-B816C** pattern (predefined type).

19. Set the Scale/Spacing to 1″ and Angle to 0.00.

20. Activate the **Layer/Color/Linetype** tab and turn the **Surface Hatch** to **Visible**.

21. Press the **OK** buttons to return to the **Wall Style Properties** dialog box.

22. Repeat the process for all the other components creating the following materials for **BLOCK**, **FRAMING**, and **FOOTING** respectively (see Figures 3-48 through 3-50).

23. Select the **Design** palette, and select the Wall icon. Drag the cursor across to the **Properties** palette. Pick the Style drop-down list to select the new **Test Wall** style. Return to the drawing editor to draw the wall.

You have now created a new wall style. Place a wall with this new style (see Figure 3-51).

Figure 3-48

Figure 3-49

Figure 3-50

Figure 3-51

Windows

When you finish this section, you should understand the following:

✔ How to place a Window object using Reference.

✔ How to place a Window object using Offset/Center.

✔ How to Change Window Sizes with Grips.

✔ How to Add Profile.

✔ How to Move the window vertically, within the wall, and along the wall.

✔ How to edit Window Styles.

Window objects can be dragged or inserted either from the **Design** tool palette, by clicking **RMB** on a wall, or by typing **window add** on the **Command line**.

Windows can be placed directly into walls by right-clicking on the wall and selecting **Insert > Window** from the contextual menu, or by selecting from the **Windows** or **Design** tool palettes and pressing **Enter**.

Number	Name	Purpose
1	Style	Change this to change to another style such as Casement, etc.
2	Standard Sizes	Select from a list of preset sizes
3	Width	Change width of window
4	Height	Change height of window
5	Measure to	Width and height are set to inside or outside of window frame
6	Opening percent	Set amount that window is open in model and elevation view
7	Position along wall	Set to **Offset/Center** or **Unconstrained**; Offset/Center automatically offsets a set distance from the wall ends, or inserts at center of wall
8	Automatic offset	Set to amount of offset when position along wall is set to **Unconstrained**
9	Vertical alignment	Set to **Head** or **Sill**; this will govern on insert
10	Head height	Set elevation for top of window if **Vertical alignment** is set to **Head**
11	Sill height	Set elevation for bottom of window if **Vertical alignment** is set to **Sill**

Hands-On

Placing a Window Object Using Reference

1. Sart a new drawing using the Architectural Building Model and View (Imperial - ctb) template.
2. Change to the **Model Layout**.
3. Set the **Object Snap** to **End Point**.
4. Change to the **Top View**.
5. Place a standard wall 10'-0" long, 10'-0" high, and 6" thick. (See Walls section for information on how to place walls.)
6. Select the **Double Hung** icon from the **Windows** tool palette and drag your cursor over the **Properties** palette to open it.
7. Enter the following data:
   a. Style = **Double Hung**
   b. Width = **3'-0"**
   c. Height = **5'-0"**
   d. Measure to = **Outside of Frame**
   e. Position along wall = **Unconstrained**
   f. Vertical alignment = **Head**
   g. Head height = **6'-8"**
8. Select the wall and enter **RE** (Reference point) in the **Command line**.
9. Select the left corner of the wall, move the cursor to the right (0°), and enter **3'** on the keyboard. Then press **Enter** to place the window 3'-0" from the left wall corner (Figure 4-1).

Figure 4-1

Hands-On

Placing a Window Object Using Offset/Center

1. Erase the window in the previous exercise.
2. Turn off all Object Snaps.
3. Select the **Double Hung** icon from the **Windows** tool palette and drag your cursor over the **Properties** palette to open it.
4. Enter the following data:
   a. Style = **Double Hung**
   b. Width = **3'-0"**
   c. Height = **5'-0"**

    d. Measure to = **Outside of Frame**

    e. Position along wall = **Offset/Center**

    f. Automatic Offset = **6"**

    g. Vertical alignment = **Head**

    h. Head height = **6'-8"**

5. Select the wall near the left end of the wall, click the mouse, and press **Enter** to complete the command and place the window.

The Window will be placed 6" from the left end of the wall (see Figure 4-2).

Figure 4-2

Note: By pressing the tab key you can cycle the 6" dimension, and enter an overriding dimension.

6. Again, select the **Double Hung** icon from the **Windows** tool palette and drag your cursor over the **Properties** palette to open it.

7. Select the wall near the center of the distance left between the previous window placement and the right-hand wall end. Click the mouse, and press **Enter** to complete the command and place the window.

The Window will be placed at the center of the distance between the second window and the right end of the wall (see Figure 4-3).

Figure 4-3

Hands-On

Changing Window Size with Grips

1. Select a window to activate its grips, and drag to the right (0°). If the window has sizes listed in its **Window Styles Properties > Standard Sizes**, it will snap at gray lines in plan. These are sizes listed in the aforementioned **Properties** (see Figure 4-4).

Figure 4-4

Hands-On

Adding a Profile

1. Erase the previous exercise.

2. Place a Standard wall 15'-0" long, 10'-0" high, and 6" thick.

3. Select the **Pivot Horizontal** icon from the **Windows** tool palette and drag your cursor over the **Properties** palette to open it.

4. Enter the following data:
   a. Style = **Pivot Horizontal**
   b. Width = **5'-0"**
   c. Height = **4'-0"**
   d. Measure to = **Outside of Frame**
   e. Position along wall = **Unconstrained**
   f. Vertical alignment = **Head**
   g. Head height = **6'-8"**

5. Place the window 2'-0" from the left edge of the wall.

6. Change to the **Front View**.

7. Place a closed Polyline as shown in Figure 4-5.

8. Select the window, **RMB**, and select **Add Profile** from the contextual menu that appears to bring up the **Add Window Profile** dialog box.

9. Select **Start from scratch** from the **Profile Definition** drop-down list, enter **TEST PIVOT WINDOW** in the **New Profile Name** data field, and press **Enter**.

A blue hatch field will appear on the window.

Figure 4-5

10. **RMB** on the blue hatch field and select **Replace Ring** from the conceptual menu that appears.

11. Select the closed polyline that you created in Step 7 of this exercise.

12. Enter **Y** (Yes) in the **Command line**, and press **Enter** to complete the command.

13. **RMB** on the blue hatch field and select **Save Changes** from the conceptual menu that appears (see Figure 4-6).

14. Mirror the window in the **Front View** (see Figure 4-7).

Figure 4-6

Figure 4-7

New Autodesk Architectural Desktop 2005 Feature

15. Delete the window you created in the previous exercise from the wall.

16. Select the **Double Hung** icon window from the **Windows** tool palette, and place a 5'-high by 3'-wide window constrained to the center of the wall (see Figure 4-8).

17. Select the window, **RMB**, and select **Add Profile** from the contextual menu that appears to bring up the **Add Window Profile** dialog box.

Figure 4-8

18. At the **Add Window** dialog box, select **Start from scratch** from the **Profile Definition** drop-down list, enter **Curved Top window** in the **New Profile Name** data field, and press the **Enter** key.

As with the editing of the previous window, a blue hatch field will appear on the window.

19. Click on the **Edge** grip, at the top enter of the window and drag upwards (see Figure 4-9).

Figure 4-9

20. Press the **Ctrl** key on your keyboard twice, and click the mouse key.

21. Press the **Save All Changes** icon in the on-screen **In-Place Edit** dialog box.

You have now created a double hung window with a curved top (see Figure 4-10).

22. Select **Format > Style Manager** from the **Main** menu.

23. Expand the multi-purpose Objects folder.

Figure 4-10

24. Expand Profiles.

25. Double click on **Curved Top window** to bring up the **Profile Definitions Properties** dialog box (see Figure 4-11).

Notice that the window profile you created in-place is now in your Style Manager.

Figure 4-11

Hands-On

Modifying Window Height

1. Use the previous exercise.
2. Change to the **Front View**.
3. Select the window to activate its grips.
4. Pick and move the square grip at the bottom of the window; a yellow dialog field appears (see Figure 4-12).

Figure 4-12

5. Press the **Ctrl** key until the dialog field reads **Move Vertically**.
6. Press the **Tab** key until the data field turns magenta in color.
7. Enter **3'-0"** in the **Command line** and press **Enter**.

The window will move vertically and be 3'-6" above the wall baseline.

8. Activate the square grip at the bottom of the window again.
9. Press the **Ctrl** key until the dialog field reads **Move Along**.
10. Enter **3'-0"** in the **Command line** and press **Enter**.

The window will move horizontally 3'-0" in the direction that the grip was moved.

11. Change to the **Top View**.
12. Activate the square grip at the center of the window.
13. Press the **Ctrl** key unril rhw dialog field reads **Move Within**.
14. Move the grip vertically.
15. Enter **2"** in the **Command line** and press **Enter**.

The window will move vertically within the wall 2" in the direction the grip was moved. Save this file.

Hands-On

Editing Window Styles

1. Use the previous exercise.
2. Change to the **Front View**.
3. Select the window, **RMB**, and select **Edit Window Style** from the contextual menu that appears to bring up the **Window Style Properties** dialog box.
4. Select the **Dimensions** tab.

This is where you set the **Frame Width** and **Depth**. Check the **Auto-Adjust** check box if you want the frame depth to match the wall in which it has been inserted.

The **Sash Width** and **Depth** plus the **Glass Thickness** are also located in the **Dimensions** tab.

5. Select the **Floating Viewer** icon at the lower left corner of the **Window Style Properties** dialog box to bring up the **Viewer**.
6. In the **Viewer**, select the **Gouraud Shaded** icon in the top **Viewer** toolbar (see Figure 4-13).

Figure 4-13

7. Enter the following data in the entry fields:
   a. Frame Width = **1"**
   b. Frame Depth = **12"**
   c. Sash Width = **4"**
   d. Sash Depth = **4"**

Press **Enter** after entering the last data field, and note the change in window in the **Viewer** (see Figure 4-14).

Figure 4-14

8. Reset the data fields to the following:
   a. Frame Width = **2"**
   b. Frame Depth = **5"**
   c. Sash Width = **1"**
   d. Sash Depth = **2"**

9. Select the **Design Rules** tab.

10. Select the **Predefined** radio button; select **Round** from the **Predefined** drop-down list, and **Awning-Transom** from the **Window Type** drop-down list.

Note the change in window in the **Viewer** (see Figure 4-15).

11. Select the **Use Profile** radio button, and select **TEST PIVOT WINDOW** from its drop-down list (**TEST PIVOT WINDOW** was the profile created in Step 9 of "Adding a Profile" in this section).

Note the change in window in the **Viewer** (see Figure 4-16).

12. Change to the **Standard Sizes** tab.

Figure 4-15

Figure 4-16

The **Standard Sizes** tab is where standardized windows are entered. These sizes allow you to change windows interactively as shown in the following exercise.

13. Press **OK** to close the **Window Style Properties** dialog box.

14. Change to the **Top View**.

15. Double-click on the window to bring up its **Properties** palette.

16. Set the style to **Double Hung**, and allow the palette to close.

17. Select the window's right arrow grip, and drag it to the right.

You will see a yellow dialog field explaining the gray and red marks that appear above the window. These marks are "snap" points corresponding to the preset width sizes set in the **Standard Sizes** tab of the **Window Style Properties** dialog box (see Figure 4-17).

Figure 4-17

18. **RMB** on the window again and select **Edit Window Style** from the contextual menu that appears.

19. Change to the **Materials** tab.

20. Activate the **Frame** field, and click on the **Material Definition** dropdown list (see Figure 4-18).

Four preset materials are shipped with the program. If you need more materials, you need to add and edit a new material.

21. To add and edit a new material, press the **Add New Material** icon at the right side of the materials tab.

22. Enter a new name for the new material in the **New Material** data field that appears, and press **OK**.

23. Activate the **New Material** field in the **Material Definition** column, and select the **Edit Material** icon above the **Add Material** icon to bring up the **Material Definition Properties** dialog box.

Figure 4-18

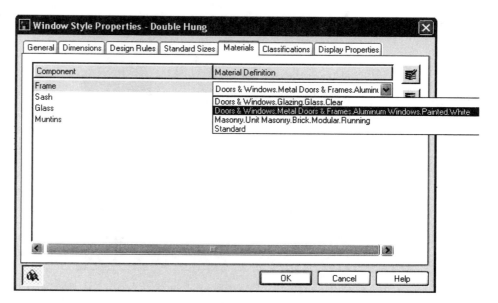

24. Check the **Style Override** check box for the **General Medium Detail** display representation to open the **Display Properties** dialog box.

25. Select the **Other** tab (see Figure 4-19).

Figure 4-19

In the **Other** tab you can control the placement of hatches on surfaces, and Browse for materials made in the VIZ Render module (see Figure 4-20).

26. Press the **OK** buttons until you return to the **Window Style Properties** dialog box.

27. Change to the **Display Properties** tab.

28. Select the **Elevation** field.

29. Press the **Edit Display** icon at the upper right side of the **Display Properties** tab to bring up the **Display Properties** dialog box.

30. Select the **Muntins** tab.

31. Press the **Add** button to bring up the **Muntins Block** dialog box.

Figure 4-20

32. Select the **Prairie - 12 Lights** from the **Pattern** drop-down list, check the **Clean Up Joints** and **Convert to body** check boxes, and then press the OK buttons to close the command and view the window (see Figures 4-21 and 4-22).

Figure 4-21

Figure 4-22

Doors

When you finish this section, you should understand the following:

- ✔ How to place a door object using **Reference**.
- ✔ How to place a door object using **Offset/Center**.
- ✔ How to change door size and swing location with **Grips**.
- ✔ How to control the door swing angle.
- ✔ How to add a profile.
- ✔ How to add a door knob.
- ✔ How to move the door within the wall, and along the wall.
- ✔ How to edit door styles.
- ✔ How to use the **Materials** tab.

Wall objects can be dragged or inserted either from the **Design** tool palette, or by typing **dooradd** in the **Command line**.

Doors

In Autodesk Architectural Desktop 2005, door objects are totally customizable. All is possible in this program—from customizing the size and shape of the door or the size and shape of the jamb to including side lights, mullions, and/or a sill. As with other features of this program, a premade library of door styles greatly enhances productivity. Hopefully, manufacturers will jump on the ADT bandwagon and place their door styles on the Web. If they do this, you will be able to quickly **idrop** or update your catalogs with premade doors and door accessories. If this happens and the manufacturer makes changes, you will be able to update your catalogs and drawings automatically directly from the Internet.

Number	Name	Purpose
1	Layer	Change this to place the door on another layer
2	Style	Change this to change to another style such as **Double Doors**
3	Standard sizes	Select from a list of preset sizes in the door style dialog box
4	Width	Set custom width
5	Height	Set custom height
6	Measure to	Set width and height to measure inside of frame or outside of frame
7	Swing Angle	Set door swing opening 0° to 90°
8	Position along	**Unconstrained** (any placement) **Offset/Center** (set offset from ends of wall or midpoint of wall)
9	Automatic Offset	Set distance for off set from wall end if **Position along** set to **Offset/Center**
10	Vertical alignment	Set to head height or threshold governs
11	Head height	Head height above wall baseline if **Vertical Alignment** set to **Head**
12	Threshold height	Head height above wall baseline if **Vertical Alignment** set to **Threshold**

Doors can be placed directly into walls by right-clicking on the wall and selecting **Insert > Door** from the contextual menu, or by selecting from the **Doors** or **Design** tool palettes and pressing **Enter**.

Hands-On

Placing a Door Object Using Reference

1. Start a new drawing using the Architectural Building Model and View (Imperial - ctb) template.
2. Change to the **Model Layout**.
3. Change to the **Top View**.
4. Set the Object snap to **End Point**.
5. Place a Standard 10'-long, 10'-high wall.
6. Select any door from the **Doors** tool palette and drag your cursor over the **Properties** palette to open the palette.
7. Enter the following data:
   a. Style = **Standard**
   b. Width = **3'-0"**
   c. Height = **6'-8"**
   d. Measure to = **Outside of Frame**
   e. Swing angle = **90**
   f. Position along wall = **Unconstrained**
   g. Vertical alignment = **Head**
   h. Head height = **6'-8"**
   i. Threshold height = **0"**
8. Select the wall and enter **RE** (Reference point) in the **Command line**.
9. Select the left corner of the wall, move the cursor to the right (0°), and enter **5'** on the keyboard. Press **Enter** to place the door 5'-0" from the left wall corner (see Figure 5-1).

Figure 5-1

Hands-On

Placing a Door Object Using Offset/Center

1. Erase the door in the previous exercise.
2. Turn off all Object Snaps.
3. Select any door icon in the **Doors** tool palette and drag your cursor over the **Properties** palette to open it.
4. Enter the following data:
   a. Style = **Standard**
   b. Width = **3'-0"**
   c. Height = **6'-8"**
   d. Measure to = **Outside of Frame**
   e. Position along wall = **Offset/Center**
   f. Automatic Offset = **6"**
   g. Vertical alignment = **Head**
   h. Head height = **6'-8"**
   i. Threshold = **0**

5. Select the wall near the left end of the wall, click the mouse, and press **Enter** to complete the command and place the door.

The door will be placed 6" from the left end of the wall (see Figure 5-2).

! **Note:** By pressing the **Tab** key, you can cycle the 6" dimension and enter an overriding dimension.

Figure 5-2

Hands-On

Changing Door Size and Swing Location with Grips

1. Select the door to activate its grips and drag the green arrow on the right door edge to the right (0°). If the door has sizes listed in its **Door Styles Properties > Standard Sizes**, it will snap at gray lines in plan.
2. To add doors to the **Standard Sizes** menu, **RMB** on the door and select **Edit Door Style** from the contextual menu that appears to bring up the **Door Style Properties** dialog box.
3. Select the **Standard Sizes** tab.
4. Press the **Add** button to bring up the **Add Standard Size** dialog box (see Figure 5-3).

5. Add the four doors shown in Figure 5-4 to the **Standard Sizes** tab, and close the **Door Style Properties** dialog box by pressing the **OK** button.

6. Again, select the door to activate its grips and drag to the right (0°). The door will now snap to the sizes you added in the **Standard Sizes** tab (see Figure 5-5).

7. Select the arrow grip shown in Figure 5-6 to flip the door swing in different directions. Save this file.

Figure 5-3

Figure 5-4

Figure 5-5

Figure 5-6

Hands-On

Controlling the Door Swing Angle

1. Using the previous exercise, change to **SW Isometric view**.

Notice that although the swing shows open in **Top View** (Plan), the door swing is closed in the **SW Isometric (Model View)**. Architectural Desktop ships from the developer with the doors closed in **Model View** (see Figure 5-7).

Figure 5-7

2. Double-click the door to bring up its **Properties** palette.

3. Notice that the swing angle is 90.

4. Change the swing angle to **45**, and press **Enter**. Note that nothing happens in the isometric view (the plan view will change).

This is because there is a model override set at 0, which prevents the door's **Properties** palette from controlling the door swing angle. To allow control from the **Properties** palette do the following:

5. Select the door, **RMB**, and select **Edit Door Style** from the contextual menu that appears to bring up the **Door Style Properties** dialog box.

6. Select the **Display Properties** tab.

7. Double-click the **Model** field (don't check the style **Override** check box because that would only control the door selected, and not all the doors) to bring up the **Display Properties** dialog box.

8. Select the **Other** tab.

9. *Clear* the **Overide Open Percent** check box, and press the **OK** buttons until you return to the Drawing Editor (see Figure 5-8).

Figure 5-8

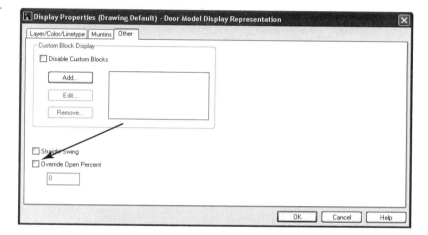

The **Override Open Percent** check box overrides the **Properties** palette. You can also change the door swing to a straight swing in the **Other** tab.

10. In the Drawing Editor, double-click the door again to bring up its **Properties** palette.

11. Change the swing angle to **90** and press **Enter**.

The door swing is open (see Figure 5-9).

Figure 5-9

Adding a Profile

1. Use the previous exercise.
2. Change to **Front View.**
3. Place the closed polylines shown in Figure 5-10 over the door.
4. Select the door, **RMB**, and select **Add Profile** from the contextual menu that appears to bring up the **Add Door Profile** dialog box.
5. Select **Start from scratch** from the **Profile Definition** drop-down list, enter **TEST PIVOT DOOR** in the **New Profile Name** data field, and press **Enter**.

A blue hatch field will appear on the door (see Figure 5-11).

Figure 5-10   Figure 5-11

6. **RMB** on the blue hatch field and select **Replace ring** from the conceptual menu that appears.
7. Select the closed polyline that you created in Step 3 of this exercise.
8. Enter **Y** (Yes) in the **Command line** and press **Enter**.
9. **RMB** again on the blue hatch field and select **Add ring** from the contextual menu that appears.
10. Select the 1'-0" circle that you created with the polyline in Step 3 of this exercise.
11. Again enter **Y** (Yes) in the **Command line**, and press **Enter** to complete the command.
12. Change to the **NE Isometric view** and select the **Hidden** icon from the **Shading** toolbar.
13. **RMB** on the blue hatch field and select **Save Changes** from the conceptual menu that appears (see Figure 5-12).

Save this exercise.

Figure 5-12

Hands-On

Adding a Door Knob

1. Use the previous exercise.
2. Draw the closed polyline shown in Figure 5-13.
3. Select **Door > Pulldowns > 3D Solids Pulldown** from the **Main** toolbar to place the **3D Solids** menu group on the **Main** toolbar.
4. Now, select **3D Solids > Revolve** from the **Main** toolbar and revolve 360° (see Figure 5-14).
5. Select **Mirror** to mirror the knob (see Figure 5-15).

Figure 5-13

Figure 5-14

Figure 5-15

6. Select **Format > Blocks > Block Definition** from the **Main** toolbar to bring up the **Block Definition** dialog box.

7. Create two blocks named **KNOB1** and **KNOB2**.

8. Select the door you created in the previous exercise, **RMB**, and select **Edit Door Style** from the contextual menu that appears to bring up the **Door Style Properties** dialog box.

9. Select the **Display Properties** tab.

10. Double-click on the **Elevation** field to bring up the next **Display Properties** dialog box.

11. Select the **Other** tab.

12. Press the **Add** button to bring up the **Custom Block** dialog box (see Figure 5-16).

Figure 5-16

13. Select the **Select Block** button to bring up the **Select A Block** dialog box.

14. Select **KNOB1** and press the **OK** button.

15. Use the settings shown in Figure 5-17 to move KNOB1 into position in the **Front View**, and then press the **OK** button to return to the **Display Properties** dialog box > **Other** tab.

16. Select the **Add** button to again bring up the **Custom Block** dialog box.

17. Press the **Select Block** button, this time select **KNOB 2**, and press **OK** to return to the **Custom Block** dialog box.

18. Use the same settings for KNOB2 that you used for KNOB1, and press the **OK** buttons until you return to the Drawing Editor (see Figure 5-18).

Save this file.

Figure 5-17

Figure 5-18

Hands-On

Moving the Door Vertically, Within the Wall, and Along the Wall

1. Use the previous exercise

2. Change to the **Front View**.

3. Select the door to activate its grips.

4. Activate the square grip at the bottom of the door—a yellow dialog field appears (see Figure 5-19).

5. Activate the square grip at the bottom of the door.

6. Drag the grip to the right until the yellow dialog field appears.

7. Enter **3'-0"** in the **Command line** and press **Enter**.

The door will move horizontally 3'-0" in the direction that the grip was moved.

Figure 5-19

Location
Press Ctrl to cycle between:
- Move along
- Move within
- Move vertically

8. Enter **3'-0"** in the **Command line** and press **Enter**.

9. Change to the **Top View**.

10. Activate the square grip at the center of the door.

11. Press the **Ctrl** key once until the dialog field reads **Perpendicular move within width**.

12. Move the grip vertically.

13. Enter **2"** in the **Command line** and press **Enter**.

The door will move vertically within the wall 2" in the direction that the grip was moved.

Save this file.

Hands-On

Editing Door Styles

1. Use the precious exercise.

2. Change to the **Front View**.

3. Select the door, **RMB,** and select **Edit Door Style** from the contextual menu that appears to bring up the **Door Style Properties** dialog box.

4. Select the **Dimensions** tab.

This is where you set the **Frame Width** and **Depth**. Please note the **Auto-Adjust** check box; check this if you want the frame depth to match the wall in which the door has been inserted.

The **Stop Width** and **Depth** plus the **Door Thickness** and **Glass Thickness** are also located in the **Dimensions** tab.

5. Select the **Floating Viewer** icon at the lower left corner of the **Door Style Properties** dialog box to bring up the **Viewer**.

6. Select the **Hidden Shaded** icon in the top **Viewer** toolbar (see Figure 5-20).

7. Enter the following data in the entry fields:

    a. Frame Width =**3"**

    b. Frame Depth =**6"**

    c. Stop Width = **1"**

    d. Stop Depth = **1"**

Press **Enter** after entering the last data field, and notice the change in door in the Viewer (see Figure 5-21).

Figure 5-20

Figure 5-21

Hands-On

Using the Materials Tab

1. Select the door in the previous exercise, **RMB**, and select **Edit Door Style** from the contextual menu.

2. Change to the **Materials** tab.

3. In the **Materials** tab, activate the **Frame** field and click on the **Material Definition** drop-down list (see Figure 5-22).

There are four preset materials that are shipped with the program. If you need more materials, you need to add and edit a new material.

Figure 5-22

4. To add and edit a new material, press the **Add New Material** icon at the right side of the **Materials** tab.

5. Enter a new name for the new material in the **New Material** data field that appears and press the **OK** button.

6. Activate the **New Material** field in the **Material Definition** column, and select the **Edit Material** icon above the **Add Material** icon to bring up the **Material Definition Properties** dialog box.

Figure 5-23

7. Check the **Style Override** check box for the **General Medium Detail** display representation to open the **Display Properties** dialog box.

8. Select the **Other** tab (see Figure 5-23).

In the **Other** tab, you can control the placement of hatches on surfaces, and browse for materials made in the VIZ Render module.

9. Press the **OK** buttons until you return to the **Door Style Properties** dialog box.

10. Change to the **Display Properties** tab.

11. Select the **Elevation** field.

12. Press the **Edit Display** icon at the upper right side of the **Display Properties** tab to bring up the **Display Properties** dialog box.

13. Select the **Muntins** tab.

14. Press the **Add** button to bring up the **Muntins Block** dialog box.

15. Select the **Prairie – 12 Lights** from the **Pattern** drop-down list, check the **Clean Up Joints** and **Convert to body** check boxes, and then press the **OK** buttons to close the command and view the door (see Figures 5-24 and 5-26).

Figure 5-24

Figure 5-25

Hands-On

New Autodesk Architectural Desktop Feature

Using In-Place Edit

1. Start a new drawing using the AEC Model (Imperial - ctb) template.
2. Change to the **Model Layout.**
3. Change to **Top View**
4. Place a Standard 10'-long, 10'-high wall.
5. Place a Standard 3'-wide x 7'-high door constrained to the center of the wall.
6. Change to the **NW Isometric View**.

Figure 5-27

7. Select the door, **RMB**, and select **Add Profile** from the contextual menu that appears to bring up the **Add Door Profile** dialog box.
8. Select **Start from scratch** from the **Profile Definition** drop-down list, enter **CURVED TOP door** in the **New Profile Name** data field, and press **Enter**.

As with the editing of the previous door, a blue hatch field will appear on the door.

9. Click on the top **Edge** grip and drag upwards (see Figure 5-27).
10. Press the **Ctrl** key on your keyboard twice and click the mouse key.
11. Press the **Save All Changes** icon in the **In-Place Edit** dialog box.

You have now created a double hung door with a curved top (see Figure 5-28).

12. Change to the **Front View**.
13. Select the door, **RMB**, and again select **Edit Profile In Place** from the contextual menu that appears.

The blue hatch fields will appear on the door again.

Figure 5-28

Figure 5-29

14. Click on the left hand edge grip, and press the **Ctrl** key to change to **Add vertex** mode.

15. Move vertically downward and click the mouse button to add a new edge grip and vertex (see Figure 5-29).

16. Select the new edge grip, drag to the right, and click the mouse button (see Figure 5-30).

17. Press the **Save All Changes** icon in the **In-Place Edit** dialog box.

18. Select **Format > Style Manager** from the **Main** menu.

19. Expand the multipurpose **Objects** folder.

20. Expand **Profiles**.

21. Double-click on **CURVED TOP DOOR** to bring up the **Profile Definitions Properties** dialog box.

Notice that the door profile you created in place is now your in your Style Manager (see Figure 5-31).

Figure 5-30

Figure 5-31

Curtain Walls

When you finish this section, you should understand the following:

✔ How to create a **Curtain Walls** tool palette.
✔ How to place a curtain wall.
✔ How to set miter angles.
✔ How to use the **Roof Line/Floor Line** command.
✔ How to apply tool properties to a layout grid.
✔ How to apply tool properties to an elevation sketch.
✔ How to edit a grid in place.
✔ How to edit curtain wall styles.

Wall objects can be dragged or inserted from the Design tool palette or by typing **curtainwall add** in the **Command line**.

Curtain wall objects can serve many purposes in Autodesk Architectural Desktop 2005. Originally created to represent storefront and nonbearing perimeter walls, curtain wall objects can be modified easily to represent many different kinds of walls. Their unique feature is their modifiable grid that can contain 3D solids, AEC polygons, and door and window assemblies. Curtain wall objects can even be modified to represent roof and floor trusses, with the curtain wall's parametrically changeable frames representing the truss members.

Besides being created from direct numerical input, **curtain wall objects** can be generated from **layout grids** and elevation **sketches.**

Once created, the resultant curtain wall styles can be applied to existing walls (the curtain wall object will replace the wall) or applied to a **reference base curve** (the curtain wall will use a curve on the ground plane as a basis for its shape in **Plan View**).

Number	Name	Purpose
1	Style	Select from available curtain wall styles
2	Segment type	Choose **Line** or **Arc** for a linear or curved wall, respectively
3	Base height	Get height of curtain wall
4	Length	Present length value of curtain wall object
5	Start Miter	Miter of curtain wall frame at corner, at start of wall (in degrees)
6	End Miter	Miter of curtain wall frame at corner, at start of wall (in degrees)
7	Roof line offset from base height	Any part of the curtain wall above the Base height such as parapet, gable end, etc.
8	Floor line offset from baseline	Any part of the curtain wall below the floor line
9	Rotation	Elevation of curtain wall base
10	Elevation	
11	Roof/Floor line	Vertex modifications for roof or floor line

Hands-On

Creating a Curtain Walls Tool Palette

1. Select the **Content Browser** icon from the **Navigation** toolbar to bring up the Catalog Library in the Content Browser (see Figure 6-1).

2. In the Catalog Library, double-click the **Design Tool Catalog - Imperial** catalog to open it (see Figure 6-2).

3. Double-click on the area shown in Figure 6-3 to open the pages with all the tool folders.

4. Change to **Page 2**, select the **Curtain wall** folder, open it, and drag all the curtain walls to a new tool palette labeled **Curtain Walls**.

Figure 6-1

Figure 6-2

Figure 6-3

Hands-On

Placing a Curtain Wall

1. Start a new drawing using the Architectural Building Model and View (Imperial - ctb) template.
2. Change to the **Model Layout**.
3. Change to the **Top View**.
4. Turn the **ORTHO** button on.
5. Click on the **Curtain Wall** icon on the **Design** tool palette and move your cursor over the **Properties** tool palette to open it.
6. Set the following parameters:
   a. Style = **Standard**
   b. Segment type = **Line**
   c. Base height = **10'-0"**
7. Click to set the curtain wall start point, drag your cursor to the right, enter **10'-0"** in the **Command line**, and press **Enter**.
8. Move your cursor vertically and again enter **10'-0"** in the **Command line**.
9. Press **Enter** twice to finish the command.

You have now created two joined sections of curtain wall.

Hands-On

Setting Miter Angles in the Contextual Menu and the Start and End Miters in the Curtain Wall Properties Toolbar

1. Press the **SE Isometric View** icon on the **Views** toolbar.
2. Press the **Flat Shaded** icon on the **Shading** toolbar to shade the curtain walls.
3. Select one of the segments of curtain wall and **RMB** to bring up the **Curtain Wall** contextual menu.
4. Select **Edit Object Display** to bring up the **Object Display** dialog box.
5. Select the Display Properties tab, select the **Model** display representation, and click the **Edit Display Properties** icon to bring up the **Display Properties** dialog box (see Figure 6-4).
6. Open the **Layer/Color/Linetype** tab, and turn the **Default Infill** light off. Press all the **OK** buttons in the dialog boxes to return to the Drawing Editor.

Notice that your curtain walls now have no glass (infill) showing.

7. Zoom close to the top corner joint between the two sections of curtain wall (see Figure 6-5).

Figure 6-4

Figure 6-5

8. Select a section of curtain wall, **RMB**, and select **Set Miter Angles** from the **Curtain Wall** contextual menu, select the other section of CurtainWall, (see Figure 6-6).

You have now mitered the corners of the curtain wall's frame.

Figure 6-6

If you select one of the curtain wall sections and double-click to bring up its **Properties** tool palette, you will see that its **Start Miter** or **End Miter** has been set. The vertical part of the frame can also be mitered, as we will see later.

9. Double-click each section of curtain wall separately to bring up its **Properties** tool palettes and check the **End Miter** for the left section, and the **Start Miter** for the right section.

The **End Miter** for the left section should now read **45**, and the **Start Miter** of the right curtain wall should read **315**.

10. Erase everything in the Drawing Editor.

11. Again, click on the **Curtain Wall** icon on the new **Curtain Walls** tool palette and move your cursor over the **Properties** tool palette to open it. This time, enter the **Start** and **End** miter values you got in the previous exercise.

12. Click to set the curtain wall start point, drag your cursor to the right, enter **10'-0"** in the **Command line**, and press **Enter**.

13. Move your cursor vertically, and again enter **10'-0"** in the **Command line**.

14. Enter **OR** (ORTHO) in the **Command line** and press **Enter**.

15. Drag your cursor to the left and click in response to the **Command line** "Point on wall in direction of close."

You have now created a four-wall enclosure with mitered corners (see Figure 6-7). Save this file.

Figure 6-7

Hands-On

Using the Roof Line/Floor Line Selections in the Contextual Menu

1. Using the walls from the previous exercise, select a wall, **RMB**, and select **Roof Line/Floor Line > Edit In Place** from the contextual menu that appears (see Figure 6-8).

When editing a curtain wall in place, an **In-Place Edit** toolbar will appear in the Drawing Editor, and blue shading will appear over the wall. This shading shape can be modified and saved back to the curtain wall (see Figure 6-9).

2. Select the blue shading, **RMB**, and select **Add Step** from the contextual menu that appears.

Figure 6-8

Figure 6-9

3. Select the floor line of the curtain wall. **The curtain wall steps** (see Figure 6-10). Repeat Step 2, this time picking **Add Gable** (see Figure 6-11).

4. Select the blue shading again, **RMB**, and select **Reverse** from the contextual menu that appears.

5. Select the floor line of the curtain wall.

The curtain wall step will reverse (see Figure 6-12).

Figure 6-10

Figure 6-11

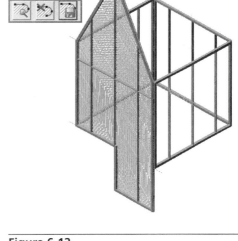

Figure 6-12

6. Select the **Left View** icon from the **Views** toolbar to change to the **Left View**.

7. Select the **Polyline** icon from the **Shapes** toolbar, and draw a polyline as shown in Figure 6-13. The polyline does not have to be in the same plane or touch the curtain wall.

8. Select the blue shading again, **RMB**, and select **Project to Polyline** from the contextual menu that appears.

9. Select the polyline that you just drew, enter **Y** for Yes in the **Command line**, and press **Enter**.

The curtain wall changes shape to match the polyline (see Figure 6-14).

10. Press the **Save All Changes** icon in the **In-Place Edit** toolbar to save the changes.

Save this file.

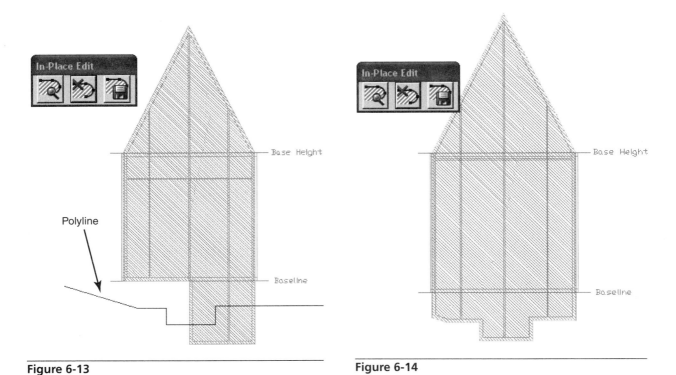

Figure 6-13

Figure 6-14

Hands-On

Applying Tool Properties to a Layout Grid

1. Start a new drawing using the Architectural Building Model and View (Imperial - ctb) template.

2. Change to the **Model Layout**.

3. Create two viewpoints, one showing **Top** View, and the other showing the **NW Isometric** View.

4. Press the **Content Browser** icon in the **Main** toolbar or enter **Ctrl + 4** on the keyboard to bring up the Content Browser.

5. In the Content Browser, select the **Autodesk Architectural Desktop Stock Tool Catalog** to open it.

6. Open the **Parametric Layout & Anchoring** folder.

7. Drag the **Layout Grid 2D** icon into the **Curtain Walls** tool palette you created, and then close the **Stock Tool Catalog**.

8. Select the **Layout Grid 2D** icon, and move your cursor over the **Properties** palette to open the palette.

9. Enter the following:
   a. Shape = **Rectangular**
   b. Boundary = ***NONE***
   c. Specify on screen = **No**
   d. X-Width = **30'-0"**

    e.   Y-Depth = **15'-0"**

    f.   (For X axis) Layout type = **Space evenly**

    g.   Number of bays = **6**

    h.   (For Y axis) Layout type = **Space evenly**

    i.   Number of bays = **3**

10. Place the grid in the **Top View** viewport, and press the Enter key twice to complete the command (see Figure 6-15).

Figure 6-15

11. Select the layout grid, **RMB**, and select **X-Axis > Layout Mode** from the contextual menu that appears.

12. Enter **M** (Manual) in the **Command line**, and press **Enter**.

13. Select the layout grid again, and move some of the grips in the X direction to change the layout (see Figure 6-16).

14. **RMB** on the **Layout Square Grid 5'x 5'** icon and select **Apply Tool Properties to > Layout Grid** from the contextual menu that appears.

15. Select the layout grid, enter **Y** (Yes) in the **Command line**, and press **Enter**.

16. Enter **V** (Vertical) in the **Command line** (to make the verticals one piece and the horizontals segments) and press **Enter**.

Figure 6-16

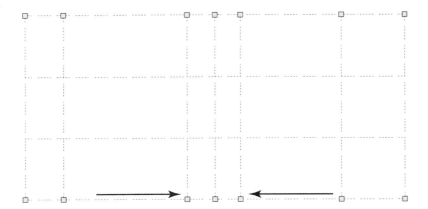

17. Give the curtain wall a new name in the **Curtain Wall Style Name** dialog box that appears and press **Enter** to create the new curtain wall (see Figure 6-17).

Save this exercise.

Figure 6-17

Hands-On

Applying Tool Properties to an Elevation Sketch

1. Start a new drawing using the Architectural Building Model and View (Imperial - ctb) template.

2. Change to the **Work Layout**.

3. Select the **Front View** and create the line drawing shown in Figure 6-18.

4. **RMB** on the **Square Grid 5'x 5' Curtain Wall** icon from the **Curtain Walls** tool palette you created to bring up its contextual menu.

5. Select **Apply Tool Properties to > Elevation Sketch** from the contextual menu.

6. Select the line drawing you made in Step 3 of this exercise, and press **Enter** twice.

7. Enter **Y** (Yes) in the **Command** line when asked to "Erase the Geometry," and press **Enter** to create the curtain wall.

Figure 6-18

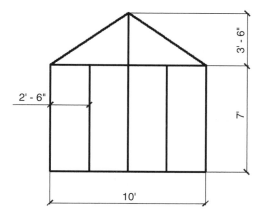

Your line work will now create a curtain (see Figure 6-19).

8. Select the new curtain wall, **RMB**, and select **Infill > Show Markers** from the contextual menu that appears.

The cell markers will now become visible (see Figure 6-20).

Figure 6-19

Figure 6-20

9. Select the new curtain wall again, **RMB**, and select **Infill > Merge** from the contextual menu that appears.

10. When the **Command line** reads, "Select cell A," select the leftmost cell marker, and press **Enter**.

11. When the **Command line** reads, "Select cell B," select the next cell marker, and press **Enter**.

The two curtain wall divisions merge into one cell.

12. Repeat Steps 8, 9, and 10 to merge the upper cell (see Figure 6-21).

13. Select the curtain wall again, **RMB**, and select **Infill > Override Assignment** from the contextual menu that appears.

14. Select the leftmost marker and press **Enter** to bring up the Infill **Assignment Override** dialog box.

15. Check the **Bottom** check box and press **OK** to remove the bottom frame (see Figure 6-22).

> **!** **Note:** For clarity, the author has removed the display of the window (infill) itself in these illustrations.

16. Select the curtain wall again, and select **Infill > Hide Markers** from the contextual menu that appears.

Figure 6-21

Figure 6-22

Hands-On

Editing a Grid in Place

1. Start a new drawing using the Architectural Building Model and View (Imperial - ctb) template.

2. Change to the **Model Layout**.

3. Change to the **Top View**.

4. Place a Square Grid 5'x 5' curtain wall 10' high and 15' long.

5. Change to the **Front View**.

6. Click on the curtain wall to activate its grips.

7. Click on the **Edit Grid** grip (see Figure 6-23).

8. Select the left edge of the grid to bring up the **In-Place Edit** toolbar.

9. **RMB** on the grid to bring up the contextual menu that appears, and select **Convert To Manual** (see Figure 6-24).

When you select **Convert To Manual**, + and – icons appear.

10. Select the + icon to add and move a horizontal mullion (see Figure 6-25).

11. Select the **Exit Editing Grid** icon to bring up the **Save Changes** dialog box, press the **New** button to bring up the **New Division Override** dialog box, enter **New Horizontal Mullion** in the **New Name** data field, and press **OK** to complete the command (see Figure 6-26).

12. Repeat this process picking a vertical mullion and creating a **New Vertical Mullion** (see Figure 6-27).

13. Change the view to **SW Isometric View** and select the **Gouraud** icon in the **Shading** toolbar (see Figure 6-28).

Save this file.

Figure 6-23

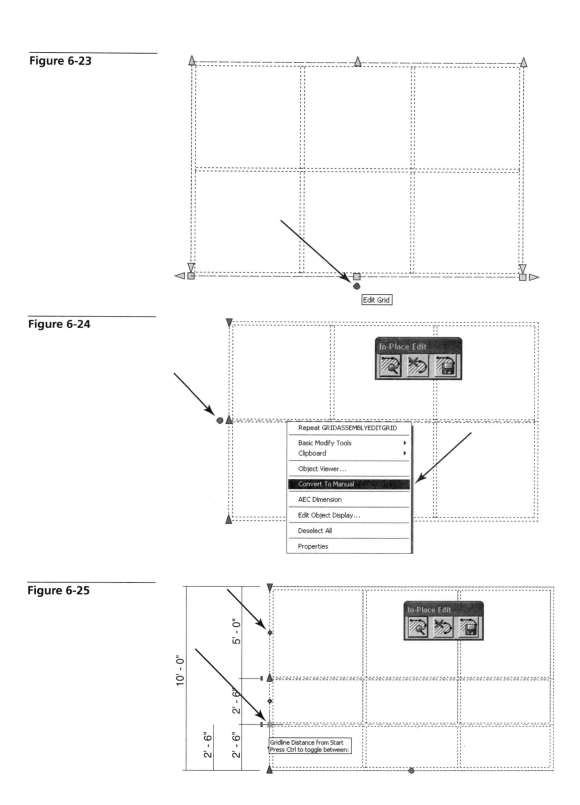

Figure 6-24

Figure 6-25

Figure 6-26

Figure 6-27

Figure 6-28

Hands-On

Editing Curtain Wall Styles

1. Use the previous exercise.

2. Select the curtain wall, **RMB**, and select **Edit Curtain Wall Style** from the contextual menu that appears to bring up the **Curtain Wall Style Properties** dialog box.

3. Select the **Design Rules** tab.

4. Select the **Floating Viewer** icon at the bottom left of the **Curtain Wall Style Properties** dialog box, and size it so that both the **Viewer** and the dialog box are open at the same time (see Figure 6-29).

5. Select the **Divisions** icon in the **Element Definitions** tree (see Figure 6-30).

Note the divisions made and saved in the previous exercise and the **New Division** icon for creating divisions in this dialog box.

6. Select the **Horizontal Division** in the tree and select **New Horizontal Mullion** from the **Division Assignment** drop-down list shown in Figure 6-31.

7. Select **Vertical Division** from the tree and select **New Vertical Mullion** from its **Division Assignment** drop-down list.

We will need a pivot window for this next part of the exercise so use the Content Browser to drag a pivot window style into your drawing. To do this: Exit the "Style" dialog box, select the "Content" Browser select **Design Tool Catalog–Imperial**. Select **Doors and Windows**, and then select the Windows folder. From the Windows folder, drag the **Pivot–Horizontal** window onto one of your palettes. Place a Pivot in some spare wall so that the style and properties of a pivot window are available to you.

Figure 6-29

Figure 6-30

8. Select **Infills** from the tree, select the **New Infill** icon, name the new infill **Pivot Window**, select **Style** from the **Infill Type** drop-down list, and pick the **Pivot - Horizontal** style from the **Style** list (see Figure 6-32).

Figure 6-31

Figure 6-32

Select the "Boxed +" symbol next to the "Horizontal Divisions" in the tree menu. This will drop down the **Vertifical Division** tree.

9. Select **Vertical Division** from the tree, select the **New Cell Assignment** icon to create a new cell assignment, select **Pivot Window** from the **New Cell Assignment Element** drop-down list, and select **End** from the **Used In** drop-down list (see Figure 6-33).

10. Press the **OK** buttons to complete the command and return to the Drawing Editor.

Figure 6-33

11. Select a pivot window that you just installed in the curtain wall, **RMB**, and select **Edit Object Display** from the contextual menu that appears to bring up the **Object Display** dialog box.

12. Make sure the **Model** field is selected, select the **Display Properties** tab, and press the **Edit Display Properties** icon at the upper right to bring up the **Display properties** dialog box.

Figure 6-34

13. Select the **Other** tab.

14. Set the **Override Open Percent** to **30**, and press the **OK** buttons in all the dialog boxes to return to the Drawing Editor (see Figure 6-34).

Door and Window Assemblies

When you finish this section, you should understand the following:

- ✔ How to create a **Primary Grid** for a Door/Window Assembly.
- ✔ How to create a door style for double doors.
- ✔ How to assign doors to a Door/Window Assembly infill.
- ✔ How to test the partially complete Door/Window Assembly.
- ✔ How to add sidelites.
- ✔ How to size the frame of a Door/Window Assembly.
- ✔ How to remove the sill of a Door/Window Assembly.
- ✔ How to use a Door/Window Assembly.

Door/window assemblies provide a grid or framework for the insertion of windows or doors that are commonly used in the design of storefront Windows. With this framework, you can create complex window or door assemblies for insertion in a wall or as repetitive elements of the curtain wall.

Window assemblies insert like doors and windows, and they are customized by using the same methods used to create curtain walls.

Hands-On

Creating a Primary Grid

1. Start a new drawing using the AEC Model (Imperial - ctb) template.

2. Change to the **Model Layout**.

3. Select **Format > Style Manager** from the **Main** menu to bring up the **Style Manager**.

4. Select **Architectural Objects > Door/Window Assembly Styles**.

5. Select the **Door/Window Assembly Styles** icon, **RMB**, and select **New** from the contextual menu that appears.

6. Name the new style **TEST DRWIN ASSEM STYLE**.

7. Double click on the **TEST DRWIN ASSEM STYLE** icon to bring up the **Door/Window Assembly Style Properties** dialog box.

8. Select the **Floating Viewer** icon and place the **Viewer** adjacent to the **Door/Window Assembly Style Properties** dialog box on the screen (see Figure 7-1).

Figure 7-1

9. Change to the **Design Rules** tab.

10. Select the **Divisions** icon and follow the directions in Figure 7-2.

11. Select the **Primary Grid** icon, and change its **Element** to the **DOUBLE DOORS DIVISION** that you just created (see Figure 7-3).

Figure 7-2

Figure 7-3

Hands-On

Creating a Door Style for Double Doors

1. Select the **Content Browser** icon to bring up the **Content Browser**.
2. Locate the **Architectural Desktop Design Tool Catalog – Imperial > Doors and Windows > Doors > Page 3** folder.
3. In the **Page 3** folder, locate the **Hinged-Single** door.
4. Drag the **Hinged-Single** door onto your **Design** toolbar. (This makes the door available as a door style in your drawing.)

Now you need a Double Door style using this door.

5. Select **Format > Style Manager** from the **Main** menu to bring up the **Style Manager**.
6. Locate the **Architectural Objects > Door Styles > Hinged-Single** icon.
7. Double-click on the **Hinged-Single** icon to bring up the **Door Styles Properties** dialog box.
8. Change to the **Dimensions** tab.
9. Set the **Frame A- Width** to 0".

This makes the door frameless.

10. In the **Door Styles Properties** dialog box, change to the **Design Rules** tab.
11. Select **Double** from the **Door Type** list, and press **OK** to return to the **Style Manager**.
12. Rename the door **DOUBLE HINGED SINGLE**, and then press the **Apply** and **OK** buttons to return to the Drawing Editor.

Hands-On

Assigning Doors to a Door/Window Assembly Infill

1. Select the **Infills** icon and follow the directions in Figure 7-4.
2. After creating the **DOUBLE DOORS** infill, press the **Primary Grid** icon again, and follow the directions in Figure 7-5.
3. Click on the **New Nested Grid** icon below the **Primary Grid** icon and follow the directions in Figure 7-6.
4. Press **OK** to return to the Drawing Editor.

Figure 7-4

Figure 7-5

Figure 7-6

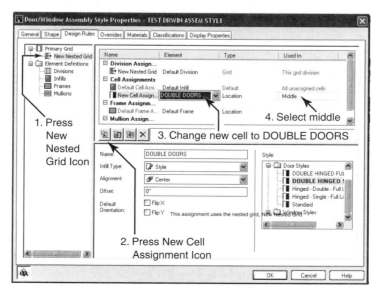

Hands-On

Testing the Partially Complete Door/Window Assembly

1. Select the **Door/Window Assembly** icon from the **Design** menu, and move your cursor over the **Properties** palette to open it.
2. Select **TEST DRWIN ASSEM STYLE** from the **Style** drop-down list.
3. In the **Top View,** press **Enter**, and place the door/window assembly.
4. Change to **SW Isometric View** (see Figure 7-7).

Figure 7-7

Hands-On

Adding Sidelites

1. Select the door/window assembly frame you just placed in the Drawing Editor, **RMB**, and select **Edit Door/Window Assembly Style** from the contextual menu that appears to bring up the **Door/Window Assembly Style Properties** dialog box.
2. Select the **Design Rules** tab again.
3. Select the **Primary Grid** icon and follow the directions in Figure 7-8.
4. Select the **SIDELITE GRID** icon below the **Primary Grid** icon and follow the directions in Figure 7-9.
5. Select the **Infill** icon and create another infill called **BASE** with a panel thickness of 1'-0" (see Figure 7-10).
6. Select the **SIDELITE GRID** icon below the **Primary Grid** and follow the directions in Figure 7-11.

Figure 7-8

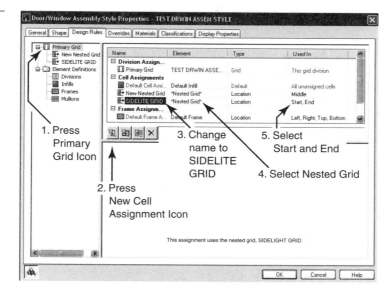

1. Press Primary Grid Icon

2. Press New Cell Assignment Icon

3. Change name to SIDELITE GRID

4. Select Nested Grid

5. Select Start and End

Figure 7-9

1. Press SIDELITE Icon

2. Select Fixed Number of cells drop down

3. Set Number of cells to 3

Figure 7-10

Figure 7-11

Hands-On

Sizing the Frame of a Door/Window Assembly

1. Click on the **Frames** icon, change the **Width** to 2" and the **Depth** to 6", and press **OK** to return to the Drawing Editor (see Figure 7-12).

Figure 7-12

Hands-On

Removing the Sill of a Door/Window Assembly and Changing the Sidelite

1. Select the door/window assembly frame, **RMB**, and select **Infill > Show Markers** from the contextual menu that appears (see Figure 7-13).

Cell Markers

Figure 7-13   **Figure 7-14**

2. Select the frame again, **RMB**, and select **Infill > Override Assignment** from the contextual menu that appears.
3. Select the cell marker in the center of the door opening, and press **Enter** to bring up the **Infill Assignment Override** dialog box.
4. Check the **Frame Removal - Bottom** check box (see Figure 7-14).
5. Press **OK** to remove the sill and return to the Drawing Editor.
6. Select the frame again, **RMB**, and select **Infill > Merge** from the contextual menu that appears.
7. Select the top two cells in each sidelite to merge the top cells.
8. Select the frame again, **RMB**, and select **Infill > Hide Markers** from the contextual menu that appears.

You now have created a new custom door/window assembly. Save this file.

Hands-On

Using the New Custom Door/Window Assembly

1. Use the previous file.
2. Change to the **Top View**.
3. Select the **Wall** icon from the **Design** tool palette, and place a 20'-0"-long Standard wall 8" thick and 10'-0" high.
4. Select the **Door/Window Assembly icon** from the **Design** tool palette.
5. Move your cursor over the **Properties** palette to open it.
6. Select the following:
   a. Style = **TEST DRWIN ASSEM STYLE**
   b. Position along the wall = **Offset/Center**
   c. Vertical alignment = **Sill**
   d. Sill Height = **0"**
7. Click on the wall to place the assembly (see Figure 7-15).

Figure 7-15

Section 8

Stairs

When you finish this section, you should understand the following:

- ✔ How to set **AEC Object Settings**.
- ✔ How to make a **Stairs** tool palette.
- ✔ How to place a stair object.
- ✔ How to modify a stair with stair grips.
- ✔ How to change an AEC stair object style.
- ✔ How add a stair rail object.
- ✔ How to edit a stair style.
- ✔ How to place a multi-landing stair.
- ✔ Interference conditions for stairs.
- ✔ How to anchor a second stair to an existing landing.
- ✔ How to project a stair edge to a polyline.
- ✔ How to project a stair edge to a wall or AEC object.
- ✔ How to generate a polyline from a stair object.
- ✔ How to create a stair tower.

Stair objects can be dragged or inserted either from the **Design** tool palette or by typing **stair add** in the **Command line**.

Stairs are an important part of almost every project, and it is here that designers often make mistakes. Autodesk Architectural Desktop 2005's stair and railing systems aid in the productivity and accuracy of these objects. Because of the complexity and variance of stairs, there is a multitude of settings. Once understood and preset, placing and modifying stairs is quite easy.

In Autodesk Architectural Desktop 2005, much refinement has been done to the stair system. Stairs styles are controlled by three factors: style, shape, and turn type. The Content Browser contains eight different preset styles. They are standard, Cantilever, Concrete, Steel, Half Wall Rail, Ramp Concrete, Ramp Concrete-Curb, and Ramp-Steel. As with the other styles in this program, there are many controls available for the styles in the **Stair Styles** dialog box. By creating your own styles, stairs can be placed into a project quickly and efficiently.

175

Properties Palette

Number	Name	Purpose
1	Style	Select from available stair styles
2	Shape	U-shaped, Multi-landing, Spiral, Straight
3	Turn type	1/2 landing, 1/2 turn, 1/4 landing, 1/4 turn
4	Horizontal Orientation	Specifies the horizontal direction in which the tair turns for spiral or u-shaped: counterclockwise or clockwise
5	Vertical Orientation	Specified whether the stair goes up or down when its height is changed
6	Width	Width of stair
7	Height	Height of stair vertically
8	Justify	Right, Center, or Left insertion points
9	Terminate with	Terminate with Riser, Tread, or Landing
10	Calculation rules	Brings up Calculation Rules dialog box
11	Straight length	Length of stair set by Calculation Rules dialog box

Number	**Name**	**Purpose**
12	Riser count	Amount of risers calculated by stair calculation rules
13	Riser	Riser height calculated by stair calculation rules
14	Tread	Length of tread set by Calculation Rules dialog box
15	Rise/tread calculation	Calculation formula used by stair calculation rules
16	Rotation	Rotation of stair
17	Elevation	Starting elevation of stair
18	Alignment type	Alignment between stairs at landings
19	Alignment offset	Offset at alignment between stairs at landings
20	Extend alignment	Extend alignment on Upper or Lower stair flight
21	Uneven tread on	Uneven tread on Upper or Lower flight
22	Top offset	Floor surface depth above top riser or top treads depending on their setting
23	Top depth	Floor surface support depth above top riser or top treads depending on their setting
24	Bottom offset	Floor surface depth below first riser
25	Bottom depth	Floor surface support depth below first riser
26	Minimum Limit type	Riser or flight height minimums
27	Maximum Limit type	Riser or Flight height maximums
28	Headroom height	Used to control interference above the stair
29	Side clearance	Used to control interference at the sides of the stair
30	Components	Information on tread and riser thickness, nosing length, etc.
31	Landing extensions	Information on landings

Before beginning to use the stair object, AEC Object Settings must be set for the stairs.

Hands-On

Setting the AEC Object Settings for Stairs

1. Select **Format > Options** from the **Main** toolbar to bring up the **Options** dialog box.

2. Select the **AEC Object Settings** tab (see Figure 8-1).

3. In the **Stair Settings** area select **Flight & Landing Corners** from the **Node Osnap** drop-down list, and **Finished Floor to Floor** from the **Measure Stair Height** drop-down list (see Figure 8-2).

Figure 8-1

Figure 8-2

Hands-On

Making a New Stairs Tool Palette

1. Create a new tool palette, and name it **Stairs**.
2. Select the **Content Browser** icon from the **Main** toolbar to launch the Content Browser.
3. In the **Architectural Desktop Design Tool Catalog - Imperial**, locate the **Stairs** folder in the **Stairs and Railings** folder.
4. Drag all the stairs into the new tool palette you created.

Hands-On

Placing a Stair

1. Start a new drawing using the Architectural Building Model and View (Imperial - ctb) template.
2. Change to the **Model Layout**.
3. Change to **Top View**.
4. Select the **Stair** icon in the **Stairs** tool palette you created and drag your cursor over the **Properties** palette to open it.
5. Set the following:
    a. Shape = **U-shaped**
    b. Turn type = **1/2 landing**
    c. Horizontal Orientation = **Clockwise**
    d. Vertical Orientation = **Up**
    e. Width = **3'-0"**
    f. Height = **10"**
    g. Top offset = **0"**
    h. Top depth = **10"**
    i. Bottom offset = **0"**
    j. Bottom depth = **10"**
    k. Headroom height = **7'-0"**
    l. Side clearance = **0**
6. Click in the viewport and drag the stair to the right, enter 10' in the command line and press **Enter** twice to complete the command and create the stair (see Figure 8-3).

Figure 8-3

Hands-On

Modifying the Stair with the Stair Grips

1. Select the stair object to activate the stair. Select the **Edit Edges** button to activate the stair grips. Place and modify six stairs using Figures 8-4 through 8-9 as examples. After placing each stair, change to **SW Isometric View** to examine your stair. Save this DWG as **STAIR**.

Figure 8-4

Figure 8-5

Figure 8-6

Figure 8-7

Figure 8-8

Figure 8-9

Hands-On

Changing Stair Styles

1. Change to **SW Isometric View**.

2. In your new **Stairs** tool palette, **RMB** on the **Half Wall Rail** icon and select **Apply Tool Properties to Stair** from the contextual menu that appears.

3. Select your stair, and press **Enter** to complete the command.

4. **RMB** in an empty space in the Drawing Editor, and select **Object Viewer** from the contextual menu that appears.

5. Select the stair, and press **Enter** to open the **Object Viewer** with the stair.

6. Expand the **Object Viewer**, and select the **Perspective** and **Flat Shaded** icons to display the stair in perspective and color (see Figure 8-10).

7. Close the **Object Viewer** to return to the Drawing Editor.

8. Repeat this process with all the other stair styles in your Stairs tool palette. Save the file.

Figure 8-10

Hands-On

Adding a Stair Rail (modifying railings is explained in the next section, "Railings.")

1. Change your stair back to the Stair style by **RMB** and applying that style to your stair.

2. Select the stair, **RMB**, and select **Add Railing** from the contextual menu that appears.

3. Move your cursor over the closed **Properties** palette to open it.

4. Click on the *** Attached to** drop-down list, and select **Stair** flight (see Figure 8-11).

5. Select the lower corners of the lower stair flight to place a rail (see Figure 8-12).

Note: If you have difficulty placing the rails in 3D or if the rails don't appear, change to **Top View**, and place the rails in that view.

6. Remove the stair rails and repeat this using the **Stair** and **NONE** options in the **Properties** palette.

Note: The **NONE** option is for custom placing of a rail. This railing option is explained in the Railings section.

Figure 8-11

Figure 8-12

Hands-On

Editing a Stair Style (this can also be done through the Style Manager)

1. Select your stair, **RMB**, and select **Edit Stair Style** from the contextual menu that appears to bring up the **Stair Styles** dialog box.

2. Select the **Design Rules** tab. This is where the **Riser Heights**, **Tread Depth**, and the stair calculator, are located (see Figure 8-13).

3. Change to the Stringers tab. This is where the stair stringers are added, removed, and modified.

Figure 8-13

4. In the **Stringers** tab, press the **Add** button and create a left stringer with the following settings:

   a. **Housed** option from the **Type** drop-down list

   b. D - Total = **12"**

   c. F - Total = **12"**

   d. E - Waist = **6"**

   e. F - Total = **12"**

5. Press **OK** to return to the Drawing Editor and see the stair changes (see Figure 8-14).

Figure 8-14

6. Select the stair, **RMB** and open the **Stair Styles** dialog box again.

7. Select the **Components** tab. This is where modifications to the tread, riser, and landing thicknesses are controlled. This is also where tread nosing length and straight or sloping risers are controlled. (Sloping risers are typically used on steel and concrete stairs.)

8. Select the **Landing Extensions** tab. This is where modifications are made relating to the landings.

9. Select the **Materials** tab. This is where the materials for the stair are set.

10. Select the **Display Properties** tab. This is where modifications are made relating to the display of stair components in different views.

Hands-On

Placing a Multi-landing Stair

1. Start a new drawing.
2. Change to the **Top View**.
3. Select the **Stair icon** from your **Stairs** tool palette.
4. Drag your cursor over the **Properties** palette to open it.
5. Set the following:
   a. Shape = **Multi-landing**
   b. Turn type = **1/2 landing**
   c. Vertical Orientation = **Up**
   d. Width = **3'-0"**
   e. Height = **10'-0"**
   f. Top offset = **0"**
   g. Top depth =**10"**
   h. Bottom offset = **0"**
   i. Bottom depth = **10"**
   j. Headroom height = **7'-0"**
   k. Side clearance = **0**
7. Click in the viewport and drag the stair vertically (90°) until 7/18 appears to the left of the stair, and click again, this starts the landing.
8. Continue to move the cursor in the direction of 90°, enter **5'** in the **Command line**, and press **Enter**, this establishes the end of the landing.
9. Drag the cursor to the right (0°) until 18/18 appears above the stair, and click the mouse to complete the stair.
10. Change to **SW Isometric View** and press the **Flat Shaded** icon in the **Shading** toolbar (see Figure 8-15). Save this file.

Figure 8-15

Hands-On

Interference Conditions

1. Using the stair from the previous exercise, change to the **Top View**.
2. Place a 20'-high wall as shown in Figure 8-16.
3. Select the wall, **RMB**, and select **Interference Condition > Add** from the contextual menu that appears.
4. Select the lower stair flight, and press **Enter**.
5. Enter **S** (Subtractive) in the **Command line** and press **Enter** to complete the command.

The wall is cut by the stair (see Figure 8-17), and the interference distance above the stair is set in the stair properties under **Interference Headroom height** (see Figure 8-18).

Note: Stair interference conditions are also available for slabs.

Figure 8-16

Figure 8-17

Figure 8-18

Hands-On

Anchoring a Second Stair to an Existing Landing

1. Use the stair created in "Placing a Multi-landing Stair" hands-on exercise.
2. Change to the **Work Layout**.

3. Change to the **Top View**.

4. Create a new straight Standard stair with **Vertical Orientation** set to **Up** (see Figure 8-19).

5. Select the original stair, **RMB**, and select **Stair landing Anchor > Anchor to Landing** from the contextual menu that appears.

6. Select the second stair.

7. Select the first stair's landing to attach the second stair to the landing.

8. Once attached, you can change to the **Top View** and move the second stair into a desired location (see Figure 8-20).

Figure 8-19

Figure 8-20

Hands-On

Projecting a Stair Edge to a Polyline

1. Start a new drawing using the Architectural Building Model and View (Imperial - ctb) template.

2. Change to the **Model Layout**.

3. Change to **Top View**.

4. Select the **Polyline** icon from the **Draw** toolbar and draw the shape shown in Figure 8-21.

5. Select the **Stair** icon from the **Stairs** tool palette and add a U-shaped stair 8' high inside the polyline as shown in Figure 8-22.

Figure 8-21

Figure 8-22

6. Select the stair, **RMB**, and select **Customize Edge > Project** from the contextual menu that appears.

7. In the **Top View** select the front of the stair landing, select the curved part of the polyline, and then press **Enter** to project the landing (see Figure 8-23).

Figure 8-23

Hands-On

Projecting a Stair Edge to a Wall or AEC Object

1. Using the previous exercise, select the polyline to activate its grips.
2. Select an end grip, and modify the polyline as shown in Figure 8-24.

Figure 8-24

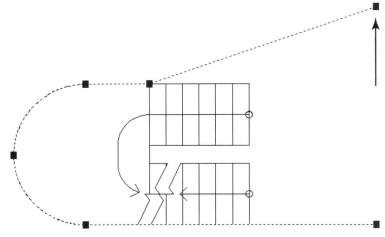

3. Select the **Wall** icon from the **Design** tool palette, **RMB**, and select **Apply Tool properties to > Linework**.
4. Select the polyline and press **Enter**.
5. Enter **Y** (Yes) in the **Command line**, and press **Enter** to create the wall.
6. While the wall is still selected, move your cursor over the **Properties** palette to open it.
7. Set the following:
    a. Style = **CMU-8 Rigid-1.5 Air-2 Brick-4**
    b. Base height = **8'-0"**
    c. Justify = **Left**

> **Note:** If you don't have the **CMU-8 Rigid-1.5 Air-2 Brick-4** style in your **Walls** tool palette, you can find it in the **Architectural Desktop Design Tool Catalog - Imperial > Walls > CMU > Page 4**.

You now have a stair within a masonry enclosure (see Figure 8-25).

Figure 8-25

8. Select the stair, **RMB**, and select **Customize Edge > Project** from the contextual menu.

9. Select the right-hand edge of the stair run, select the wall opposite it, and then press **Enter** to complete the command.

The stair run projects itself to the wall (see Figure 8-26).

Figure 8-26

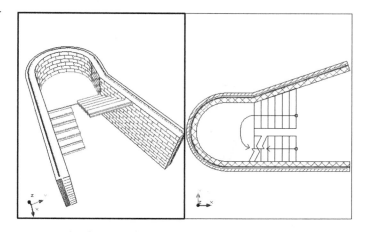

Hands-On

Generating a Polyline from a Stair Object

The Generate Polyline command is very useful when you have created a stair, and need a polyline to create walls, or to create an opening in a slab.

1. Use the previous exercise.

2. Erase the walls leaving just the stair.

3. Select the **Slab** icon from the **Design tool** palette, and place a Standard 6", Direct-mode, top-justified slab underneath the stair as shown in Figure 8-27.

Figure 8-27

4. Select the stair, **RMB**, and select **Customize Edge > Generate Polyline** from the contextual menu that appears.

5. Select the outer edge of the stair, repeat Step 4, and touch the inside of the lower stair run. Press **Enter** to complete the command, and then place a line at the inner edge of the stair run (see Figure 8-28).

Figure 8-28

6. Select the **Layers** icon from the **Object Properties** toolbar and **Freeze** the **Stair** layer (A-Flor-Strs) to hide the stair.

7. Using **Extend** and **Trim**, clean up the polylines created by the **Generate Polyline** option of **Customize Edges** in Steps 4 and 5.

8. Type **Pedit** in the **Command line** and create two polylines as shown in Figure 8-29.

Figure 8-29

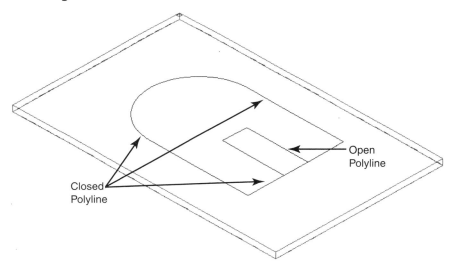

9. Select the slab object, **RMB**, and select **Hole > Add** from the contextual menu that appears.

10. Select the closed polyline, and press **Enter**.

11. Enter **Y** (Yes) in the **Command line** and press **Enter** to create the hole in the slab.

You have now made a hole in the slab exactly matching the stair through the use of the **Generate poly** option of the **Customizing Edge** command.

Finishing the Stairway

12. Un-freeze the stair layer to unhide the stair.

13. Select the **Wall** icon from the **Design** tool palette, **RMB**, and select **Apply Tool Properties to > Linework** from the contextual menu that appears.

14. Select the open polyline, enter **Y** (Yes) in the **Command line**, and press **Enter** to create a wall.

15. While the wall is still selected, move your cursor over the **Properties** palette to open it.

16. Set the following:
    a. Style = **Standard**
    b. Width = **6"**
    c. Base height = **8'-0"**
    d. Justify = **Left**

You have now created a stair, a slab, and walls (see Figure 8-30).

Figure 8-30

17. Select the **Railing** icon from the **Design** tool palette, and move your cursor over the **Properties** palette to open it.

18. Select the following:
    a. Style = **Standard**
    b. Attached to = **Stair**
    c. Side offset = **2"**
    d. Automatic placement = **Yes**

19. Select the stair to create the railing, then press **Enter** to complete the command.

Hands-On

Creating a Stair Tower

You create a stair tower from one stair, which is replicated on selected levels in the building. You can create a stair tower with all stair shapes except spiral. The floor-to-floor height and starting elevation of each stair are adjusted to match those for each selected level. The X,Y coordinates for each stair start point are fixed.

> **Note:** To create a stair tower, the stair must be in a construct with multiple levels.

1. Select **File > Project Browser** from the **Main** menu to bring up the **Project Browser** dialog box.

2. Select the **New Project** icon at the bottom left of the dialog box, and create a new project. Name the new project **STAIR TOWER TEST**, and press the OK button.

3. Press the **Close** button in the **Project Browser** dialog box to bring up the **Project Navigator** dialog box.

4. Select the **Edit Levels** icon in the **Levels** icon to bring up the **Levels** dialog box.

5. Press the **Add Level** icon five times to create five levels. Set the **Floor Elevations** and **Floor to Floor Heights** as shown in Figure 8-31, and press the **OK** button to return to the Drawing Editor.

6. In the **Project Navigator**, select the **Constructs** tab, **RMB** on the **Constructs** icon, and select **New > Construct** from the contextual menu that appears to bring up the **Add Construct** dialog box.

7. Enter **STAIR TOWER** in the **Name** field.

8. Check all check boxes in the **Division** column and press the **OK** button (see Figure 8 -32).

9. In the **Project Navigator**, select the **Constructs** tab and double-click on the **STAIR TOWER** construct you just created to open it in the Drawing Editor.

10. Place a Standard U-shaped stair with the following property settings:
    a. Shape = **U-shaped**
    b. Turn type =**1/2 landing**
    c. Horizontal Orientation = **Clockwise**
    d. Vertical Orientation = **Up**
    e. Width = **3'-0"**
    f. Height = **10'**
    g. Justify = **Outside**
    h. Top offset = **0"**
    i. Top depth = **10"**
    j. Bottom offset = **0"**
    k. Bottom depth =**10"**
    l. Headroom height = **7'-0"**
    m. Side clearance = **0"**

11. Make the overall width of the stair **7'-0"**.

Figure 8-31

Figure 8-32

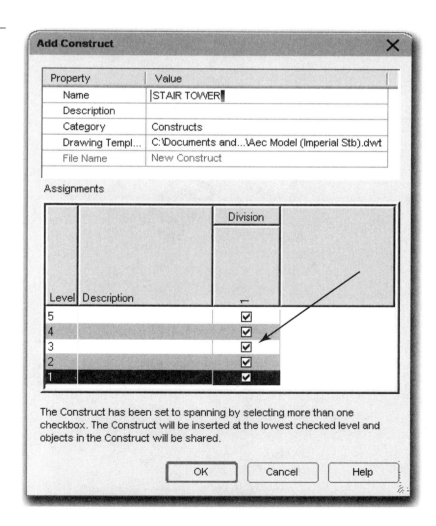

12. Place an 8' x 12' rectangle as shown in Figure 8-32.

13. In the **Design** tool palette, **RMB** on the **Slab** tool, and select **Apply tool properties to > Linework and Walls**.

14. Select the rectangle you just created and press **Enter**.

15. Enter **Y** (Yes) in the **Command line** and press **Enter**.

16. Enter **P** (Protected) in the **Command line** and press **Enter**.

17. Enter **10'** in the **Command line** and press **Enter**.

18. Enter **T** (Top) in the **Command line** and press **Enter** .

You have you how placed a slab at the top of the stair (see Figure 8 -33).

19. Change to the **SW Isometric View**.

20. In the **Design** tool palette, select the **Stair Tower Generate** tool, select the stair and then the slab you just created, and press **Enter** to bring up the **Select Levels** dialog box (see Figure 8 -34).

21. Press the **OK** button in the **Select Levels** dialog box to generate the stair tower (see Figure 8 -35).

Figure 8-33

Figure 8-34

Figure 8-35

Figure 8-36

Railings

When you finish this section, you should understand the following:

- ✔ How to make a **Railing** tool palette.
- ✔ How to place a railing.
- ✔ How to edit a railing style.
- ✔ How to modify balusters.
- ✔ How to add a railing to a stair and stair flight.
- ✔ How to add a railing to a landing.
- ✔ How to add a railing and landing support—**Anchor to Object**.
- ✔ How to create a railing using a polyline.
- ✔ How to edit a railing profile in place.

Number	Name	Purpose
1	Style	Select from available railing styles
2	Rail locations	Set locations of rails fixed by **Style**
3	Post locations	Set locations of posts fixed by **Style**
4	Attached to	Set **None**, **Stair**, or **Stair Flight**
5	Rotation	Set rotation of railing
6	Elevation	Set elevation of railing

Hands-On

Making a New Railing Tool Palette

1. Create a new tool palette, and name it **Railings**.
2. Select the **Content Browser** icon from the **Main** toolbar to launch the Content Browser.
3. In the **Architectural Desktop Design Tool Catalog - Imperial**, locate the **Stairs** folder in the **Stairs and Railings** folder.
4. From the **Railings** folder, drag all the railings into the new tool palette you created.
5. Click and hold on the tab of your new tool palette and drag a copy to **My Tool Catalog** in the Content Browser.

Hands-On

Placing a Railing

1. Start a new drawing using the AEC Model and View (Imperial - ctb) template.
2. Change to the **Model Layout**.
3. Change to **Top View**.
4. Select any **Railing** icon in the **Railings** tool palette you created and drag your cursor over the **Properties** palette to open it.
5. In the **Properties** palette select **Standard** from the **Style** drop-down list and ***NONE*** from the **Attached to** drop-down list.
6. Click in the Drawing Editor, drag your cursor to the right (0°), enter **10'** in the **Command line**, and press **Enter** three times to complete the command.

You have now placed a 10'-0"-long Standard railing.

Note: When you select ***NONE***, you can use your railing as a fence, porch rail, and so on.

Hands-On

Editing a Railing Style

1. Select the railing you placed in the previous exercise, **RMB**, and select **Edit Railing Style** from the contextual menu that appears to bring up the **Railing Styles** dialog box.
2. Press the **Floating Viewer** icon to bring up the **Viewer**.
3. Resize the **Viewer** so that both **Viewer** and **Railing Styles** dialog box are side by side, and open at the same time. In the **Viewer**, set the drop-down list to **SW Isometric View**, and press the **Flat Shading** icon (see Figure 9-1).
4. In the **Railing Styles** dialog box, select the **Rail Locations** tab.
5. Check and uncheck **Guardrail, Handrail,** and **Bottomrail** check boxes and view the changes in the **Viewer**.
6. Change the **Side for Offset** by clicking on the **Side for Offset** drop-down lists and view the changes in the **Viewer**.
7. Enter **8** in the **Number of Rails** value entry field, and **4"** in the **Spacing of Rails** value entry field. Press **Enter**, and view the changes in the **Viewer** (see Figure 9-2).
8. Reset to all the original settings.
9. Change to the **Post Locations** tab.
10. Check and uncheck **Guardrail, Handrail,** and **Bottomrail** check boxes and view the changes in the **Viewer**.

Figure 9-1

Figure 9-2

11. Check and uncheck **Fixed Posts**, **Dynamic Posts**, and **Balusters** check boxes and value entry fields. View the changes in the **Viewer**.

12. Change to the **Post Locations** tab.

13. Check the **Fixed Posts** check box, and change the value in the **Extension of ALL Posts from Top Railing** value entry field to **18"**.

14. Check the **Dynamic Posts** check box, and change the value in the **Maximum Center to Center Spacing** value entry field to **2'-0"**. View the changes in the **Viewer** (see Figure 9-3).

15. Reset to all the original settings.

16. Change to the **Components** tab.

17. Select the **D - Fixed Post** field.

18. Select ***circular*** from the drop-down list under **Profile Name**, and press **Enter**. Set its width to **1'-0"**, and again press **Enter**.

19. View the changes in the **Viewer** (see Figure 9-4).

Figure 9-3

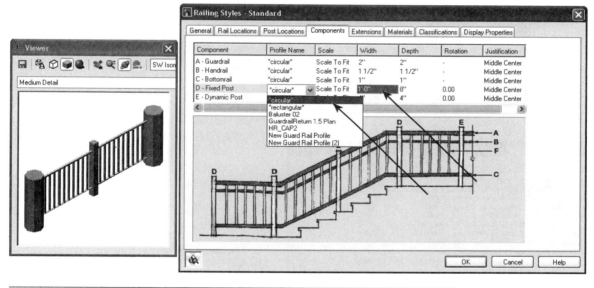

Figure 9-4

20. Reset to all the original settings.

21. Change to the **Extensions** tab.

The settings in this tab are used to set the extensions to the railings when the rails are connected to stairs. These extension dimensions are usually governed by the building codes (see Figure 9-5).

22. Change to the **Materials** tab.

23. Select the **Fixed Post** field and press the **Edit Material** icon to bring up the **Material Definition Properties** dialog box. Press the **Edit Display Properties** icon to bring up the **Display Properties** dialog box (see Figure 9-6).

24. Select the **Other** tab. Select **Woods & Plastics > Architectural Woodwork > Wood Stairs and Railings > Ash** from the **Surface Rendering - Rendering Material** drop-down list (see Figure 9-7).

Figure 9-5

Figure 9-6

Figure 9-7

25. Press the **OK** buttons in the **Display Properties** and **Material Definition Properties** dialog boxes to return to the **Railing Styles** dialog box. View the material changes in the **Viewer** (see Figure 9-8).

Figure 9-8

Hands-On

Modifying Balusters

1. Return to the Drawing Editor.
2. **RMB** on the **Guardrail - Wood Balusters 02** icon in the **Railings** tool palette you created, and select **Apply Tool Properties to > Railing** from the contextual menu that appears. (If this railing style is not available in the tool palette, get it from the **Architectural Desktop Design Tool Catalog - Imperial**).
3. Select the railing that you placed in "Placing a railing" in this section, and press **Enter**.

The railing changes to the new railing style.

4. Select the railing again, **RMB**, and select **Edit Railing Style** from the contextual menu that appears to bring up the **Railing Styles** dialog box.
5. Press the **Floating Viewer** icon to bring up the **Viewer**.
6. Again resize the **Viewer** so that the **Viewer** and **Railing Styles** dialog box are side by side, and open at the same time. In the **Viewer**, set the drop-down list to **SW Isometric View**, and press the **Flat Shading** icon.
7. View the railing (see Figure 9-9).
8. In the **Railing Styles** dialog box select the **Display Properties** tab and press the **Edit Display Properties** icon to bring up **Display Properties** dialog box. Select the **Other** tab (see Figure 9-10).
9. Press the **Remove** button to remove the Baluster 02 block.
10. Press **OK** and view the railing in the **Viewer** again. This time the balusters are the default balusters (see Figure 9-11).

If you press the **Edit** button in the **Display Properties** dialog box, you can add your own balusters made from 3D solid model or surface model blocks.

Figure 9-9

Figure 9-10

Figure 9-11

Hands-On

Adding a Railing to a Stair and Stair Flight

1. Start a new drawing using the Architectural Building Model and View (Imperial - ctb) template.
2. Change to the **Work Layout**.
3. Change to **Top View**.
4. Place a Standard-style U-shaped stair with 3'-0"-wide stair flights, a total of 9'-0" overall in width, and 10' height.
5. Select the **Guardrail** icon in the **Railings** tool palette you created and move your cursor over the **Properties** palette to open it.
6. Select **Stair** from the **Attached to** drop-down list.
7. Select the outside side of the stair and inside side of the stair to place the rail (see Figure 9-12).

Figure 9-12

Note: You can add a railing to a stair in the **3D View**, but it is easier in the **Top View**.

8. Erase the railing, and repeat this process using the **Stair flight** option from the **Attached to** drop-down area of the **Properties** palette (see Figure 9-13).

Figure 9-13

Hands-On

Adding a Railing to a Landing

1. Erase the previous railing.

2. Activate the **SW Isometric View**.

3. Type **UCS** in the command line and press **Enter** twice to make sure the **SW Isometric View** is in the World UCS.

4. Measure the railing landing. Type ID in the command line, press **Enter**, and snap to any top corner of the landing. Read the Z dimension (5'-0" for my landing). See Figure 9-14.

Figure 9-14

5. Activate the **Top View**.

6. Turn the **End Point Osnap** on.

7. Select the **Guardrail** icon in the **Railings** tool palette you created and move your cursor over the **Properties** palette to open it.

8. Select ***NONE*** from the **Attached to** drop-down list.

9. Start at the corner, and place a rail as shown in Figure 9-15.

Figure 9-15

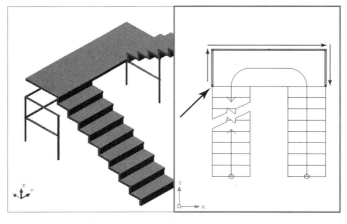

10. Double-click on the railing to bring up the **Properties** palette for the railing.

11. Enter 5' in the **Elevation** data entry field—the railing will move to the top of the landing (see Figure 9-16). Save the file.

Figure 9-16

You can return to the Top View and use the Stretch command to adjust the railing lengths.

Hands-On

Adding a Railing and Landing Support—Anchor to Object

1. Undo the previous exercise to Step 9.
2. Select the railing, **RMB**, and select **Railing Anchor > Anchor to Object** from the contextual menu that appears.
3. Select the landing and press **Enter**.
4. Enter **Y** (Yes) in the command line and press **Enter**.
5. Enter **F** (Follow surface) in the command line and press **Enter**. Save the file.

The railing moves to the top of the landing, but the posts extend to the ground (see Figure 9-17).

Figure 9-17

Hands-On

Creating a Railing Using a Polyline

1. Clear the Drawing Editor.
2. Using the **Polyline** tool, create the shape shown in Figure 9-18.

Figure 9-18

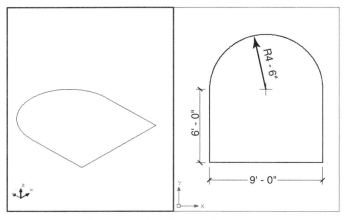

3. **RMB** on the **Guardrail - Cable** icon in your **Railings** palette and select **Apply Tool Properties to > Polyline** from the contextual menu that appears.
4. Select the polyline and press **Enter**.
5. Enter **Y** (Yes) in the **Command line** to erase the layout geometry and press **Enter** to create the railing (see Figure 9-19).

Figure 9-19

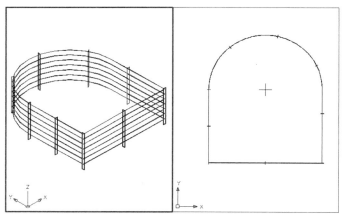

6. Select the railing, **RMB**, and select **Edit Railing Style** from the contextual menu that appears to bring up the **Railing Styles** dialog box.
7. Select the **Post Locations** tab.
8. Check the **Dynamic Posts** check box and enter **1'-0"** in the **Maximum Center to Center Spacing** data entry field.

Your railing changes to include more posts (see Figure 9-20).

Figure 9-20

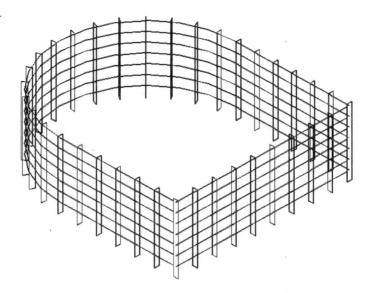

Hands-On

Editing a Railing Profile in Place

1. Clear the Drawing Editor.
2. Change to the **Model Layout**.
3. Change to **Top View**.
4. Select the **Guardrail - Wood balusters 01 Railing** icon in the Railings tool palette you created and drag your cursor over the Properties palette to open the palette.
5. Select **Standard** from the **Style** drop-down list and ***NONE*** from the Attached to drop-down list.
6. Click in the Drawing Editor, drag your cursor to the right (0°), enter **12'** in the **Command line**, and press **Enter** three times to complete the command.
7. Change to the **Right View**.
8. In the **Right View**, select the railing, **RMB,** and select **Edit Profile In-Place** from the contextual menu that appears.
9. Select the top rail of the railing. You will get an AutoCAD message that the profile shape must be converted. Press the **Yes** button.
10. The top rail end will turn light blue with magenta grips (see Figure 9-21).

You can drag on the grips to edit the profile, or do the following:

11. Draw a circle and a rectangle similar to that shown in Figure 9-22.
12. Select the blue-shaded top rail, **RMB**, and select **Add Ring** from the contextual menu that appears.
13. Select the circle you drew in Step 10, enter **Y** (Yes) in the **Command line** and press **Enter**.

Figure 9-21

Figure 9-22

14. Enter **J** (Join) in the **Command line** and press **Enter**.

15. Repeat Steps 11 through 13 of this exercise for the rectangle.

16. Select the blue-shaded top rail again, **RMB**, and select **Save As New Profile** from the contextual menu that appears to bring up the **New Profile** dialog box.

17. In the **New Profile** dialog box, type the name **TEST RAIL PROFILE**, and press the **OK** button.

You have now edited the top rail in place (see Figure 9-23).

18. Select the top rail you just created, **RMB**, and again select **Edit Profile In-Place** from the contextual menu that appears.

19. Select the top rail, and again the top rail end will turn light blue with magenta grips.

20. Grab the lower right **Edge** grip, drag to the right and press the **Ctrl** button on your keyboard until the tool tip message reads **Convert line to arc**, and click the mouse button (see Figure 9-24).

Figure 9-23

Figure 9-24

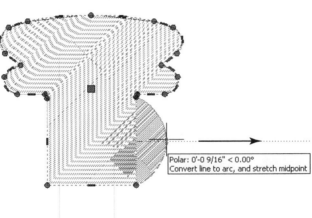

Polar: 0'-0 9/16" < 0.00°
Convert line to arc, and stretch midpoint

21. Repeat the process for the lower left **Edge** grip.

22. **RMB** in the blue field and select **Save As New Profile** from the contextual menu that appears to bring up the **New Profile** dialog box.

23. In the **New Profile** dialog box, type the name **TEST RAIL PROFILE 2**, and press the **OK** button to create the new profile (see Figure 9-25).

Figure 9-25

10

Roofs and Roof Slab Objects

When you finish this section, you should understand the following:

- ✔ How to make a **Roof** and **Roof Slabs** tool palette.
- ✔ How to place a roof object.
- ✔ How to modify a roof object.
- ✔ How to edit a roof edge.
- ✔ How to convert to roof and surfu.
- ✔ How to use the **Convert to Roof Slabs** command.
- ✔ How to use the **roofslabmodifyedges** command.
- ✔ How to use **Apply Tool Properties**.
- ✔ How to cut a hole in a roof slab.
- ✔ How to add edge profiles in place.
- ✔ How to create a roof dormer.

Roofs

Number	Name	Purpose
1	Thickness	Thickness of the roof structure
2	Edge cut	**Square** (perpendicular to the roof) or Plumb (parallel to the walls)
3	Shape	**Single slope**, **Double slope**, or **Gable**
4	Overhang	Distance beyond roof edge
5	Lower Slope—Plate height	Height above elevation
6	Lower Slope—Rise	Vertical rise per foot dimension
7	Lower Slope—Run	Horizontal dimension
8	Slope	Angle in degrees of slope
9	Rotation	Rotation of roof
10	Elevation	Elevation

Roof Slabs

Number	Name	Purpose
1	Style	Style created in the **Style Manager**
2	Mode	**Projected** (elevated) or **Direct** (at 0 elevation)
3	Thickness	Thickness of the roof structure
4	Vertical offset	Offset from wall top
5	Horizontal offset	Offset from wall edge
6	Justify	**Top, Center, Bottom, Slopeline**
7	Base height	Height above 0 elevation
8	Direction	Direction of slope
9	Overhang	Distance beyond wall edge
10	Baseline edge	Edge type at baseline
11	Perimeter edge	Edge type at perimeter
12	Slope—Rise	Vertical height per foot dimension
13	Slope—Run	Horizontal run per foot dimension
14	Slope	Slope angle in degrees
15	Rotation	Rotation of roof slab
16	Elevation	Elevation of roof slab

Roofs

Roof Slabs

Making a New Roof and Roof Slabs Tool Palette

1. Create a new tool palette, and name it **Roof & Roof Slabs**.
2. Select the **Content Browser** icon from the **Main** toolbar to launch the Content Browser.
3. In the **Autodesk Architectural Desktop Stock Tool Catalog** locate the **Roof in Architectural Object Tools**.
4. Drag all the roof objects into the new tool palette you created.
5. In the **Architectural Desktop Design Tool Catalog - Imperial**, locate the **Roof Slabs** folder in the **Roof and Roof Slabs** folder.
6. Drag all the roof slabs into the new tool palette you created.
7. Click and hold on the tab of your new tool palette and drag a copy to **My Tool Catalog** in the Content Browser.

Roofs are intelligent AEC Objects. There are several ways to place them, and many controls to modify them. It is probably easiest to place a roof, then modify it rather than set the roof controls before placement.

Do the following lesson to experience how to add, convert, and modify roof objects.

Placing a Roof Object

1. Start a new drawing using the AEC Model (Imperial - ctb) template.
2. Change to the **Model Layout**.
3. Change to **Top View**.
4. Using the wall object, place the floor plan shown in Figure 10-1. Make the walls 6' wide and 9'-0" high.
5. Set Object Snap to **End Point**.
6. Select the **Roof** icon in the **Roof and Roof Slabs** tool palette you created and drag your cursor over the **Properties** palette to open it.
7. Set the following:
    a. Thickness = **10"**
    b. Edge cut = **Square**
    c. Shape = **Single slope**
    d. Overhang = **1'**
    e. Plate height = **9'-0"**
    f. Rise = **1'-0"**
    g. Run = **12**
    h. Slope = **45.00**

Figure 10-1

8. Starting at the top left outside corner shown in Figure 10-2, move clockwise until you get back to the last point shown in the figure. Then press **Enter** or the space bar on your keyboard. You have now placed a roof object.

Figure 10-2

Hands-On

Modifying a Roof Object

1. Change to the **Work Layout**, and zoom extents in both viewports.
2. In the **SW Isometric View**, select the **Flat Shaded, Edges On** icon from the **Shade** menu to shade the **SW Isometric View**.
3. Change the other viewport to **Front View** (see Figure 10-3).
4. Double-click on the roof to bring up its **Properties** palette.

Figure 10-3

5. In the **Properties** palette, change the **Shape to Double**, and the **Upper slope's Upper height** to **12'**, and **Slope** to **55.00**. Notice the change to the roof (see Figure 10-4).

Figure 10-4

6. In the **Front View** viewport, zoom close to the edge of the roof.

7. Again, double-click on the roof to bring up its **Properties** palette.

8. Change the **Edge cut to Plumb**, and notice the change (see Figure 10-5).

Figure 10-5

Hands-On

Editing a Roof Edge

1. Double-click and reset the roof object to single slope in the **Properties** palette.

2. Select the roof, **RMB**, and select **Edit Edges/Faces** from the menu that appears.

3. Select a roof edge and press **Enter** to bring up the **Roof Edges and Faces** dialog box (see Figure 10-6).

Figure 10-6

4. Set Slope to **90**, and press **OK** to return to the Drawing Editor.

The roof now has a gable end, but there is no infill between the top of the lower end wall and the underside of the roof (see Figure 10-7).

Figure 10-7

5. Select the end wall, **RMB**, and select **Modify Roof line** from the contextual menu that appears.

6. Enter **A** (Auto project) in the command line and press **Enter**.

7. Select the wall again and press **Enter**.

8. Select the **Roof** object and press **Enter** twice to end the command.

The wall now meets and closes the gable end (see Figure 10-8).

This same process can be done with a curtain wall (see Figure 10-9). To get this image you must select the **Design** tool palette, and select the **Curtain Wall** icon. RMB the icon, and select **Apply tool property to > Walls**. Select the appropriate wall, accept Baseline for the Curtain wall baseline alignment, and enter Y(yes) to erase layout geometry.

Figure 10-8

Figure 10-9

9. Change to the **Work Layout**.

10. In the **Top View** viewport, select the roof and pull on the vertex shown in Figure 10-10.

You have now created a simple roof and roof overhang. Save this file.

Figure 10-10

Hands-On

Using Apply Tool Properties to Roof and Surfu

Another way to create a roof is to use **Apply Tool Properties to**. In the following exercise **Apply Tool Properties to** was used because of the curved walls.

1. Using the AEC Arch Imperial template, select the **Work** viewport tab.
2. Activate the **Top View** viewport.
3. Create the floor plan with 6"-wide walls 9' high as shown in Figure 10-11.

Figure 10-11

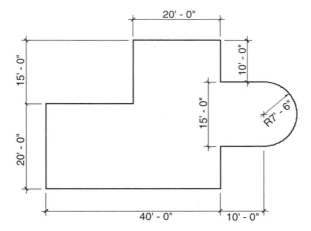

4. Type **_surfu** on the **Command line** and press **Enter**.
5. Set the new value to 4 in the command line and press the **space bar** or **Enter** key.

_Surfu is the variable that controls the smoothness of the roof curves. This variable must be set before the roofs are placed or reapplied.

6. Select the **Roof** icon from the **Roof and Roof Slabs** tool palette you created previously, **RMB**, and select **Apply Tool Properties to** from the contextual menu that appears.
7. Select all the walls.

8. At the **Command line** question "Erase layout geometry?" type **N** (No) and press **Enter** to create a roof.

9. While the new roof is still lit (grips showing), move your cursor over the **Properties** palette to open it.

10. Change the **Edge cut to Plumb** and **Elevation** to **9'-0"**.

You have now created a roof with one command. This technique is very useful when you have rounded roofs (see Figure 10-12).

11. Erase the roof.

12. Type **_surfu** on the **Command line** and press **Enter**.

13. Set the new value to **24** on the **Command line** and press **Enter**.

14. Again use **Apply Tool Properties to** in order to make a roof, and save this file.

Figure 10-13 shows the effects of increasing the **surfu** variable to **24** (more facets).

Figure 10-12

Figure 10-13

Hands-On

Converting to Roof Slabs

 Note: Roofs can also be created by adding roof slab objects. This system is identical to that for creating slabs (see the next section, "Slabs and Slab Objects," for exercises on creating, modifying, and editing slabs).

Converting roofs to slabs allows you the flexibility to adjust one slab or cut holes inherent in slabs. For pitched roofs it is often best to start with a standard roof object, and then convert it to roof slabs.

1. Use the previous exercise.

2. Select the roof, **RMB**, and select **Convert to Roof Slabs** from the contextual menu that appears.

3. Type **Y** (Yes) at the **Command line** question "Erase layout geometry" and press **Enter**. Accept the Standard roof, and again press **Enter** to complete the command.

The roof color should now change because the roof will now be made of roof slab objects, and is now on the A-Roof-Slab layer.

Hands-On

roofslabmodifyedges

Although not documented in the manual, **roofslabmodifyedges** allows you to adjust all the roof slab edges at one time.

1. Use the previous exercise.
2. Type **Slabmodifyedges** in the **Command line** and press **Enter**.
3. Type **All** at the **Command line** request to select slabs to modify, and press **Enter**.
4. Select the **Baseline** option in the **Command line** and press **Enter**.
5. Enter **OV** (Overhang) in the **Command line** and press **Enter**.
6. Enter **3'-0"** in the **Command line**, and press **Enter**.

You have now adjusted the overhang for all the roof slab objects (see Figure 10-14).

Figure 10-14

Hands-On

Applying Tool Properties to a Roof Slab

1. Select the roof slabs (this can be done by selecting the **Quick Select** icon at the top of the **Properties** palette to bring up the **Quick Select** dialog box and selecting **Roof Slab** from the **Object type** drop-down list).
2. **RMB** on any **Roof Slab** icon in the **Roof and Roof Slabs** toolbar that you created.
3. Select **Apply Tool properties to > Roof Slab** from the contextual menu that appears and press **Enter**. Press the **Gouraud** icon in the **Shading** toolbar. Save this file.

The roof slabs change to the new applied roof slabs style, and the roof slab material is displayed (see Figure 10-15).

Figure 10-15

Hands-On

Cutting a Hole in a Roof Slab

1. Zoom close to a roof slab in which you wish to place a hole.
2. Select the **Object UCS** icon from the **UCS** toolbar.
3. Select the roof slab in which you wish to place a hole.

The UCS now matches the surface of the roof slab.

4. Select the **Rectangle** icon in the **Draw** toolbar and place a rectangle on, over, or under the roof slab (see Figure 10-16).
5. Select the roof slab in which you wish to place a hole, **RMB**, and select **Hole > Add** from the contextual menu that appears.
6. Select the rectangle created in Step 4 of this exercise, and press **Enter**.
7. Enter **Y** (Yes) in the **Command line** and press **Enter** to complete the command.

You have now created a hole in the roof slab (see Figure 10-17).

Figure 10-16

Figure 10-17

Hands-On

Adding Edge Profiles in Place

1. Select **Format > Style Manager** from the Main toolbar to bring up the **Style Manager** dialog box.

2. Expand the **Architectural Objects** tree, select **Slab Edge Styles, RMB,** and select **New** from the contextual menu that appears.

3. Rename the new style to **SLAB EDGE TEST,** and press **OK** to return to the Drawing Editor.

4. Select a roof slab **RMB** and select **Add Edge Profiles** from the contextual menu that appears.

5. Select an edge of the roof slab, and a dialog box will appear (see Figure 10-18).

Figure 10-18

NOTE: This dialog box may not appear and you will immediately go to the dialog box shown in (Figure 10-19)

6. Press the **Yes** button to bring up the **Edit Roof Slab Edges** dialog box.

7. Select **Standard** for the **Edge Style** and press **OK** (see Figure 10-19).

8. The **Add Fascia/Soffit Profiles** dialog appears.

Figure 10-19

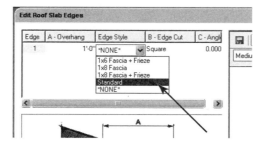

9. Check the **Fascia Profile** check box, select **Start** from scratch from the drop-down list, enter the name **FASCIA PROFILE TEST** as the **New Profile Name**, and press **OK** to enter the **In-Place Edit** mode (see Figure 10-20).

10. Change to the **Right View**, and zoom close to the blue shading that signifies the **In-Place Edit** area.

11. Create a gutter from a closed polyline as shown in Figure 10-21.

12. Select the blue area and grips will appear.

Figure 10-20

Figure 10-21

13. **RMB** on the blue area and select **Replace ring** from the contextual menu that appears.

14. Select the gutter drawn in Step 11 of this exercise, enter **Y** (Yes) in the command line, and press **Enter**.

The blue hatch will be replaced by the gutter in blue hatch.

15. Select the blue gutter, **RMB**, and select **Save Profile** from the contextual menu that appears.

The **FASCIA PROFILE TEST** is now the gutter.

Hands-On

Creating a Roof Dormer

Dormers are in vogue today, and ADT 2005 has a command that aids in the creation of these objects.

1. Start a new drawing using the AEC Model (Imperial - ctb) template.
2. Change to the **Model Layout**.
3. Change to the **Top View**.
4. Select the **Wall** icon from the **Design** tool palette, and create a 43'-0" × 31'-wide structure 8'-0" high with 6"-wide Standard walls.
5. Add a 15' × 8' enclosure 14'-0" high with 6"-wide Standard walls.
6. Add a **Gable** roof to the 43' × 31' enclosure with a 30° slope (see Figure 10-22).

Figure 10-22

15' x 8' enclosure

8' - 0"

43' - 0"

16' - 0"

31' - 0"

7. Select the **Roof Slab** icon from the **Design** menu, **RMB**, and select **Apply Tool Properties to > Linework, Walls, and Roof** from the contextual menu.
8. Select the left wall of the 15' × 8' enclosure and press **Enter**.
9. Enter **N** (No) in the **Command line** and press **Enter**.
10. Enter **B** (Bottom) in the **Command line** and press **Enter**.
11. Enter **R** (Right) in the **Command line** and press **Enter**.
12. Enter **L** (Left) in the **Command line** and press **Enter** to create the first roof slab of the dormer (see Figure 10-23).

NOTE: Steps 11 and 12 may be reversed depending on which direction the walls were drawn.

13. Again, select the **Roof Slab** icon from the **Design** menu, **RMB**, and select **Apply Tool Properties to > Linework, Walls, and Roof** from the contextual menu.
14. Select the right wall of the 15' × 8' enclosure and press **Enter**.
15. Enter **N** (No) in the **Command line** and press **Enter**.
16. Enter **B** (Bottom) in the **Command line** and press **Enter**.

17. Enter **L** (Left) in the **Command line** and press **Enter**.

18. Enter **R** (Right) in the **Command line** and press **Enter** to create the first roof slab of the dormer.

> **Note:** If your roof slab doesn't follow the above rules, reverse the wall direction and repeat (see Figure 10-24).

19. Select both new roof slabs, and move your cursor over the **Properties** palette to open it.

20. Change the **Slope** to **25** (25°).

21. Select one of the roof slabs, **RMB**, and select **Miter** from the contextual menu.

22. Accept the default **<Intersection>** in the **Command line** and press **Enter**.

23. Select the lower part of the slab at the intersection of the two slabs, and then select the lower part of the other slab.

The two roof slabs will now miter, forming the roof of the dormer. This could also have been done with the roof object, making it a gable roof.

24. Change to the **Top View** and drag each roof slab 2'-0" (see Figure 10-25).

25. Select the main gable roof over the 43' × 31' enclosure, **RMB**, and select **Convert to Roof Slabs** from the contextual menu.

Figure 10-25

26. Enter **N** (No) in the **Command line**, and press **Enter** twice to change the roof object into roof slabs.

27. Press the **ESC** key to deselect the slabs.

28. Select the roof slab shown in Figure 10-26, **RMB**, and select **Roof Dormer** from the contextual menu.

29. Select the 15′ × 8′ enclosure and its roof slabs and then press **Enter.**

30. Enter **Y** (Yes) in the **Command line**, and press **Enter** to form the dormer.

31. Erase any unneeded walls (see Figure 10-27).

Figure 10-26

Figure 10-27

11

Slabs and Slab Objects

When you finish this section, you should understand the following:

- ✔ How to make a **Slabs** tool palette.
- ✔ How to use **Direct Mode** and **Direction**.
- ✔ How to use **Projected** mode.
- ✔ How to apply tool properties to slabs.
- ✔ How to cut slabs.
- ✔ How to modify a slab object.
- ✔ How to make a new edge from a Profile.
- ✔ How to change a slab edge profile.

Number	Name	Purpose
1	Style	Select from available slab styles
2	Mode	Specifies whether the slab is created in **Direct** or **Projected** modes
3	Thickness	Specifies the thickness of the slab
4	Vertical offset	Slopeline offset Specifies the vertical offset of the slab
5	Horizontal offset	Specifies the horizontal offset of the slab while sicking points
6	Justify	Specifies the slab justification—**Top**, **Bottom**, **Center**, or **Slopeline**
7	Direction	Specifies the **Left** or **Right** direction for the slab
8	Overhang	Distance of overhang; Specifies the overhang depth for the slab
9	Perimeter edge	Specifies the edge style along the perimeter of the slab
10	Rotation	Rotation reference angle for the slab
11	Elevation	Elevation of the slab

Hands-On

Creating a New Slab Tool Palette

1. Create a new tool palette, and name it **Slab**.
2. Select the **Content Browser** icon from the **Main** tool bar to launch the Content Browser.
3. In the **Desktop Design Tool Catalog – Imperial**, locate the **Slabs** folder in the **Roof Slabs and Slabs** folder.
4. From the **Slabs** folder, drag all the slabs into the new tool palette you created.
5. Click and hold on the tab of your new tool palette and drag a copy to **My Tool Catalog** in the Content Browser.

Hands-On

Using Direct Mode and Direction

Slabs can be either **Direct** or **Projected** modes. **Direct** mode allows you to place a Flat slab, **Direct Projected** mode allows you to place a slab at a location in space with a given slope. **Direction** is used when using **Ortho Close.**

The first point establishes slab origin and pivot point. The first line establishes the base line.

1. Start a new drawing using the AEC Model (Imperial - ctb) template.
2. Change to the **Model Layout**.
3. Change to **Top View**.
4. Select the **Slab** icon from the **Design** toolbar.
5. Move your cursor over the **Properties** palette to open it.
6. Set the following parameters:
   a. Style = **Standard**
   b. Mode = **Direct**
   c. Thickness = **to 12"**
   d. Overhang = **0"**
   e. Mode = **Direct**
   f. Justify = **Bottom**
   g. Direction = **Left**
7. Set the first point of your slab.
8. Moving clockwise, set the second point at **10'** to the right.
9. Enter **O** (Ortho close) in the **Command line**, and press **Enter**.

10. Repeat Steps 5, 6, 7, 8, and 9 slightly below the first slab in the **Top** viewport, but change the direction arrow to the **Right** direction arrow.

11. Select each slab, and change the slope of each slab to **45** (45 degrees)

Ortho Close works differently for slabs than for walls. For slabs, only one line is drawn so the direction arrow dictates in which direction the slab is cast (see Figures 11-1 and 11-2).

Figure 11-1

Figure 11-2

Hands-On

Projected Model

1. Create a new drawing.
2. Again select the **Slab** icon from the **Design** tool palette.
3. Move your cursor over the **Properties** palette to open it.
4. Set the following parameters:
   a. Style = **Standard**
   b. Mode = **Projected**
   c. Thickness = **to 12"**
   d. Justify = **Bottom**
   e. Base height = **0**
   f. Direction = **Right**
   g. Overhang = **0"**

Notice that selecting the **Projected** mode causes the **Slope** option to now be available in the **Properties** palette.

5. In the **Properties** palette under **Slope**, set **Rise** to **6** and, **Run** to **12**.

6. Set a point, and moving clockwise, set the second point at **10'** to the right.

Notice that the **Pivot** symbol is at your starting point. Also notice that selecting the **Projected** mode causes the **Slope** option to be available.

7. Enter **O** (Ortho close) in the **Command line**, and press the **Enter** key.

8. Repeat Steps 5, 6, and 7, but change the **Direction** to **Left** (see Figure 11-3).

You only change the **Rise** numbers. Leave **Run** at **12.000**, and the **Angle** will automatically calculate.

Figure 11-3

Hands-On

Applying Tool Properties to Slabs

Convert to Slab uses closed polylines or walls as a basis for creating slabs. You don't need closed walls to use **Convert to Slab**; one wall will work just fine. The default location for slabs created by **Convert to Slab** using walls is at the top of the wall.

1. Start a new drawing using the AEC Model (Imperial - ctb) template.

2. Change to the **Model Layout**.

3. Change to **Top View**.

4. Select the **Wall** icon from the **Design** tool palette.

5. Starting at the bottom left and moving clockwise, place a 8' × 8' enclosure (see Figure 11-4).

6. Select the **Slab** icon from the **Design** tool palette, **RMB**, and select **Apply Tool properties to > Linework and Walls** from the contextual menu that appears.

Figure 11-4

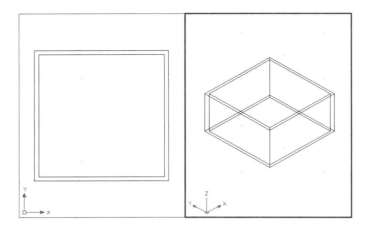

7. In the **Top View**, select all the walls of the 8' × 8' enclosure starting at the bottom wall and moving counterclockwise.

Note: The first wall you pick becomes the pivot wall.

8. In the **Command line**, accept **N** to leave the **Walls** in place.

9. For **Slab Justification**, select **Bottom**; for **Wall Justification** select **Right**; for **Slope Direction**, select **Right** or **Left** (either is OK); and accept the **Standard** slab style.

You have now placed a Standard slab object at the top of the wall enclosure (see Figure 11-5).

Figure 11-5

10. Repeat the above exercises, changing the **Wall Justification, Slab Justification,** and **Slope Direction** until you feel comfortable with the controls.

11. Save your exercise.

Hands-On

Cutting Slabs

1. Use the previous exercise.
2. In the **Top View**, place and **Offset** several polylines as shown in Figure 11-6.)

Figure 11-6

We are going to cut the slab with the polylines, even though the polylines are at 0" elevation, and the slab is at 8'-0" elevation.

3. Select the slab, **RMB**, and select **Cut** from the contextual menu that appears.
4. Select one of the polylines, and press **Enter**.
5. Enter **Y** (Yes) in the **Command line**, and press **Enter**.
6. Repeat Steps 3 through 5 for the other polylines.

You should now have three slab sections.

7. Select each slab section, and move your cursor over the **Properties** palette to open it.
8. Set the elevation for each section 8" lower than the previous one (see Figure 11-7). Save this file.

Figure 11-7

Hands-On

Modifying the Slab Object

Once you have placed a slab object, there are many controls to manipulate the object.

1. Erase the slabs created in the previous exercise, and place a new slab 12" slab starting at the upper left corner and moving clockwise.

2. Make the **Wall Justification Left**.

Making the justification **Left** moves the edges of the slab to the outside of the enclosure.

3. Double-click the slab to open the **Properties** palette.

4. Set the slope **Rise** to **12** (12") (see Figure 11-8).

Figure 11-8

5. Select **Edges** from the **Properties** palette to bring up the **Slab Edges** dialog box.

6. Change the **Edge Cut** to **Plumb** (see Figures 11-9 and 11-10).

Figure 11-9

Figure 11-10

Making a New Edge from a Profile

7. Return the slab object to its original position by changing the **Rise** to **0.00**, and change the **Edge Cut** back to **Square**.

8. In the **Top View**, select and drag the slab's grips and move each edge 1'-0" as shown in Figure 11-11.

9. Create a profile polyline shape by drawing the polyline shown in Figure 11-12.

Figure 11-11

Figure 11-12

10. Select the polyline, **RMB**, and select **Convert to > Profile Definition** from the contextual menu that appears.

11. Select the upper left corner of the polyline you just created.

12. Press **Enter** to bring up the **Profile Definition** dialog box.

13. Enter **CURVED EDGE PROFILE**, and press the **OK** button.

14. Select **Format > Style Manager** to bring up the **Style Manager**.

15. Select **Architectural > Slab Edge Styles**, **RMB**, and select **New** from the contextual menu that appears.

16. Rename the new style **CURVED EDGE STYLE**.

17. Double-click on the **CURVED EDGE STYLE** icon you just created to bring up the **Slab Edge Styles** dialog box, and select the **Design Rules** tab.

18. Check the **Fascia** check box, select **CURVED EDGE PROFILE** from the **Fascia Profile** drop-down list, and press the **OK** and **Apply** buttons to return to the Drawing Editor (see Figure 11-13).

Figure 11-13

19. Double-click the slab to bring up the **Properties** palette.

20. Select **Edges** to bring up the **Slab Edges** dialog box.

21. Select all the edges, select **CURVED EDGE STYLE** from the **Edge Style** drop-down list, and then press the **OK** button.

You have now placed a new curved edge on all the slab edges (see Figure 11-14).

Figure 11-14

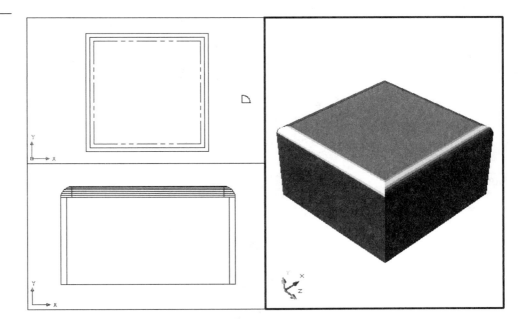

Hands-On

Changing the New Slab Edge Profile

1. Return to the profile you created in the last exercise.
2. Add a rectangle as shown in (see Figure 11-15).
3. **RMB** on an empty place in the Drawing Editor, and select **AEC Modify Tools > Merge** from the contextual menu that appears.
4. Select the rectangle and press **Enter**.
5. Select the original profile and press **Enter**.
6. Enter **Y** (Yes) in the **Command line** and press **Enter** (see Figure 11-16).

Figure 11-15

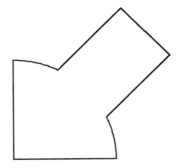

Figure 11-16

7. Select the changed profile, **RMB**, and select **Convert To > Profile Definition** from the contextual menu that appears.

8. Select the lower left corner of the profile and press **Enter**.

9. Enter **E** (Existing) in the **Command line**, and press **Enter** key to bring up the **Profile Definitions** dialog box.

10. Select **CURVED EDGE PROFILE** (the one you created in the last exercise), and press **OK**.

The slab edge now reflects the changed profile (see Figure 11-17).

Figure 11-17

Structural Members, Column Grids, Grids and Anchors

Structural Column

Structural Brace

Structural Beam

Structural Column Grid

Node Anchor

Layout Curve

Layout Grid 2D

Column Bubble

Structure

TOOL PALETTES

When you finish this section, you should understand the following:

✔ How to make a **Structure** palette.

✔ How to place a column and column grid.

✔ How to modify structural members.

✔ How to create a round composite concrete and steel column.

✔ How to add bar joists.

✔ How to label a grid.

✔ How to add and label a layout grid (2D).

✔ How to create and use a layout curve.

✔ How to use a wall as a layout curve.

All buildings have a structural system. In the design of commercial buildings, the understanding and documentation of the structural system is of utmost importance. In Autodesk Architectural Desktop 2005, structural members give control over this phase of construction.

Structural members can be used as columns, beams, and braces, and can be configured in many ways not originally intended by the developers of the program. In reality, columns, beams, and braces are the same AEC object used in different work planes. When understood, structural members can be some of the most important AEC objects in your portfolio of tools.

Column grids are a variant on grids; they can be planar (flat) or volumetric (three-dimensional). Columns can be attached to any grid, but column grids can have columns attached upon input of the grid.

Number	Name	Purpose
1	Style	Select from available structural member styles
2	Member type	**Column**, **Beam**, or **Brace**
3	Start offset	Distance offset from the start end of member
4	End offset	Distance offset from the end of member
5	Logical length	Actual length of structural member
6	Specify roll on screen	Specify roll angle around the main axis through member
7	Roll	Roll angle around the main axis through member
8	Justify	Insertion node location
9	Justify using overall extents	
10	Rotation	Rotation of the structural member
11	Elevation	Elevation of the structural member
12	Trim planes	Planes used to modify end conditions of the structural member

Hands-On

Making a New Structure Tool Palette

1. Create a new tool palette named **Structure**.

2. Select the **Content Browser** icon from the **Main** toolbar to launch the **Content Browser**.

3. In the **Stock Tool Catalog** locate the **Structural Beam, Structural Brace, Structural Column,** and **Structural Grid Object** in the **Architectural Object Tools** folder.

4. From the **Architectural Object Tools** folder, drag the objects into the new tool palette you created.

5. In the **Stock Tool Catalog** locate the **Cell Anchor, Node Anchor, Layout Curve,** and **Layout Grid (2D)** tools in the **Parametric Layout & Anchoring** folder, and drag these tools to the **Structure** palette you created.

6. Click and hold on the tab of your new tool palette and drag a copy to **My Tool Catalog** in the Content Browser.

7. In the **Sample Palette Catalog - Imperial** locate the **Column Bubble** tool in the **Annotation** folder, and drag these tools to the **Structure** palette you created.

Hands-On

Placing a Column and Grid

1. Start a new drawing using the Architectural Building Model and View (Imperial - ctb) template.

2. Change to the **Work Layout**.

3. Erase the existing viewports.

4. Select **View > Viewports > 3 Viewports** from the **Main** menu.

5. Enter **L** (Left) on the **Command line**, and press **Enter**.

6. Enter **F** (Fit) on the **Command line**, and press **Enter**.

7. Activate the **Top View,** in the upper left viewport.

8. Set the Object Snap to **NODE**.

9. Select **Structural Column Grid** from the **Structure** tool palette you created and drag your cursor over the **Properties** palette to open it.

10. Enter the following data:
    a. Shape = **Rectangular**
    b. Boundary = ***NONE***
    c. Specify on screen = **No**
    d. X - Width = **60'**

e. Y - Depth = **40'**

f. XAXIS Layout type = **Repeat**

g. Bay size = **20'-0"**

h. YAXIS Layout Type = **Repeat**

i. Bay size = **20'-0"**

j. Column Style = **Standard**

k. Column Logical Length = **10'-0"**

l. Justify = **Middle Center**

11. Click in the Drawing Editor to place the grid and columns, and press Enter twice to complete the command (see Figure 12-1).

Figure 12-1

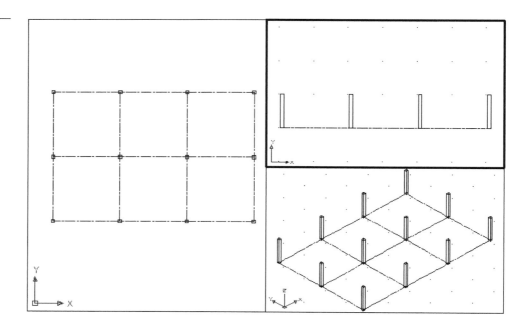

Hands-On

Modifying Structural Members

1. Select all the middle row of columns, and move your cursor over the **Properties** palette to open it.

2. Set the **Logical length** to 14'-0", and press **Enter**.

3. Select the **Structural Beam** icon from the **Structure** toolbar, set the **Style** to **Standard**, and **Justify** to **Bottom Center**.

Note: Bottom center is the location of the grips now set for the beam.

4. Click at the top of the first center column, then at the top of the second center column.

5. Repeat the above process with the top center nodes of the columns (see Figure 12-2).

Figure 12-2

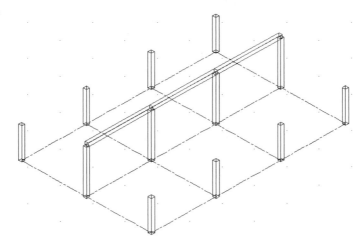

6. Repeat the process for the other columns to create the frame illustrated in Figure 12-3.

7. Select the end beams on the left side and right sides, and move your cursor over the **Properties** palette to open it.

8. Set the **Start Offset** to –2'-0" (see Figure 12-4).

9. Repeat this process on the beams at the opposite end. Use +2'-0" for the **End Offset.**

Figure 12-3

Figure 12-4

10. Select **Format > Structural Member Catalog** from the **Main** toolbar.

11. In the left panel select **Imperial | Steel | AISC | Channels | MC, Miscellaneous Channels**.

12. Double-click the **MC12x10.6** channel.

13. When the **Structural Member Style** dialog box appears, accept the default **MC12x10.6** name (see Figure 12-5).

Figure 12-5

14. Select all the outer beams, **RMB**, and select **Properties** from the contextual menu. In the structural **Properties** dialog box, select the **Style** tab, and change the style to **MC12x10.6** (see Figure 12-6).

15. Repeat the above process for the beams on the other side. This time also change **Roll** to **180**, and **Justification** to **Top Center**. This will cause the other channels to rotate 180° with the grip on the bottom.

Figure 12-6

Hands-On

Creating a Round Composite Concrete and Steel Column

1. Select **Format > Structural Member Catalog** from the **Main** toolbar.
2. Select **Imperial > Concrete > Cast - in place > Circular Columns**.
3. Double-click the 14″ diameter.
4. When the **Structural Member Style** dialog box appears, enter **14 DIA COL** and then press **OK**.
5. Select **Imperial | Steel | AISC | I Shaped, Wn Wide-Flange Shapes**.
6. Double-click **W6x25**.
7. When the **Structural Member Style** dialog box appears, accept **W6x25** and then press **OK**.
8. Close the **Structural Member Catalog**.
9. Select **Format > Style Manager** to bring up the **Style Manager** dialog box.
10. **RMB** on the **Structural Member Styles** icon in the **Architectural Objects** folder in the display tree and select **New** from the contextual menu that appears.
11. Rename the new style **COMPOSITE COL** and press **OK**.
12. Double-click on the icon adjacent to the new **COMPOSITE COL** style to bring up the **Structural Members Style Properties** dialog box.
13. Select the **Design Rules** tab.
14. Name the unnamed component **CONC**.
15. Under **Start Shape Name,** select **14″-Diameter** from the drop-down list.
16. Press the **Add** button, and rename the next component **W6x25**.
17. Select **W6x25** under **Start Shape Name,** and press **OK** (see Figure 12-7).

Figure 12-7

You have now created the composite round concrete column with steel shape inside.

18. Select all the columns in the Drawing Editor, and move your cursor over the **Properties** palette to open it.
19. Select **COMPOSITE COL Structural Beam** from the **Style** drop-down list. All the columns change to composite columns (see Figure 12-8).

Figure 12-8

Hands-On

Adding Bar Joists

1. Select the **Content Browser** icon from the **Main** toolbar to launch the **Content Browser**.

2. In the **Design Tool Catalog - Imperial** locate the **Bar Joists** in the **Structural** folder.

3. From the **Bar Joists** folder, drag the **Steel Joist 24** into the **Structure** tool palette you created, and close the Content Browser.

4. Select **Line** from the **Draw** toolbar, and place a line from the middle beam to the top/outside edge of the channel (see Figure 12-9).

Figure 12-9

5. Select the **Steel Joist 24** icon from the **Structure** palette you created, **RMB**, and select **Apply Tool Properties to > Linework** from the contextual menu that appears.

6. Select the line you placed in Step 4 of this exercise and press **Enter**.

7. Enter **Y** (Yes) in the **Command line** and press **Enter**.

The line changes to a 24" steel bar joist. If it is on its side, change the **Roll** to **0** in the **Properties** palette while it is still selected (see Figure 12-10).

8. Change to the **Model Layout**.

Figure 12-10

9. Change to the **Left View,** and zoom window around the location of the joist seat and the channel (see Figure 12-11).

Figure 12-11

10. Select the bar joist, **RMB,** and select **Edit Member Style** from the contextual menu that appears to bring up the **Structural Member Style** dialog box.

11. Select the **Design Rules** tab. This is where you control the components of the bar joist.

12. Set the settings shown for the **TopChord** and **JoistSeat-End** and press **OK** (see Figure 12-12).

The bar joist top chord and joist seat changes (see Figure 12-13).

Figure 12-12

Figure 12-13

13. **RMB** in an empty space in the Drawing Editor and select **Basic Modify Tools > Array** from the contextual menu that appears to bring up the **Array** dialog box.

14. Set the following:

    a.   Rectangular array = **Selected**

    b.   Columns = **33**

    c.   Rows = **1**

    d.   Column offset = **2'-0"**

15. Select the bar joist that you created, and press **OK**.

16. Mirror the bar joists to the other side of the structure, and you are finished (see Figure 12-14). Save this exercise.

Figure 12-14

Labeling a Column Grid

1. Use the previous exercise.

2. Change to the **Top View**.

3. Select the **Layer Manager** icon from the **Layer Properties** toolbar to bring up the **Layer Manager**.

4. Turn the **S-Beam** and the **S-Cols** layers off, and press **OK** to return to the Drawing Editor.

The column grid will now be exposed.

5. Select the column grid, **RMB**, and select **Label** from the contextual menu that appears to bring up the **Column Grid Labeling** dialog box.

6. Select the **X - Labeling** tab.

7. In the **Number** list enter the letter **A** and press **Enter** to fill the other letters automatically.

8. Also do the following on the same tab:

   a. Check the **Automatically Calculate Values** for **Labels** check box.

   b. Select the **Ascending** radio button.

   c. Check the **Bottom** check box for **Bubble Parameters**.

   d. Enter **4'-0"** for **Extension** under **Bubble Parameters**.

   e. Check the **Generate New Bubbles On Exit** check box.

9. Change to the **Y - Labeling** tab.

10. In the **Number** list enter the number **1** and press **Enter** to fill the other numbers automatically.

11. Also do the following in the same tab:

   a. Check the **Automatically Calculate Values** for **Labels** check box.

   b. Select the **Ascending** radio button.

   c. Check the **Right** check box for **Bubble Parameters**.

   d. Enter **4'-0"** for **Extension** under the **Bubble Parameters**.

   e. Check the **Generate New Bubbles On Exit** check box.

12. Press **OK** to return to the Drawing Editor (see Figure 12-15).

13. Select the bubble containing the letter **A** to activate its grips.

14. Drag the grip above the bubble to the right; the leader will follow (see Figure 12-16).

Figure 12-15

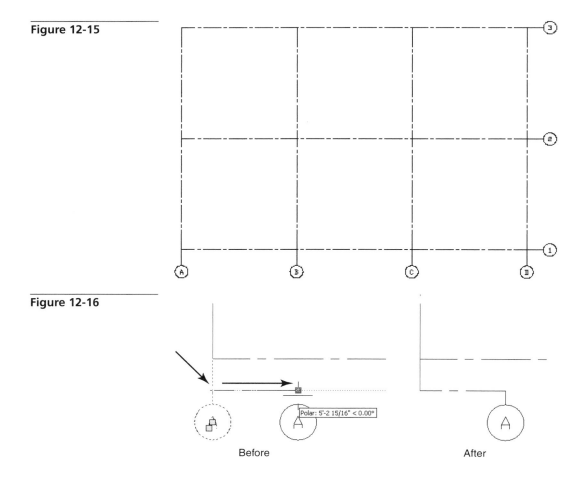

Figure 12-16

Before

After

Hands-On

Adding and Labeling a Layout Grid 2D

1. Start a new drawing using the AEC Model (Imperial - ctb) template.
2. Activate the **Top View**.
3. With various tools from the **Draw** menu, create the plan shown in Figure 12-17.

Figure 12-17

4. Select the **Layout Grid 2D** icon from the **Structure** palette that you created, **RMB**, and select **Apply Tool Properties > Linework** from the contextual menu that appears.

5. Select the plan you created in Step 4 of this exercise and press **Enter**.

6. Enter **Y** (Yes) in the **Command line**, and press **Enter** to erase the linework.

7. Select the **Column Bubble** from the **Structure** tool palette, and click the bottom left node of the plan to bring up the **Create Grid Bubble** dialog box.

8. Enter **A1** in the **Label** data field, **4'-0"** in the **Extension** data field, uncheck the **Apply at both ends of gridline** check box, and press the **OK** button.

9. Repeat for the following right-hand nodes (see Figure 12-18).

If a column bubble is misplaced or at an angle, do the following:

10. Select the column bubble, **RMB**, and select **Leader Anchor > Set Direction** from the contextual menu that appears.

11. For this example, enter **270°** and press **Enter** (see Figure 12-19).

Figure 12-18

Figure 12-19

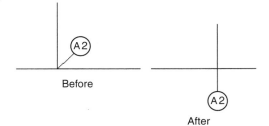

Layout Curves

Layout curves are not necessarily curves. Straight lines and many AEC objects such as walls, stairs, and doors can also be used as layout curves. If a line was placed on a wall, changed to a layout curve, and then moved vertically 24" up the wall, attached content would move with the layout curve. If the wall had been used as a layout curve, the nodes would have been at its base.

Use a layout curve to anchor objects along a path. You can define the following objects as layout curves:

n   Walls

n   Curtain walls

n   Window assemblies

n   Spaces

n   Mass elements

n   Roofs

n   Lines

n   Arcs

n   Circles

n   Ellipses

n   Polygons

n   Polylines

n   Splines

Hands-On

Creating and Using a Layout Curve

1. Create a new drawing.
2. Select **Spline** from the **Draw** menu, and place a spline.
3. Select the **Layout Curve** icon from the **Structure** palette.
4. Select the spline, enter **S** (Space evenly) in the **Command line**, and press **Enter**. Enter **0"** for Start and End offsets.
5. Enter **5** in the **Command line** for the **Number of** nodes and press **Enter**.
6. Change to the **SW Isometric View**.
7. Turn on the **Node** Object Snap.
8. Select **Structural Column** from the **Structure** tool palette, select one of the nodes on the spline, and click the mouse to place it.
9. Select **Node Anchor** from the **Structure** tool palette.
10. Enter **C** (Copy to each node) in the **Command line**, and press **Enter**.
11. Select the column you placed and press **Enter,** as the object to be copied.
12. Select any other node on the spline and press **Enter**.

13. Enter **Y** (Yes) in the **Command line** and press **Enter**.

All the nodes on the spline now have columns (see Figure 12-20).

Figure 12-20

Hands-On

Using a Wall as a Layout Curve

1. Select the **Wall** icon from the **Design** menu and place a **Standard** 15'-0"-long 10'-high, 6"-wide wall.

2. Select the **Layout Curve** icon from the **Structure** palette, and select the wall you just created.

3. Enter **S** (Space evenly) in the **Command line**, and press **Enter**.

4. Enter **24"** for the **Start offset** and press **Enter**.

5. Enter **24"** for the **End offset** and press **Enter**.

6. Accept **3** as the **Number of nodes**, and press **Enter** to place the nodes.

7. Select the **Content Bowser** icon from the **Main** toolbar and select and drag into the drawing the **Regular** drinking fountain from the **Design Tool Catalog - Imperial > Mechanical > Plumbing Fixtures > Fountain** folder (see Figure 12-21).

8. Select the **Node Anchor** icon from the **Structure** palette.

9. Enter **C** (Copy to each node) in the **Command line** and press **Enter**.

10. Select the drinking fountain, and then select one of the nodes anchored to the wall as the layout tool.

The fountains are now anchored to the wall.

11. Select all the fountains and move your cursor over the **Properties** palette to open it.

12. Select the **Anchor** field to bring up the **Anchor** dialog box.

13. Change the **Insertion Offset Z** to **3'-0"**, the **Rotation Z** to **270**, and press **OK** to return to the Drawing Editor.

All the fountains move vertically up the wall 3'-0" (see Figure 12-22).

Figure 12-21

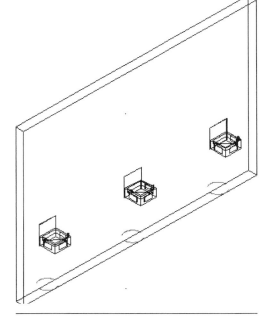

Figure 12-22

Hands-On

Layout Grid (2D)

1. Start a new drawing using the AEC Model View (Imperial - ctb) template.

2. Change to the **Model Layout**.

3. Change to the **Top View**.

4. Create a 40'-long × 30'-wide building with a 6"-rise roof.

5. Select the **Roof Slab** icon from the **Design** tool palette, **RMB**, and select **Apply Tool Properties to > Linework, Walls, and Roof** from the contextual menu that appears.

6. Select the roof object, Enter **N** (No) in the **Command line**, and press **Enter** to change the roof object to roof slabs.

7. Select the **Object UCS** from the **UCS** toolbar, and select the front roof slab. Make sure the **ucsicon** OR **option** is on (see Figure 12-23).

8. Select the **Layout Grid (2D)** icon from the **Structure** tool palette.

9. Center a 15' × 10' grid on the front roof slab with three divisions in the X direction, and two divisions in the Y direction. The grid will lie parallel to the roof because the UCS was set parallel to the roof in Step 7 (see Figure 12-24).

10. Place a 5'-0"-high × 1'-0"-radius mass element cylinder in a convenient place in your drawing.

11. Select the **Cell Anchor** icon from the **Structure** tool palette.

12. Type **C** at the **Command line** to copy to each cell, and press **Enter**.

13. Select the mass object, and then select the layout grid on the roof slab (see Figures 12-25 and 12-26).

Figure 12-23

Figure 12-24

Figure 12-25

Figure 12-26

Note in Figures 12-25 and 12-26 that the mass elements in the cells of the layout grid match the size of the grid.

14. Select the grid, and move your cursor over the **Properties** palette to open it.

15. Change the grid size to **5'-0"** in the **X-Width** and **5'-0"** in the **Y-Depth**.

Note that the mass elements in the cells automatically change size (see Figures 12-27 and 12-28).

16. Place another grid on the roof, **9'x6'** will fit.

17. Select the **Node Anchor** icon from the **Structure** tool palette.

18. Enter **C** (Copy to each node) in the **Command line** and press **Enter**.

19. Select the mass element, and then select the layout grid (see Figure 12-29).

Note that the mass elements attached to the nodes of the layout grid. Moving or modifying the grid will then move the anchored objects.

The layout volume grid (3D) works and is modified in a similar manner to the 2D layout grid.

Figure 12-27

Figure 12-28

Figure 12-29

Experiment with all the different settings, and try anchoring and rotating different kinds of content to AEC objects and AutoCAD entities. Don't forget that you can use the layout grid to put a series of skylights or windows on a roof or wall.

AEC Dimensions

When you finish this section, you should understand the following:

- ✔ How to set the text style.
- ✔ How to create a dimension style.
- ✔ How to create an AEC dimension style.
- ✔ How to use and modify an AEC dimension style.
- ✔ How to dimension doors and windows with AEC dimension styles.
- ✔ How to add a manual AEC dimension.
- ✔ How to detach objects from AEC dimensions.
- ✔ AEC dimension chains.
- ✔ The Dimension Wizard.

AEC Dimensions

AEC dimensions are automatic dimensions based on styles. Because there are so many variables in the dimension system, there are many dialog boxes. To make it easier, the developers have also added a Wizard to aid in variable setup.

Standard AutoCAD dimensions can be converted into AEC dimensions, and AEC dimensions can be mixed with the manual AEC and standard AutoCAD dimensioning systems.

AEC dimensions can dimension only AEC objects such as walls, windows, stairs, structural members, and so on. If you add non-AEC objects to AEC objects, you have to add manual dimension points to the automatic AEC dimension, or create manual AEC or standard AutoCAD dimensions.

The following table describes the difference between the three available dimensioning systems.

Automatic AEC Dimensions	Manual AEC Dimensions	AutoCAD Dimensions
Logical dimension points taken from object	Manual dimension points taken from drawing	Manual dimension points taken from drawing
Dimension AEC objects	Dimension picked points in drawing	Dimension picked points in drawing
Associative towards building elements	Associative or nonassociative towards points, depending on user settings	Associative towards points
Dimension groups	Dimension groups	Single dimensions
Support superscripting, variable extension line length	Support superscripting, variable extension line length	Supports no superscripting, variable extension line length
Dimension texts cannot be edited	Dimension texts cannot be edited	Dimension texts can be edited
Defined by AEC dimension style and AutoCAD dimension style	Defined by AEC dimension style and AutoCAD dimension style	Defined by AutoCAD dimension style

 Tip Since the AEC dimensions are based on AutoCAD's standard dimensioning variables, it is imperative that you have a good understanding of that system and its operation. This includes an understanding of the relationship between dimensioning and Model - Paperspace. This book assumes that understanding.

Hands-On

Setting the Text Style

Before setting the dimension styles, change the **Standard** text style. I prefer Stylus BT which comes with Architectural Desktop.

1. Start a new drawing using the AEC Model (Imperial - ctb) template.
2. Select **Format > Text Style** from the **Main** toolbar to bring up the **Text Style** dialog box.
3. Select the **New** button and create a new style name called **NEW Text**.
4. Set the **NEW Text** font to **Stylus BT** in the **Font Name** drop-down list, apply, and close (see Figure 13-1).

You have now created a Text style that you can use with AutoCAD Dimensions and Architectural Desktop AEC dimensions. Save this file.

Figure 13-1

Hands-On

Creating a Dimension Style

1. Select **Format > Dimension Style** from the **Main** toolbar to bring up the **Dimension Style Manager** dialog box.

2. Press the **New** button to bring up the **Create New Dimension Style** dialog box.

3. Set the following:

   a.   New Style Name = (put your name here)

   b.   Start With = **Standard**

   c.   Use for = **All dimensions**

4. Press the **Continue** button to bring up the **New Dimension Style** dialog box.

5. Select the **Text** tab.

6. Set the following:

   a.   Text style = **NEW Text**

   b.   Text height = **1/8"**

   c.   Text Placement Vertical = **Above**

   d.   Text Placement Horizontal = **Centered**

   e.   Text Alignment = **Aligned with dimension line**

7. Change to the **Lines and Arrows** tab.

8. Set the following:

   a.   Extend beyond dim lines = **1/16"**

   b.   Offset from origin = **1/16"**

   c.   Arrowheads 1st = **Architectural tick**

   d.   Arrowheads 2nd = **Architectural tick**

   e.   Leader = **Closed filled**

   f.   Arrow size = **1/16"**

9. Change to the **Fit** tab, and set **Use overall scale of:** to **48.0**.

10. Change to the **Primary Units** tab, and set the **Unit** format to **Architectural**.

11. Press **Set Current** and press **OK** to close the dialog boxes and return to the Drawing Editor.

Hands-On

Creating an AEC Dimension Style

1. Select **Format > AEC Dimension Styles** from the **Main** toolbar.

2. At the **Style Manager** dialog box, select the **New Style** icon in the top toolbar, and rename the new style (your name) (see Figure 13-2).

Figure 13-2

3. Select (your name) **DIM, RMB,** and select **Edit** from the contextual menu that appears to bring up the **AEC Dimension Style Properties** dialog box.

4. Select the **Display Properties** tab.

5. Double-click on **Plan** in the **Display Representations** column to bring up the **Display Properties** dialog box.

6. Select the **Contents** tab.

7. Select **Wall** from **Apply to**, check the **Length of Wall** check box, check the **Chain 1** check box, and select **Wall Length** from the **Length of Wall** drop-down list (see Figure 13-3).

8. Select the **Other** tab, and select (your name) **DIM** at the **Dimension Style** drop-down list. Make sure the check boxes are unchecked, and then press the **OK** buttons to return to the Drawing Editor.

You have now created an AEC dimension style called (your name) **DIM**. Save this file.

Figure 13-3

Hands-On

Using and Modifying an AEC Dimension Style

1. Use the previous exercise.
2. Change to the **Work Layout**.
3. Clear the viewports and create one viewport.
4. Change to the **Top View**.
5. Change to **Paper space**, select the viewport frame, and move your cursor over the **Properties** palette to open it.
6. Set the following:
a. Standard scale = **1/4" = 1'-0"**
7. Change to **Model** space.
8. Select the **Wall** icon from the **Design** tool palette, and move your cursor over the **Properties** palette to open it.
9. Set the following settings:
   a.   Style = **Standard**
   b.   Width = **6"**
   c.   Justify = **Left**
10. Create the walls shown in Figure 13-4. Don't include dimensions shown.

Figure 13-4

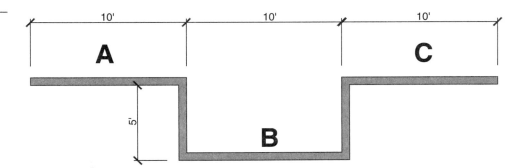

11. Select all wall segments, **RMB**, and select **AEC Dimension** from the contextual menu that appears.

12. Move your cursor over the **Properties** palette to open it.

13. Set the **Style** to **HEGRA AEC DIM** from the **Style** drop-down list.

14. Drag your cursor above the walls, and click to place dimensions for the walls.

15. Select the dimension string you just placed, **RMB**, and select **Remove Dimension Points** from the contextual menu that appears.

16. Select the dimension extension lines that you want removed, and they will turn red (see Figure 13-5).

Figure 13-5

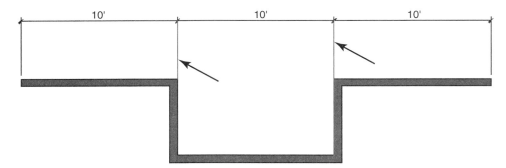

17. Press **Enter**. The extension lines will disappear, and the dimension string will show the total width between walls (see Figure 13-6).

Figure 13-6

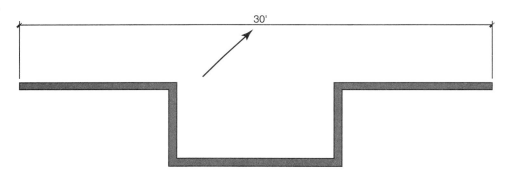

18. Select the dimension string again, **RMB**, and select **Add Dimension Points** from the contextual menu that appears.

19. Using an Object Snap, snap on a point you wish to add, press **Enter**, and then select the dimension chain to complete the command (see Figure 13-7).

Figure 13-7

20. Select the dimension string again, **RMB**, and select **Edit AEC Dimension Style** from the contextual menu that appears to bring up the **AEC Dimension Style** Properties dialog box.

21. Select the **Display Properties** tab.

22. Double-click on **Plan** in the **Display Representations** column to bring up the **Display Properties** dialog box, and select the **Contents** tab.

23. Check the **Wall Intersections** check box, and press the **OK** buttons to close the dialog boxes and return to the Drawing Editor.

The AEC dimension string now shows the wall intersections (see Figure 13-8). Save this file.

Figure 13-8

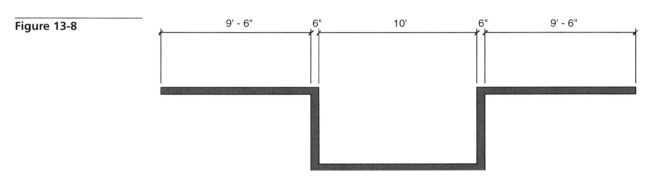

Hands-On

Dimensioning Doors and Windows with AEC Dimension Styles

1. Start a new drawing.

2. Select **Format > AEC Dimension Styles** from the **Main** toolbar again to bring up the **Style Manager**.

3. Double-click on (your name) **DIM** to bring up the **AEC Dimension Style Properties** dialog box.

4. Select the **Display Properties** tab.

5. Double-click on **Plan** in the **Display Representations** column to bring up the **Display Properties** dialog box.

6. Select the **Contents** tab, and select **Opening/Door/Window** from the **Apply to** list.

7. Check the **Center** check box, and clear the other check boxes (see Figure 13-9).

8. Select **Opening in Wall** from the **Apply to** list.

9. Check the **Center** checkbox, and clear the other check boxes.

10. Select the wall (see Figure 13-10), **RMB**, and select **Insert > Window** from the contextual menu that appears.

11. In the Properties tool palette make sure to check the **Automatic Offset/Center** checkbox, and insert a Standard 3'-wide, 5'-high window in the center of the wall.

12. Select all the walls, **RMB**, and select **AEC Dimension** from the contextual menu that appears.

Figure 13-9

13. Drag your cursor vertically above the horizontal walls, and click the mouse to place the dimension string.

The window will now be dimensioned by its center (see Figure 13-10).

Figure 13-10

14. Select the dimension string again, **RMB**, and select **Edit AEC Dimension Style** from the contextual menu that appears to bring up the **AEC Dimensional Style Properties** dialog box.

15. Select the **Display Properties** tab.

16. Double-click on **Plan** in the **Display Representations** column to bring up the **Display Properties** dialog box.

17. Select the **Contents** tab, and select **Opening/Door/Window** from the **Apply to** list

18. Check the **Center** checkbox, and clear the other check boxes (see Figure 13-11).

Figure 13-11

If there is some problem where dimension text overlaps, or if you want to modify the location of the text, you must do the following:

You can only display and move the **Edit in Place** grips of an AEC dimension text if the underlying AutoCAD dimension style has the correct text placement settings. To do this, select the AEC dimension string, **RMB**, and select **Edit AEC Dimension Style** from the contextual menu that appears. Then, select the display representation where you want the changes to appear, and check the **Style Override** check box to bring up the **Display Properties** dialog box. Click **Edit**, and in the **Dimension Style Manager**, click **Modify**. Click the **Fit** tab, and select **Over the dimension line, without a leader** for **Text Placement** (see Figure 13-12).

Figure 13-12

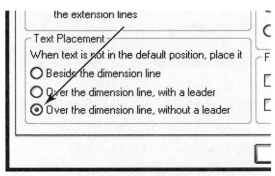

Now when you select the **Edit in Place** button for the AEC dimensions, a grip will appear on the dimension itself. You can grab that grip and move the dimension text anywhere you wish.

19. Move the window **24'-0"** to the left. (Use the move command, or activate the window's grips.)

Note that the AEC dimensions move with the window.

20. Select wall **B**, **RMB**, and again select **Insert > Window** from the contextual menu that appears.

21. Move your cursor over the **Properties** palette to open it.

22. Set the **Automatic Offset/Center** to **18"**, and pick a spot near the right side of wall B.

You should now have two windows centered in wall B, and the AEC dimensions should show the dimensions for the new window (see Figure 13-13).

Figure 13-13

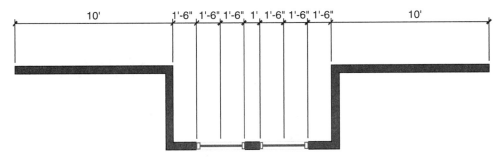

Explore the other Display Props for dimension styles. Save this exercise. Sometimes you will want to create an AEC dimension manually. Perhaps you want to dimension somewhere else than the built-in logical points.

Save this file.

Hands-On

Adding a Manual AEC Dimension

1. Use the previous exercise.

2. Lock your viewport.

3. Be sure the **MODEL** space button is activated.

4. Zoom in close to the two windows inserted in the B wall.

5. Select **Format > Point Style** from the **Main** menu.

6. In the **Point Style** dialog box, select the **X** (see Figure 13-14).

7. Type **dimpointmode** in the **Command line**, and press the space bar or **Enter**.

8. Type **T** in the **Command line**, and press the space bar or **Enter**.

This sets the dimension points to transformable. Transformable dimension points move and are updated with the object; static points stay in place.

9. Set the **Intersection** Object Snap.

10. Select the **AEC Dimension (1) - Manual** icon from the **Annotation** tool palette.

11. Pick the two corners of the two window jambs, and press the space bar or **Enter**.

12. Pick a point to place the dimension string, and then pick a second point to complete the command (see Figure 13-15).

Figure 13-14

Figure 13-15

13. Select the **Move** icon from the **Modify** toolbar, and select the left window with a window marquee (see Figure 13-16), and move it to the left 1'-0". Repeat with the right window (see Figure 13-17).

You must move the points with the window to maintain the associative dimensions. Repeat Steps 7 through 12, but enter **S** (Static) when prompted for dimpointmode points. Note that the dimensions don't move.

14. The point style you set in Step 6 will cause the points to show as X when you plot. To stop this, bring up the **Point Style** dialog box again, and change the point style to **NONE** (see Figure 13-18). Save this file.

Figure 13-16

Figure 13-17

Figure 13-18

Hands-On

Detaching Objects from AEC Dimensions

1. Use the previous exercise.

2. Zoom Extents (since the viewport is locked, the **Paperspace View** will zoom extents).

3. Select the AEC dimension string, **RMB**, and select **Detach Objects** icon from the contextual menu that appears.

4. Select the top AEC dimension group (dimension string), and press the space bar or **Enter**.

5. Select the left window object, and press the space bar or **Enter** (see Figure 13-19).

You have now detached the left window from the top AEC Dimension Group. Save this file.

Figure 13-19

Hands-On

AEC Dimension Chains

In order to clarify dimension strings, architects and architectural drafts-people often add additional dimension strings. Architectural Desktop 2005 calls these *chains*. The chain nearest the AEC Object is called "Chain1," the next is "Chain2," and so forth up to ten chains.

1. Use the previous exercise, and adjust the windows and AEC dimension settings to match Figure 13-20.

Figure 13-20

2. Select the AEC dimension string, **RMB**, and select **Edit AEC Dimension Style** from the contextual menu that appears to bring up the **AEC Dimensional Style Properties** dialog box.
3. Select the **Chains** tab.
4. Change the **Number of Chains** to **2**.
5. Change to the **Display Properties** tab.
6. Double-click on **Plan** in the **Display Representations** column to bring up the **Display Properties** dialog box.
7. Select the **Contents** tab.

Notice that two **Chain** check boxes now appear at the lower right of the **Contents** tab (see Figure 13-21).

Figure 13-21

8. Activate the **Chain1** field, select the **Wall** icon in the **Apply to** field, and clear all the **Wall** check boxes.

9. Select the **Opening/Door/Window** icon in the **Apply to** field, and check the **Opening/Door/Window Center** check box.

10. Activate the **Chain2** field, select the **Wall** icon in the **Apply to** field, and check the **Length of Wall** check box.

11. Press the **OK** buttons to return to the Drawing Editor (see Figure 13-22).

Figure 13-22

12. Select the AEC dimension string, **RMB**, and select **Add Dimension Points** and add a point to locate the windows.

13. Repeat Step 12, selecting **Remove Dimension points**, and remove the two **Chain2** dimension extension lines to create the image shown in Figure 13-23.

Figure 13-23

Hands-On

The AEC Dimension Wizard

Although you can set the AEC Dimension display manually as shown at the beginning of this section, Autodesk Architectural Desktop 2005 has provided a Wizard to aid you in setting the display.

Selecting the **Format** > **AEC Dimension Style Wizard** from the **Main** toolbar activates the dialog boxes shown in Figures 13-24 through 13-27.

Figure 13-24

Figure 13-25

Figure 13-26

Figure 13-27

14

Elevations

When you finish this section, you should understand the following:

- ✔ How to make a new **Elevations** tool palette.
- ✔ How to create a simple building.
- ✔ How to make an elevation.
- ✔ How to modify and update a 2D elevation.
- ✔ How to understand elevation subdivisions work.
- ✔ How to work with material boundaries.

Hands-On

Making a New Elevation Tool Palette

1. Create a new tool palette and name it **Elevations**.
2. Select the **Content Browser** icon from the **Main** toolbar to launch the Content Browser.
3. Locate the **Documentation Tool Catalog - Imperial**.
4. Locate the **Callouts > Elevation Marks** folder.
5. Drag all the elevation marks into the new tool palette you created.
6. Click and hold on the tab of your new tool palette and drag a copy to **My Tool Catalog** in the Content Browser.

For the following exploration of elevations, first create a simple three-story building.

Hands-On

Creating a Sample Building for the Elevation Exercises

1. Start a new drawing using the AEC Model (Imperial - ctb) template.

2. Change to **Top View**, and create the outline shown in Figure 14-1.

Figure 14-1

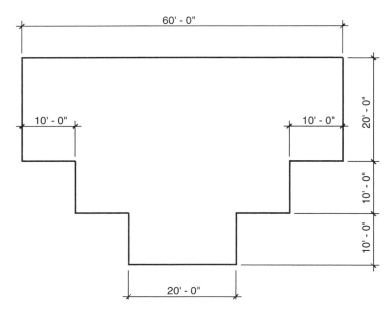

3. Select the **Wall** icon from the **Design** tool palette, **RMB**, and select **Apply Tool properties to > Linework** from the contextual menu that appears.

4. Select the outline you created.

5. Enter **Y** (Yes) in the command line to erase the geometry, and press **Enter** to create walls from the outline.

6. While the walls are still selected, move your cursor over the **Properties** palette to open it.

7. Set the following:
   a. Style = **Standard**
   b. Wall Width = **8"**
   c. Base Height = **10'-0"**
   d. Justify = **Baseline**

8. Save the drawing as **Floor 1**.

9. Save the drawing two more times as **Floor 2** and **Floor 3**.

10. Open **Floor 3**, select the **Roof** icon from the **Design** tool palette, **RMB**, and select **Apply Tool Properties to > Linework and Walls** from the contextual menu that appears.

11. Select all the walls in the **Floor 3** drawing.

12. Enter **N** (No) in the **Command line**, and press **Enter** to create the roof.

13. While the roof is still selected, move your cursor over the **Properties**

palette to open it.

14. Set the roof to the following:
    a. Thickness = **10"**
    b. Edge cut = **Square**
    c. Shape = **SingleSlope**
    d. Plate height = **10'-0"**
    e. Rise = **6"**

15. Save **Floor 3**.

16. Start a new drawing and save it as **Composite**.

17. Using **Insert > Xref Manager** from the **Main** toolbar, **Attach** the three floors at Z elevation of 0' for Floor 1, 10' for Floor 2, and 20' for Floor 3 in the Composite drawing.

You have now created the building in Figure 14-2.

18. Select **Floor 1** in the **Composite** drawing, **RMB**, and select **Edit Xref in place** from the contextual menu that appears to bring up the **Reference Edit** dialog box.

19. Press **OK** to return to the Drawing Editor.

20. Select different walls in the floor, **RMB**, and insert windows and a door.

21. Press the **Save back changes to reference** icon in the **Refedit** dialog box, and press the **OK** button that appears.

22. Repeat for each floor until you have a building similar to that shown in Figure 14-3. Save this exercise.

Figure 14-2

Figure 14-3

Hands-On

Making an Elevation

Using the previous exercise, select the Composite drawing.

1. Select the **Model Layout**, activate the **Top View,** and then pan the building to the left until it takes up a little less than half the page. Change the scale to **1/8" = 1'-0"** in the **Scale** pop-up list (see Figure 14-4).

Figure 14-4

2. Select the **Elevation Mark A1** from the **Elevations** tool palette, and click and place an elevation line starting at the lower center in front of the building. Drag your cursor as shown in Figure 14-5.

3. Click your mouse again to bring up the **Place Callout** dialog box.

4. Check the **Generate Section/Elevation** check box. Make sure the scale is set to the same scale you set in the **Scale** pop-up list, and press the **Current Drawing** icon (see Figure 14-6).

5. Select the region of the elevation you wish to generate (see Figure 14-7).

6. Move your cursor to an insertion point for your generated elevation, and click the mouse button. Your elevation will now appear (see Figure 14-8).

Save this exercise, and all its files.

Figure 14-5

Figure 14-6

Figure 14-7

Figure 14-8

Hands-On

Modifying and Updating the 2D Elevation

1. Open the Composite drawing from the previous exercise.
2. Change to the **SW Isometric View**.
3. Select the first floor in the Composite drawing, **RMB,** and select **Edit Xref in place** from the contextual menu that appears to bring up the **Reference Edit** dialog box.
4. Press **OK** to return to the Drawing Editor.
5. Select the front wall of the first floor, **RMB,** and insert windows on either side of the front door.
6. In the **Refedit** dialog box, press the **Save back changes to reference** icon button, and press **OK** at the AutoCAD message.
7. Change back to the **Top View,** and select the 2D elevation that you created.
8. **RMB** the 2D elevation, and select **Refresh** from the contextual menu that appears.

The 2D elevation now reflects the changes made in the 3D model (see Figure 14-9). Save this exercise.

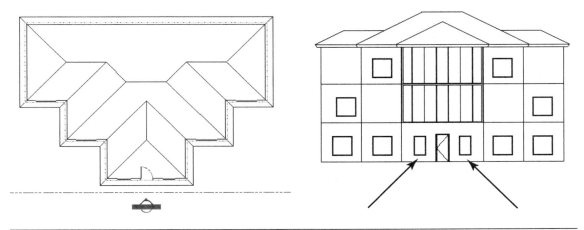

Figure 14-9

Hands-On

Understanding Subdivisions

1. Using the previous exercise, select the elevation line object, and move your cursor over the **Properties** palette to open it.

2. Click in the **Subdivisions** field to open the **Subdivisions** dialog box.

3. Press the **Add** button, add a 10'-0" subdivision, and press **OK** to return to the Drawing Editor.

You have now created Subdivision 1 (see Figure 14-10).

 Note: Once you have a subdivision, you can select the elevation, and move the subdivision with grips.

4. Move the Subdivision 1 line so that the front extension of the building is within the first subdivision (see Figure 14-11).

5. Select the 2D elevation, **RMB**, and select **Edit Object Display** from the contextual menu that appears to bring up the **Object Display** dialog box.

6. Select the **Display Properties** tab, and check the **Override** check box to bring up the **Display Properties** dialog box.

7. Select the **Layer/Color/Linetype** tab.

8. Change the Subdivision 1 **Color** to **blue**, select **OK**, and close all the dialog boxes.

9. Select the elevation, **RMB**, and select **Refresh** from the contextual menu.

You have now changed Subdivision 1 to a blue color. Anything between the defining line and Subdivision 1 will be blue in the elevation. You can also set the line width to be different in a subdivision (see Figure 14-12).

10. Select the elevation line object, **RMB**, and add two more subdivisions.

11. In the **Top View**, move the topmost boundary to the back of the building.

Subdivision 1

Figure 14-10

Figure 14-11

Distance of Subdivision 0

Front Extension

12. Select the elevation, **RMB,** and again select **Edit 2D Section/Elevation Style** from the contextual menu that appears.

13. Change the Subdivision 2 **Color** to **green,** and Subdivision 3 **Color** to **black** (black will say "white" in the dialog box). Change the

subdivision 1

Figure 14-12

Figure 14-13

Lineweight of Subdivision 3 to **.30 mm**, select **OK**, close all the dialog boxes, and return to the Drawing Editor (see Figure 14-13).

14. Select the elevation line to activate it, and using the grips (be sure your Object Snap is turned off) move the subdivisions to look like Figure 14-14.

15. Select the elevation, **RMB**, and select **Refresh** from the contextual menu that appears. Make sure the **LTW** button at the bottom of the screen is active (to visually show lineweights in the drawing).

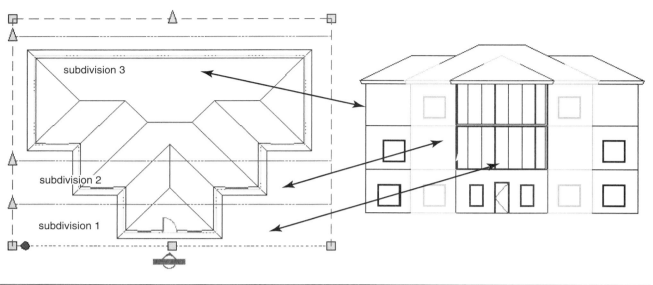

Figure 14-14

Notice that the back outline of the building is black with a .30 mm out-line. This is because everything between Subdivision 2 and 3 will have the attributes of Subdivision 3. Notice that there is a problem at the roof. Because the roof is pitched, it crosses both Subdivision 2 and 3. You might also want the roof pitch between Subdivision 1 and 2 to be all one color (see Figure 14 -15).

To fix these problems, you will use the **Linework > Edit** command.

1. Select the 2D elevation, **RMB**, and select **Linework > Edit** from the con-textual menu that appears (see Figure 14-16).

Figure 14-15

Figure 14-16

2. Select the segment of lines that you wish to edit, and erase them.

3. Using the **Line** command, replace the line with new lines (see Figure 14-17).

4. After placing the new lines, press the **Save All Changes** icon in the **In-Place Edit** dialog box shown in Figure 14-17.

5. Select the elevation again, **RMB**, and select **Linework > Merge** from the contextual menu that appears.

6. Select the two lines you just placed and press **Enter**.

7. The **Select Linework Component** dialog box will now appear.

Figure 14-17

8. Select **Subdivision 3** from the **Linework Component** drop-down list, and press the **OK** button (Figure 14-18).

The lines will merge with the subdivision lines and have the same lineweight (see Figure 14-19).

Figure 14-18

Figure 14-19

To fix the roof pitch between Subdivision 1 and 2 do the following:

9. Select the elevation again, **RMB**, and select **Linework > Edit** from the contextual menu that appears.

10. Select the two lines at the top of the front roof pitch, **RMB**, and select **Modify Component** from the contextual menu that appears (see Figure 14-20).

Figure 14-20

11. The **Select Linework Component** dialog box will appear again.

12. Select **Subdivision 1** from the **Linework Component** drop-down list, and press the **OK** button. The lines will now turn blue to match Subdivision 1.

Add the remaining lines, select **Linework > Edit**, and complete the elevation.

Save this file.

Hands-On

Working with Material Boundaries

1. Close the Composite drawing.

2. Reopen the drawings for Floors 1, 2, and 3.

3. In each drawing, select all the walls, **RMB** on the **Brick4 Brick 4** icon in the **Walls** tool palette and select **Wall** from the option that appears. The walls will turn into brick walls.

4. Save all the drawings you just changed, and reopen the Composite drawing. All the walls in the building model are now brick.

5. Select the generated elevation, **RMB**, and select **Refresh** from the contextual menu that appears. The elevation now contains brick walls (see Figure 14-21).

6. Zoom in close to the generated elevation, and using the polyline command, create the closed polyline shown in Figure 14-22.

Figure 14-21

Figure 14-22

closed Polyline

7. Select the generated elevation, **RMB**, and select **Material Boundary > Add** from the contextual menu that appears.

8. Select the closed polyline, enter **Y** (Yes) in the **Command line**, and press **Enter** to bring up the **2D Section/Elevation Material Boundary** dialog box.

9. Select **Limit** from the **Purpose** drop-down list, and Surface **Hatching Only** from the **Apply to:** drop-down list.

10. Press the **OK** button to create the material boundary (see Figure 14-23).

Figure 14-23

Hands-On

New Autodesk Architectural Desktop 2005 Feature

Showing Common Materials as One Surface and Showing Objects Hidden behind Other Objects in Generated Elevations

1. Start a new drawing using the AEC Model (Imperial - ctb) template.

2. Change to the **Top View**.

3. Select the **Concrete-8** icon from the **Walls** tool palette and create a 10' x 10' enclosure 8' high.

4. Select the **Slab** icon from the **Design** tool palette, **RMB**, and select **Linework and Walls** from the contextual menu that appears.

5. Select all the walls of the enclosure you just created and press **Enter**.

6. Enter **N** (No) in the **Command line** and press **Enter**.

7. Enter **B** (Bottom) in the **Command line** and press **Enter**.

8. Enter **R** (Right) in the **Command line** and press **Enter**.

9. Enter **L** (Left) in the **Command line** and press **Enter**.

10. Select the slab you have just created, move your cursor over the **Properties** palette to open it, and set the **Thickness** to **8"**, and **Elevation** to **0**.

11. Change to the **Front View** and using the **Array** command, array your enclosure and slab three rows high (see Figure 14-24).

12. Change to the **Top View** and, using the **Elevation Mark A1**, generate an elevation in the current drawing. Notice the floor division lines (see Figure14-25).

Floor Lines

Figure 14-24   **Figure 14-25**

13. Select **Format > Material Definitions** from the **Main** menu to bring up the **Style Manager**.

14. Double-click on **Concrete.Cast-in-place.Flat** to bring up the **Material Definition Properties** dialog box.

15. Double-click on **General Medium Detail** to open the **Display Properties** dialog box.

16. Change to the **Other** tab.

17. Check the **Merge Common Materials** check box, press the **OK** button, and close all the dialog boxes (see Figure 14-26).

18. Select the generated elevation, **RMB**, and select **Refresh** from the contextual menu that appears. The floor lines disappear (see Figure 14-27).

19. Repeat Steps 13 through 17, this time checking the **Display Hidden Edges for this Material** check box in the **Display Properties** dialog box.

20. Again, select the generated elevation, **RMB**, and select **Refresh** from the contextual menu that appears. The hidden wall lines appear (see Figure 14-28).

21. Because the slabs are using standard material, repeat Steps 13 through 17, selecting the standard material and checking the **Display Hidden Edges for this Material** check box in the **Display Properties** dialog box.

22. Again, select the generated elevation, **RMB**, and select **Refresh** from the contextual menu that appears. The hidden slab lines appear (see Figure 14-29).

Figure 14-26

Figure 14-27   **Figure 14-28**   **Figure 14-29**

Section 15

Sections

When you finish this section, you should understand the following:

- ✔ How to make a new **Section** tool palette.
- ✔ How to create a simple building.
- ✔ How to place a section object.
- ✔ How to generate a section.
- ✔ How to change the section arrow appearance.
- ✔ Live section definitions.
- ✔ Creating a sample building for a live section.
- ✔ How to create a Live section.
- ✔ How to modify a Live section.

Sections

There are two different types of sections you can create in Architectural Desktop: Standard sections and Live sections.

Live sections cut only in Model Views and are limited to the following AEC Objects only:

- n Walls
- n Doors, Windows, and Door and Window assemblies
- n Mass elements and mass groups
- n Stairs and railings
- n Roofs and roof slabs
- n Spaces and space boundaries
- n Curtain wall layouts and units
- n Structural members

Hands-On

Making a New Section Tool Palette

1. Create a new tool palette, and name it **Section**.
2. Select the **Content Browser** icon from the **Main** tool bar to launch the Content Browser.
3. Locate **Documentation Tool Catalog - Imperial**.
4. Locate the **Callouts > Section Marks** folder.
5. Drag all the section marks into the new tool palette you created.
6. Click and hold on the tab of your new tool palette and drag a copy to **My Tool Catalog** in the Content Browser.

For the following exercise create a sample residence.

Hands-On

Creating the Sample Building

1. Start a new drawing using the AEC Model (Imperial - ctb) template.
2. Change to the **Model Layout**.
3. Change to **Top View**, select the **Wall** icon from the **Design** tool palette, and move your cursor over the **Properties** palette to open it.
4. Set the following:
   a. Style = **Standard**
   b. Wall Width = **8"**
   c. Base Height = **8'-0"**
   d. Justify = **Baseline**
5. Place the walls as shown in Figure 15-1.

Figure 15-1

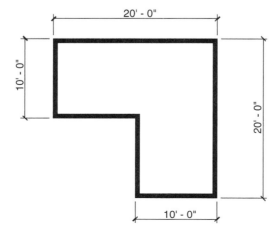

6. Select the **Roof** icon from the **Design** tool palette, **RMB**, and select **Apply Tool Properties to > Linework and Walls** from the contextual menu that appears.

7. Select all the walls in your drawing.

8. Enter **N** (No) in the command line, and press **Enter** to create the roof.

9. While the roof is still selected, move your cursor over the **Properties** palette to open it.

10. Set the roof to the following:
    a. Thickness = **10"**
    b. Edge cut = **Square**
    c. Shape = **SingleSlope**
    d. Plate height = **8'-0"**
    e. Rise = **12"**

11. Select the **Slab** icon from the **Design** tool palette, **RMB**, and select **Apply Tool Properties to > Linework and Walls** from the contextual menu that appears.

12. Again, select all the walls in your drawing, and press **Enter**.

13. Enter **N** (No) in the command line and press **Enter**.

14. Enter **T** (Top) in the command line and press **Enter**.

15. Enter **R** (Right) in the command line and press **Enter** twice to place the slab.

16. While the slab is still selected, move your cursor over the **Properties** palette to open it.

17. Set the following:
    a. Style = **Standard**
    b. Thickness = **4"**
    c. Elevation = **0"**

18. Select the **Quick Select** icon in the **Properties** palette, select all the walls, and press **OK**.

19. With the walls selected, **RMB** anywhere in the Drawing Editor, and select **Insert > Window** from the contextual menu that appears.

20. Place 2' × 4'-high Standard windows on each wall as shown in Figure 15-2.

21. With the walls still selected, **RMB** anywhere in the Drawing Editor, and select **Insert > Door** from the contextual menu that appears.

22. Place a 3'-0" × 6'-8"-high Standard door as shown in Figure 15-2.

Figure 15-2

Hands-On

Placing the Standard Section Object

1. Select the **Section Mark A1** from the **Section** tool palette, click and drag through a window, and then click again through another window.

2. Press **Enter**, move your cursor in the view direction you wish to cut the section, and click the mouse button to bring up the **Place Callout** dialog box.

3. Name the view, check the **Generate Section/Elevation** check box, set the **Scale** to **1/8″ = 1′-0″**, and press the **Current Drawing** icon.

4. Move your cursor to an insertion point for the generated section, and click the mouse button to create the generated section.

! ***Note:*** If you want to show the section object constantly in the Drawing Editor, do the following:

    a. Select the section line, **RMB**, and select **Edit Object Display** from the contextual menu that appears to bring up the **Object Display** dialog box.

    b. Check the **Object Override** check box for the **Plan** display representation to bring up the **Display Properties** dialog box.

    c. Turn on the visibility of the boundary, press **OK,**and close all the dialog boxes to return to the Drawing Editor (see Figure 15-3).

Figure 15-3

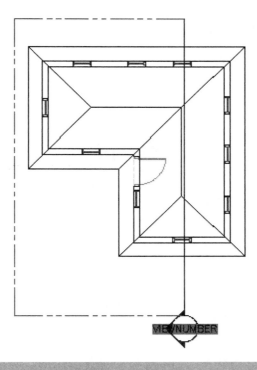

Hands-On

Reversing the Section Direction

1. Select the section line, **RMB**, and select **Reverse** from the contextual menu that appears.

2. Using the **Mirror** command, select the direction arrow and view number and reverse them.

3. Select the generated section, **RMB**, and select **Refresh** from the contextual menu that appears (see Figure 15-4).

Figure 15-4

Hands-On

Modifying the Section

1. Reverse the section again.

2. Double-click the roof to open the **Properties** palette.

3. Change the **Rise** to **4"**.

4. Select the generated section, **RMB**, and select **Refresh** from the contextual menu that appears. Notice that anything you change in the building model will change in the generated section when you refresh it (see Figure 15-5).

Figure 15-5

Hands-On

Customizing the Section Arrow Appearance

1. Select the **VIEWNUMBER** text, **RMB**, and select **Edit Block in-place** from the contextual menu that appears to bring up the **Reference Edit** dialog box.

2. Press **OK** to return to the Drawing Editor.

3. Erase the circle and add a rectangle (see Figure 15-6).

4. Press the **Save back changes to reference** icon in the **Refedit** dialog box that appeared near the arrow.

5. Select the direction arrow, **RMB** and select **Edit Block in-place** from the contextual menu that appears to bring up the **Reference Edit** dialog box.

6. Press **OK** to return to the Drawing Editor.

7. Erase the existing arrow and add a new arrow. You could even add your company logo. You now have a custom section line object arrow (see Figure 15-7).

Figure 15-6

Figure 15-7

Live Sections

Unlike generated sections, Live sections retain the original objects after sectioning, can set display properties for all objects in section, and can set hatching for section boundaries.

Note: Each new Live section is displayed in a separate display configuration created specifically for that section. See the explanation of display configurations in this book.

Live section AEC objects consist of six components (see Figure 15-8).

n **Cutting boundary** - Outside limit of the section (section line)

n **Hatch** - Graphic indication of area inside the cutting boundary

n **Inside cutting boundary** - Remaining object cut by cutting boundary *inside* cutting boundary

n **Outside cutting boundary** - Remaining object cut by cutting boundary *outside* cutting boundary

Figure 15-8

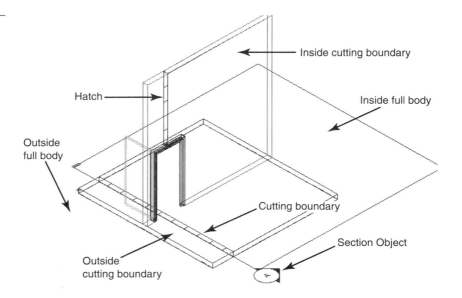

n **Inside full body** - Object completely *inside* section

n **Outside full body** - Object completely *outside* section

Before a live section or any section can be created, a section mark or section line must be placed in your drawing to identify where the section is to take place.

Hands-On

Creating a Sample Building for a Live Section

1. Start a new drawing using the AEC Model (Imperial - ctb) template.

2. Change to **Top View**.

3. Select the **CMU-8 Rigid-1.5 Air-2 Brick-4 Furring Wall** icon from the **Walls** tool palette in the **Autodesk Architectural Desktop Sample Palette Catalog - Imperial**, and create a 10'-0"x 10'-0" enclosure.

4. Select the left wall, **RMB**, and select **Insert Door** from the contextual menu.

5. Place a 3'-0" Standard door centered in the left wall, swinging inward (see Figure 15-9).

Figure 15-9

6. Select **Sections Mark A1** from the **Section** tool palette.

7. Place the start point at the left of the door, place the second point to the right of the right wall, and press **Enter**. Move your cursor in the view direction you wish to cut the section, and click the mouse button to bring up the **Place Callout** dialog box.

8. Name the view, check the **Generate Section/Elevation** check box, set the **Scale** to **1/8" = 1'-0"**, and press the **Current Drawing** icon.

9. Move your cursor to an insertion point for the generated section, and click the mouse button to create a generated section (see Figure 15-10).

Figure 15-10

It is a good idea to show the section object constantly in the Drawing Editor (follow the directions mentioned in the earlier section, "Placing the Standard section object").

Hands-On

Creating the Live Section

1. Use the previous exercise.

2. Select the section object, (the cutting plane) **RMB,** and select **Enable Live Section** from the contextual menu that appears.

A 3D sectioned model of the enclosure appears (see Figure 15-11) in the Axonometric viewport.

3. Change to the **Work Layout**.

4. Place one viewport of the enclosure in **Top View** and the other in **Front View**.

5. Change to the **Front View**.

6. Select the **Hidden** icon in the **Shading** toolbar to display the Live section in hidden display.

Figure 15-11

7. Notice that the sectioned view displays symbols of all the materials set for the wall components (see Figure 15-12).

Figure 15-12

8. Double-click on the front wall to open its **Properties** palette.

9. Change the **Style** to **Standard**.

10. Return to the Drawing Editor, and notice that the front wall in the **Top View (Plan View)** has changed (see Figure 15-13).

11. Open the Content Browser (by pressing **Ctrl + 4**).

12. Add the **Bow Window Set** from the **Design Tool Catalog** to your tool palette.

13. Click the **Bow Window Set** icon in your tool palette, and select the wall illustrated in Figure 15-14.

14. Insert the **Bow Window Set** into the live section in the **Front View**. Notice that the window now also appears in the **Top View** (see Figure 15-15).

Figure 15-13

Figure 15-14

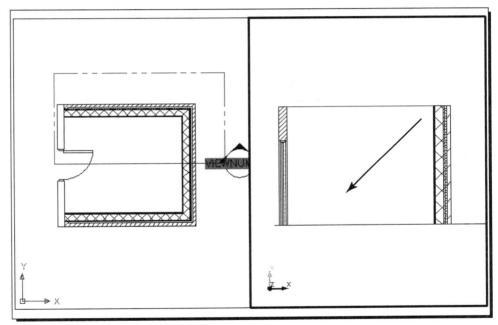

All the AEC components in a live section such as door size, hatching, etc. can be changed in the section, and will reflect in the 2D plan drawing.

Figure 15-15

Hands-On

Modifying a Live Section

1. Select the section line object and move it so that it does not pass through the door. See that the Live section changes (see Figure 15-16).

Figure 15-16

2. Select the section line object and rotate it. See that the Live section changes (see Figure 15-17).

Using the Live section concept, you can adjust your sections automatically, even in another drawing, by changing the plan or changing the Live section.

Figure 15-17

16

Drawing Management

When you finish this section, you should understand the following:

- ✔ The Drawing Management concept.
- ✔ How to use the **Project Browser**.
- ✔ How to create constructs and elements in the **Project Navigator**.
- ✔ How to work with constructs and elements in the **Project Navigator**.
- ✔ How to assign constructs and elements in the **Project Navigator**.
- ✔ How to create views in the **Project Navigator**.
- ✔ How to create plotting sheets in the **Project Navigator**.

Autodesk Architectural Desktop 2005's Drawing Management feature automates the building design and document process. With this feature, all your project document files are codified in a central location from which you can call up and modify any drawing. This feature allows you to manage projects, automatically control levels, and create views and sheets. See Figure 16-1.

Figure 16-1

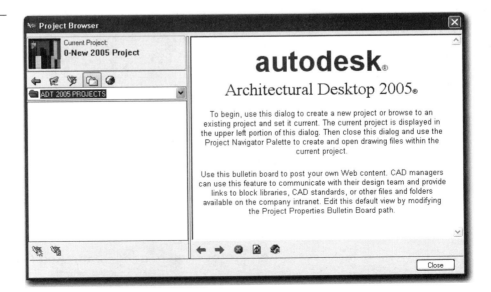

In reality, the new Drawing Management feature is an advanced form of external referencing (XREF), which has been a feature of AutoCAD and Architectural Desktop for many releases. Using XML programming in conjunction with XREF, the programmers have created a very comprehensive system for automating this process.

Because the Drawing Management system is so closely related to the XREF system, those who understand how to use the conventional XREF will find the learning curve for this advanced feature easily comprehendible. For those who are totally new to AutoCAD or Architectural Desktop, this author suggests that you first read the online help on XREF before going on to the Drawing Management system.

The Drawing Management Concept

The Drawing Management system is based on a hierarchy starting with the project, which is made of constructs, elements, views, and plot sheets. Through sophisticated automated XREF commands, elements are XREFed into constructs, which are XREFed into views and then XREFed into plot sheets. See Figure 16-2.

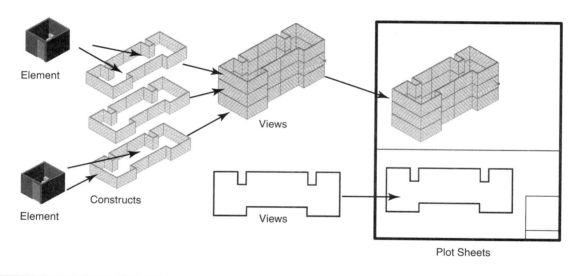

Figure 16-2

Hands-On

Using the Project Browser

1. In **Windows Explorer,** create a Microsoft Windows file directory and name it **ADT 2005 Projects**.

2. Start **Autodesk Architectural Desktop 2005**.

3. Start a new drawing using the AEC Model (Imperial - ctb) template.

4. Select **File > Project Browser** from the **Main** menu to bring up the **Project Browser** dialog box (see Figure 16-3).

5. Locate the **ADT 2005 Projects** directory from the drop-down list.

6. Press the **Add Project** icon to bring up the **Add Project** dialog box.

Figure 16-3

7. Enter the following information (see Figure 16-4):

   a.   Number = **100**

   b.   Name = **TEST PROJECT**

   c.   Description: **3 Story Building**

   d.   Bulletin Board = (Any Intranet or leave Default directory)

   e.   Project Image = (Any small GIF image or leave Default directory)

   f.   Prefix Filenames with project Number = **Yes** (from drop-down list)

   g.   Default Construction Template = (accept default - AEC Model (Imperial - stb).dwt)

   h.   Default Element Template = (accept default - AEC Model (Imperial - stb).dwt)

   i.   Default View Template = (accept default - AEC Model (Imperial - stb).dwt)

   j.   Default Sheet Template = (accept default - Architectural Sheet (Imperial - stb).dwt)

   k.   Default Section/Elevation View Template = (accept default - AEC Model (Imperial - stb).dwt.)

   l.   Default View Template = (accept default - AEC Model (Imperial - stb).dwt.)

   m.   Default Sheet Set Template = (accept default - AEC Sheet Set (Imperial - stb).dst.)

   n.   Default Project Details Template = (accept default - AEC Project Details.apj)

Figure 16-4

8. Press Edit to bring up the **Project Details** dialog box. Here you can add information such as telephone numbers, billing addresses, and owner's representative (see Figure 16-5).

Figure 16-5

9. Press the **OK** buttons to return to the **Project Browser**.

10. Press the **Project History** icon to open the past created projects.

11. Select the drop-down list shown in Figure 16-6 to locate past projects by the **Most Recently Used, By Date, By Project**, or **By Location** options.

12. **RMB** on **TEST PROJECT** in the list and select **Set Project Current** from the contextual menu that appears.

The project will now appear in the Project Browser's header (see Figure 16-7).

13. Press the **Close** button to return to the Drawing Editor, and automatically open the **Project Navigator** palette (see Figure 16-8).

Figure 16-6

Figure 16-7

Figure 16-8

Edit
Levels Icon

Hands-On

Creating Constructs and Elements in the Project Navigator

This project will have three floors with a basement. The second and third floors will each have two apartments, and the apartments will have bathrooms.

1. In the **Project** tab, select the **Edit Levels** icon in the top right corner of the levels information to bring up the **Levels** dialog box.

2. In the **Levels** dialog box, press the **Add Level**, create four levels, and enter the information as shown in Figure 16-9. Be sure to check the **Auto-Adjust** check box so that the **Floor Elevation** adjusts when you enter the **Floor to Floor Height**.

3. Press **OK** to return to the **Project Navigator** palette.

4. Select the **Constructs** tab.

The **Constructs** tab contains the **Constructs** and **Elements** folders, plus preview and detail screens to view their contents (see Figure 16-10).

Figure 16-9

Figure 16-10

5. In the **Constructs** tab, select the **Constructs** folder, **RMB**, and select **New > Construct** from the contextual menu that appears to bring up the **Add Construct** dialog box.

6. Enter **BASEMENT WALLS** in the **Name** field.

7. Check the **Basement** check box and press **OK** (see Figure 16-11).

8. In the **Constructs** tab, select the **Elements** folder, **RMB**, and select **New > Element** from the contextual menu that appears to bring up the **Add Element** dialog box.

9. Enter **COLUMN GRID** in the **Name** field and press **OK**.

10. Create new elements, and name them **APARTMENT WALLS** and **BATH ROOM** (see Figure 16-12).

Figure 16-11

Figure 16-12

Hands-On

Working with Constructs and Elements in the Project Navigator

1. After the constructs and elements have been labeled, double-click on the **Column Grid** icon to bring up the **COLUMN GRID** drawing.

2. Allow the **Project Navigator** palette to close in order to provide more room to work in the Drawing Editor.

3. In the **COLUMN GRID** drawing, change to the **Top View**, and place a structural column grid 120' wide by 60'-deep with 20'-0" bays in both directions, and 10' columns.

4. Select the column grid, **RMB**, and select **Label** from the contextual menu that appears.

5. Label the bottom and right of the grid with letters and numbers respectively (see Figure 16-13).

Figure 16-13

6. Select **File > Save** from the **Main** toolbar, and save the **COLUMN GRID** drawing.

7. Move your cursor over the **Project Navigator** palette (to open it) and double-click on the **Basement Walls** icon to open the BASEMENT WALLS drawing.

8. Open the **Project Navigator** again, select the **Column Grid** icon, and drag the icon into the **BASEMENT WALLS** drawing.

The grid you made previously will now be XREFed into the **BASEMENT WALLS** drawing.

9. Turn the **Node** Object Snap on.

10. Using the **Node** snap, place Standard 12"-wide, 10'-high walls as shown in Figure 16-14.

11. Delete the **COLUMN GRID** XREF and save the **BASEMENT WALLS** drawing.

12. Move your cursor over the **Project Navigator** palette to open it, select the **BASEMENT WALLS** construct, **RMB,** and select **Copy Construct to Levels** from the contextual menu that appears to bring up the **Copy Construct to Levels** dialog box.

13. Check the **First Floor**, **Second Floor**, and **Third Floor** check boxes, and then press **OK**.

The **Project Navigator Constructs** tab now contains three copies of the basement walls labeled BASEMENT WALLS (2), (3), and (4) (see Figure 16-15).

Figure 16-14

Figure 16-15

14. Select the **BASEMENT WALLS (2)**, **(3)**, and **(4)**, and rename them **FIRST FLOOR WALLS**, **SECOND FLOOR WALLS**, and **THIRD FLOOR WALLS** respectively.

15. Change to the **Views** tab in the **Project Navigator**.

16. Press the **Add View** icon to bring up the **Add View** dialog box.

17. Select the **General View** radio button (see Figure 16-16).

18. Press **OK** to bring up the **Add General View** dialog box.

19. Enter **TOTAL PERSPECTIVE** in the **Name** field and press **Next**.

20. In the next dialog box, check all **Level** check boxes and press **Next** again.

21. In the next dialog box, make sure that all the check boxes are checked, and press **Finish** to return to the Drawing Editor.

Figure 16-16

A new view called **TOTAL** will now appear in the **Views** tab of the **Project Navigator**.

22. Double-click on **TOTAL** in the **Views** tab to open it in the Drawing Editor.

23. Select the **Hidden** icon on the **Shading** toolbar, change to the **SW Isometric View**, and save the drawing.(see Figure 16-17).

24. Change back to the **Constructs** tab in the **Project Navigator**.

25. Double-click on **APARTMENT WALLS** under **Elements** to bring up the **APARTMENT WALLS** drawing in the Drawing Editor.

Figure 16-17

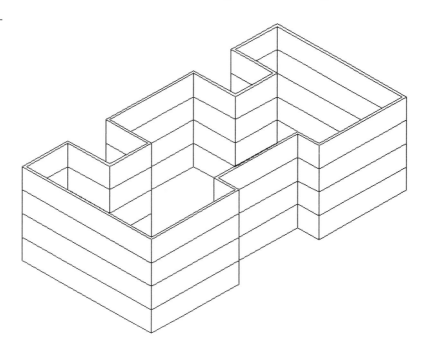

26. Drag the **Second Floor Walls** icon into the **APARTMENT WALLS** drawing.

27. Select the **Standard** wall from the **Design** tool palette, and place 4"-wide × 8'-high walls and 3'-0" doors as shown in Figure 16-18.

Figure 16-18

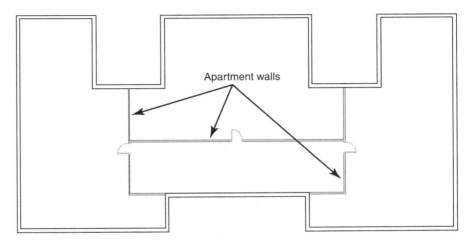

Apartment walls

28. Delete the **SECOND FLOOR WALLS** and save the **APARTMENT WALLS** drawing.

29. In the **Constructs** tab of the **Project Navigator**, create two new elements called **COLUMNS** and **FLOORS**.

30. Double-click the **Column Grid** icon to bring up the **COLUMN GRID** drawing in the Drawing Editor.

31. Select all the columns, **RMB**, and select **Node Anchor > Release** from the contextual menu that appears.

32. Select all the columns, and select **Edit > Cut** from the **Main** menu.

33. In the **Constructs** tab of the **Project Navigator**, double-click on **COLUMNS** to open the **COLUMNS** drawing in the Drawing Editor.

34. Select **Edit > Paste to Original Coordinates** from the **Main** menu, and save the **COLUMNS** drawing.

35. Double-click on the **FLOORS** element to bring it up in the Drawing Editor.

36. Drag the **BASEMENT** construct into the **FLOORS** element drawing in the Drawing Editor.

37. Enter **BPOLY** in the command line and press **Enter**.

38. Click in the middle of the **BASEMENT WALLS** that have been XREFed into the **FLOORS** construct to create a polyline.

39. Delete the **BASEMENT WALLS** from the **FLOORS** element drawing leaving only the polyline.

40. RMB the **Slab** tool in the **Design** tool palette, and select **Apply Tool Properties to > Linework and Walls** from the contextual menu that appears.

41. Select the polyline you just created and press **Enter**.

42. Enter **Y** (Yes) in the command line and press **Enter**.

43. Enter **D** (Direct) in the command line and press **Enter**.

44. Enter **B** (Bottom) in the command line and press **Enter**.

You have now created the floor slab.

45. While the slab is still selected, change its Thickness to **4″** in the **Properties** palette.

46. Save the file.

47. Open the **Project Navigator** again, and double-click on the **BATH ROOM** icon under the **Elements** folder to bring up the **BATHROOM** drawing in the Drawing Editor.

48. In the **BATHROOM** drawing, create a 10′-0″ square enclosure using Standard 4″-wide x 8′-0″-high walls.

49. Select one wall, **RMB**, and insert a Standard door 2′-6″ wide by 6′-8″ high.

50. Place a vanity, toilet, and spa tub from the **Design Tool Catalog – Imperial > Mechanical > Plumbing Fixtures** catalog.

51. Select the **Ceiling Grid** icon from the **Design** tool palette, center a 2′-0″ × 2′-0″ ceiling grid at 7′-6″ elevation, and save the file (see Figure 16-19).

You have now created all the parts for your building.

Figure 16-19

Hands-On

Putting the Elements and Constructs Together

1. In the **Constructs** tab of the **Project Manager**, double-click on the **BASEMENT WALLS** construct to open it in the Drawing Editor.

2. Drag the **FLOORS** and **COLUMNS** elements into the Drawing Editor, and save the file.

3. In the **Constructs** tab of the **Project Manager**, double-click on the **FIRST FLOOR WALLS** construct to open it in the Drawing Editor.

4. Drag the **FLOORS** and **COLUMNS** elements into the Drawing Editor, and save the file.

5. In the **Constructs** tab of the **Project Manager**, double-click on the **SECOND FLOOR WALLS** construct to open it in the Drawing Editor.

6. Drag the **FLOORS**, **COLUMNS**, **APARTMENT WALLS**, and **BATH ROOM** elements into the Drawing Editor.

7. Copy the **BATHROOM** element twice, arrange as shown in Figure 16-20, and save the file.

Figure 16-20

8. Select the apartment walls and bath rooms you just dragged into the **SECOND FLOOR WALLS** drawing.

9. While selected, open the **Properties** palette and set the Insertion point Z to **4"** (this places these elements on top of the 4"-thick FLOORS).

10. Repeat Steps 5 to 9 of this for the third floor walls, and save that file.

11. In the **Views** tab of the **Project Navigator**, double-click on the **Total View** to open it in the Drawing Editor.

Note: If the **Total View** is already in the Drawing Editor, and changes have been made to any of the xref that comprise this view, you will get a yellow message reminding you to reload. To do this, **RMB** on the icon shown in Figure 16-21, and select **Reload Xref** from the contextual menu that appears to create the updated **Total View** (see Figure 16-22).

Figure 16-21

Figure 16-22

Hands-On

Modifying the Constructs and Their Effects on the Views

1. In the Constructs tab of the **Project Navigator**, double-click on the **FIRST FLOOR WALLS** construct to open it in the Drawing Editor.

2. **RMB** the **Curtain Wall** tool in the **Design** menu, select **Apply Tool Properties to > Walls**, and select the indented front wall of the **FIRST FLOOR WALLS** construct.

3. For the curtain wall alignment, choose **Baseline**, and choose **Y** (Yes) to erase the layout geometry.

4. Drag the new curtain wall to a height of 35'.

5. Change to **Front View**.

6. Select the curtain wall, press the **Edit Grid** button, click the left edge of the curtain wall, **RMB**, and select **Convert To Manual** from the contextual menu that appears.

7. Adjust the curtain wall as shown in Figure 16-23 and save its in-place edit changes.

The curtain wall needs to span the first, second, and third floors. To coordinate these, do the following:

Figure 16-23

8. In the **Constructs** tab of the **Project Navigator**, **RMB** on the **FIRST FLOOR WALLS** construct, and select **Properties** from the contextual menu that appears to bring up the **Modify Construct** dialog box.

9. Select the **First Floor**, **Second Floor**, and **Third Floor** check boxes. This will allow the curtain wall to span all three floors (see Figure 16-24).

Figure 16-24

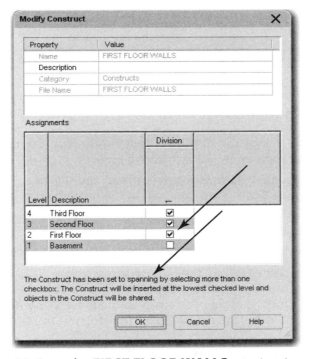

10. Save the **FIRST FLOOR WALLS** construct.

11. Open the **SECOND FLOOR WALLS** and **THIRD FLOOR WALLS** constructs, delete their front indented walls, and save those files.

12. In the **Views** tab of the **Project Navigator**, double-click on the **Total View** to bring it up in the Drawing Editor (see Figure 16-25).

Figure 16-25

! **Note:** If the **Total View** is already in the Drawing Editor, and changes have been made to any of the xref that comprise this view, you will get a yellow message reminding you to reload.

Hands-On

Creating Named Views and Plotting Sheets

1. In the **Views** tab of the **Project Navigator**, double-click on the **Total View** to open it in the Drawing Editor.
2. Change to the **SW Isometric View**, and set the scale to 1/8″ = 1′-0″ from the **Scale** drop-down list at the bottom right of the Drawing Editor.
3. Select **View > Named Views** from the **Main** menu to bring up the **View** dialog box.
4. Select the **New** button to bring up the **New View** dialog box.
5. Enter **SW PERSPECTIVE** in the **View Name** field, select the **Define Window** radio button, select the building with a window selection, and click the mouse to return to the **New View** dialog box, and press **OK** and close the dialog boxes to return to the Drawing Editor.
6. Change to the **Front View**, and repeat the previous process naming the view **FRONT VIEW**.
7. Change to the **Top View**, and again repeat the process naming the view **TOP VIEW**.
8. Save the **Total View**.

Notice that in the **Views** tab of the **Project Navigator**, the **TOTAL VIEW** drawing contains your new named views (see Figure 16-26).

Figure 16-26

9. In the **Sheets** tab of the **Project Navigator**, **RMB** on **Plans** and select **New > Sheet** from the contextual menu that appears (see Figure 16-27).

10. Enter **A-001** in the **Number** field, enter **TEST PROJECT** in the **Sheet title** field, and press **OK** to add the sheet to the **Plans** folder in the **Sheet** tab.

11. Double-click on **TEST PROJECT** to bring it up in the Drawing Editor (see Figure 16-28).

12. While the **TEST PROJECT** drawing is showing in the Drawing Editor, change to the **Views** tab in the **Project Navigator** and drag the **SW ISOMETRIC**, **FRONT**, and **TOP Views** into the **TEST PROJECT** drawing.

While dragging, you can **RMB** and select a scale for the view from a drop-down list (see Figure 16-29).

You have now completed your plot sheet (see Figure 16-30). You will learn more ways to insert views into sheets in the Callouts section.

Figure 16-27

Figure 16-28

Figure 16-29

Figure 16-30

When you finish this section, you should understand the following:

✔ How to create plotting sheets in the **Project Navigator**.

✔ How to create a new project with the **Project Browser**.

✔ How to creating a new construct in the **Project Navigator**.

✔ How to create elevations with the **MARK A3 Elevation** callout.

✔ How to create details with the **Detail Boundary** callout.

✔ How to place elevations in an **ELEVATION SHEET**.

✔ How to place details into a **DETAIL SHEET**.

✔ How to place floor plans in a **PLAN SHEET**.

New Feature for Autodesk Architectural Desktop 2005

In the last two sections you learned about elevations and sections as well as elevation and section objects. In those exercises, you placed the elevation or section with a callout. In this section, you will learn the new advanced coordination capabilities of the callouts

With Autodesk Architectural Desktop 2005, details, elevations, and sections are views of the building model and part of the construction documentation. They can be created with callouts. Callouts tools create a callout that is referenced to a model space view containing a user-defined part of the building model, such as a section, an elevation, or a detail. They are coordinated across the complete construction document set with the help of projects and sheet sets.

Because callouts operate in conjunction with project management and the sheet sets, it is a good idea to review those sections before doing theses exercises.

The following callout tools are provided with Autodesk Architectural Desktop 2005.

A detail callout tool with a circular boundary that optionally can insert a title mark. The callout symbol has field placeholders for the sheet number and a detail number, which are resolved when the detail is placed on the sheet.

A detail callout tool with a rectangular boundary that optionally can insert a title mark. The callout symbol has field placeholders for the sheet number and a detail number, which are resolved when the detail is placed on the sheet.

A detail callout tool with a free-form boundary that optionally can insert a title mark. The callout symbol has field placeholders for the sheet number and a detail number, which are resolved when the detail is placed on the sheet.

A detail tool with a leader line. The callout symbol has a field placeholder for the detail number that gets resolved when the detail is placed on the sheet.

A detail tool with a leader line and tail. The callout symbol has a field placeholder for the detail number that gets resolved when the detail is placed on the sheet.

A detail tool with a leader line. The callout symbol has field placeholders for the detail number and the sheet number, which are resolved when the detail is placed on the sheet.

A detail tool with a leader line and tail. The callout symbol has field placeholders for the detail number and the sheet number, which are resolved when the detail is placed on a sheet.

A single elevation mark tool. The elevation mark has a field placeholder for the elevation number that gets resolved when the elevation is placed on the sheet.

A single elevation mark tool. The elevation mark has field placeholders for the elevation number and the sheet number, which are resolved when the elevation is placed on the sheet.

A four-way interior elevation mark tool in the format 1/2/3/4. The elevation mark's callout symbol has a field placeholder for the sheet number that gets resolved when the elevations are placed on the sheet.

A four-way interior elevation mark tool in the format N/E/S/W. The elevation mark's callout symbol has a field placeholder for the sheet number that gets resolved when the elevations are placed on the sheet.

A four-way exterior elevation mark tool in the format 1/2/3/4. The elevation mark's callout symbol has field placeholders for the detail number and the sheet number that gets resolved when the elevations are placed on the sheet.

A single interior elevation mark tool. The elevation mark contains field placeholders for the sheet number and the elevation number, which are resolved when the elevation is placed on the sheet.

A single interior elevation mark tool with inverted text. The elevation mark contains field placeholders for the sheet number and the elevation number, which are resolved when the elevation is placed on the sheet.

A single section mark tool with a leader line. The section mark contains a field placeholder for the section number that gets resolved when the section is placed on the sheet.

A single section mark tool with a leader line and a tail. The section mark contains a field placeholder for the section number that gets resolved when the section is placed on the sheet.

A single section mark tool with a leader line. The section mark contains field placeholders for the section number and the sheet number, which are resolved when the section is placed on the sheet.

A section mark tool with a leader line in a tail. The section mark contains field placeholders for the section number and the sheet number, which are resolved when the section is placed on the sheet.

A double section mark tool with a section line. The section marks contain field placeholders for the section number and the sheet number, which are resolved when the section is placed on the sheet.

The Callout Methodology

Callouts are meant to work within the Autodesk Architectural Desktop Drawing Management System. They automatically will reference the drawings in which they are placed. This automatic referencing system is said to be "resolved" when a view is placed on a plotting sheet. *Callouts are meant to only work with 2D details and 2D elevations.*

Hands-On

Creating a New Project with the Project Browser

1. Using the **Windows Explorer** or **My Computer**, create a new folder called **CALLOUTS**.

2. Select **File > Project Browser** from the **Main** menu to bring up the **Project Browser**.

3. Locate the **CALLOUTS** folder from the drop-down list and select the **New Project** icon to bring up the **Add Project** dialog box.

4. Enter the number **001** in the **Number** field, **CALLOUTTEST** in the **Name** field, and press **OK** to return to the **Project Browser** (see Figure 17-1).

5. In the **Project Browser**, **RMB** on **CALLOUTTEST**, select **Set Project Current** from the contextual menu that appears, and press the **Close** button to close the **Project Manager** and bring in the **Project Navigator**.

In order for the Drawing Manager system to work, you must have a drawing file in the Drawing Editor. This file is a dummy file, and will not be used. The term dummy file refers to the fact that a file must be in the Drawing Editor for the menu bars to appear.

Figure 17-1

Hands-On

Creating Plotting Sheets in the Project Navigator

1. In the **Project Navigator**, change to the **Sheets** tab.

2. In the **Sheets** tab of the **Project Navigator**, select the **Plans** icon, and then press the **Add Sheet** icon to bring up the **New Sheet** dialog box.

3. Enter **A-101** in the **Number** field, **PLAN SHEET** in the **Sheet title** field, and press **OK.**

4. In the **Sheets** tab of the **Project Navigator**, select the **Elevations** icon, and then press the **Add Sheet** icon to bring up the **New Sheet** dialog box.

5. Enter **A-201** in the **Number** field, **ELEVATION SHEET** in the **Sheet title** field, and press **OK**.

6. In the **Sheets** tab of the **Project Navigator**, select the **Details** icon, and then press the **Add Sheet** icon to bring up the **New Sheet** dialog box.

7. Enter **A-401** in the **Number** field, **DETAILS SHEET** in the **Sheet title** field, and press **OK** (see Figure 17-2).

Figure 17-2

Hands-On

Creating a New Construct in the Project Navigator

1. In the **Project Navigator**, change to the **Constructs** tab.
2. Select the **Add Construct** icon to bring up the **Add Construct** dialog box.
3. Enter **STAIR** in the **Name** field, and press **OK** to return to the Drawing Editor.
4. In the **Constructs** tab of the **Project Navigator**, double-click on the STAIR drawing you created in the previous step to bring that drawing into the Drawing Editor.
5. In the Drawing Editor place a wall with windows, a door, and a stair similar to that shown in Figure 17-3.

Figure 17-3

Hands-On

Creating a New Plan View Drawing in the Project Navigator

1. In the **Project Navigator**, change to the **Views** tab.
2. Select the **Add View** icon to bring up the **Add View** dialog box.
3. Select the **General** radio button, and press **OK** to open the **Add View** dialog box.
4. Enter **STAIR PLAN**, and press the **Next** button to bring up the **Context** screen.
5. Check the **Level** check box, and press the **Next** button to bring up the **Content** screen.
6. Make sure the **STAIR CONSTRUCT** check box is checked—this will add the stair construct to your STAIR PLAN drawing. Finally press the **Finish** button in the **Content** screen to return to the Drawing Editor, and create the STAIR PLAN drawing (see Figure 17-4).
7. In the **Views** tab of the **Project Navigator**, double-click on the **STAIR Plan** icon to bring the **STAIR PLAN view** drawing into the Drawing Editor.

Figure 17-4

> **Note:** The STAIR PLAN drawing will contain the stair created in **STAIR** in the **Constructs** tab (it has been XREFed into the **STAIR PLAN** drawing automatically).

Hands-On

Creating Elevations with the MARK A3 Elevation Callout

1. Select **Elevation Mark Elevation Mark A3** from the **Callouts** tool palette (see Figure 17-5).

Figure 17-5

2. In the STAIR PLAN drawing in the **Top View**, place a window selection around the stair construct and click to bring up the **Place Callout** dialog box.

3. Check the **Generate Section/Elevation** check box, select **1/2"** from the **Scale** drop-down list, and press the **New View** drawing icon to bring up the **Add Section/Elevation View** dialog box (see Figure 17-6).

4. Enter **ELEVATION VIEWS** in the **Name** field, (this will appear as the drawing file name in the **Project Navigator**) and press the **Next** button to bring up the **Context** screen

5. Check the **Level** check box, and press the **Next** button to bring up the **Content** screen.

Figure 17-6

6. Make sure the **STAIR CONSTRUCT** check box is checked, and press the **Finish** button to return to the Drawing Editor.

7. In the Drawing Editor, click to the right of stair (where you click doesn't matter because you are creating the elevations in the new drawing file).

8. Move your cursor down 10' vertically again, (this will dictate the distance between the four elevations) and click your mouse button. The **Generate Elevation Progress** dialog screen will appear telling you when the elevations have been created in a new file.

Notice that the **ELEVATION VIEWS** file appears in the **Views** tab of the **Project Navigator**.

9. In the **Views** tab of the **Project Navigator**, double-click on the **ELEVATIONS VIEWS** file to bring that file up in the Drawing Editor (see Figure 17-7).

Figure 17-7

Hands-On

Placing Elevation Views in the A-201 ELEVATION Sheet

1. In the **Sheets** tab of the **Project Navigator**, double-click the **A-201 ELEVATION SHEET** icon, to bring it up in the Drawing Editor.

2. In the **Project Navigator**, change to the **Views** tab.

3. Drag the **ELEVATION VIEWS** icon into the **A-201 ELEVATION SHEET** that is open in the Drawing Editor.

4. Click a spot in the A-201 ELEVATION SHEET to place the first elevation. The other three elevations will appear in sequence automatically—place them also (see Figure 17-8).

Figure 17-8

Note: You can place single elevations by dragging the individual elevations from the Views tab into a plotting sheet.

5. Press **Ctrl + S** on your keyboard or select **File > Save** from the **Main** menu to save the A-201 ELEVATION SHEET.

Hands-On

Creating Details with the Detail Boundary Callout

1. In the **Project Navigator**, change to the **Views** tab and double-click the **East Elevation** to bring it up in the Drawing Editor.

2. Select the **Detail Boundary B** tool from the **Callouts** tool palette (see Figure 17-9).

Figure 17-9

3. Click in the EAST ELEVATION drawing, and select with a window selection the area for your detail (see Figure 17-10).

Figure 17-10

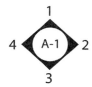

4. Move the leader line location and click to bring up the **Place Callout** dialog box.

5. Enter **DETAIL 1** in the **New Model Space View Name** field, un-check the **Generate Section/Elevation** check box, select **1" = 1'-0"** from the **Scale** drop-down list, and press the **New View** drawing icon to bring up the **Add Detail View** dialog box.

6. Enter **DETAILS** in the **Name** field, (this will appear as the drawing file name in the **Project Navigator**) and press the **Next** button to bring up the **Context** screen.

7. Check the **Level** check box, and press the **Next** button to bring up the **Content** screen.

8. Make sure the **STAIR CONSTRUCT** check box is checked, and press the **Finish** button to return to the Drawing Editor.

9. In the Drawing Editor, click in the drawing to create the new detail view drawing.

10. In the **Views** tab, expand the DETAILS drawing that you just created to see the **DETAIL 1 View** (see Figure 17-11).

Figure 17-11

11. Repeat the previous process to create a new detail called **DETAIL 2**.

12. Press **Ctrl + S** on your keyboard or select **File > Save** from the **Main** menu to save the ELEVATION VIEWS drawing.

Hands-On

Placing Details into the A-401 DETAIL SHEET

1. In the **Project Navigator**, change to the **Sheets** tab and double-click **A-401 DETAIL SHEET** to bring the A-401 DETAIL SHEET drawing into the Drawing Editor.

2. In the **Project Navigator**, change to the **Views** tab.

3. Drag the **DETAILS** icon into the A-401 ELEVATION SHEET that is open in the Drawing Editor.

4. Click a spot in the A-401 DETAIL SHEET to place the first detail. The other details will appear in sequence automatically–place them also (see Figure 17-12).

Figure 17-12

Note: You can place single details by dragging the individual details from the Views tab into a potting sheet.

5. Press **Ctrl + S** on your keyboard or select **File > Save** from the Main menu to save the A-401 DETAIL SHEET.

Hands-On

Placing the Floor Plan into the A-101 PLAN SHEET

1. In the **Project Navigator**, change to the **Sheets** tab and double-click **A-101 PLAN SHEET** to bring the A-101 PLAN SHEET drawing into the Drawing Editor.

2. In the **Project Navigator**, change to the **Views** tab.

3. Drag the **FLOOR PLAN** into the A-101 PLAN SHEET that is open in the Drawing Editor (see Figure 17-13).

4. Press **Ctrl + S** on your keyboard or select **File > Save** from the **Main** menu to save the A-101 PLAN SHEET.

Figure 17-13

Close all the drawings.

In the **Sheets** tab, double-click on **A-101**, **A-201**, and **A-401**, and look at the callouts. The callout numbers have been coordinated automatically to the sheet, plan, elevation, and detail numbers (see Figures 17-14 through 17-17).

Figure 17-14

Figure 17-15

Figure 17-16

Figure 17-17

Detail Components and the Detail Component Manager

When you finish this section, you should understand the following:

✔ The detail component concept.

✔ How to create a wall detail using detail components.

✔ How to place detail components.

✔ How to use the **Detail Component Manager.**

✔ How to place keynotes.

The Detailer has been around since the beginnings of Autodesk Architectural Desktop. In Autodesk Architectural Desktop 2005, Detailing has been totally revamped with new routines that are meant to aid in the creation of 2D details.

Detail components represent specific building materials and products and are made up of simple two-dimensional line work entities such as lines, polylines, arcs, circles, and hatches. In most cases, the detail component is a collection of such entities grouped as a block, which can be easily copied or moved as a single entity. The following are examples of detail components that are inserted as blocks:

- Bolt heads
- Fixed length nails
- Section reviews of beams and columns
- Most selection views of framing members
- Units such as CMUs, bricks, and pavers
- Connectors
- Materials with reviews generated from interrelating parameters, for example, trusses, precast concrete, and hollow metal frames.

Hands-On

Inserting Detail Components

All detail components are inserted into drawings using the same basic tool, which performs the insertion routine associated with a selected component. Each detail component tool provided on the sample tool palettes represents a different configuration of the basic tool. You can activate the tool insertion tool in five different ways:

1. Click a detail component tool icon on a tool palette.

2. Click on the **Detail Component** icon on the **Navigation** tool bar (see Figure 18-1), and select a component from the **Detail Component Manager** (see Figure 18-2).

Figure 18–1

3. Drag and drop a detail component that has been placed in a drawing from that drawing into a tool palette (see Figure 18-3).

4. Select a component in a drawing, right-click, and click **Add selected**. This reruns the tool with the same property settings used to insert the existing component, so that one can quickly insert additional copies of the same component.

5. Select a component in a drawing, right-click, and click **Replace selected**. This erases the selected component and reruns the tool with the same property settings used to insert the erased component. However, you can modify the tool to insert a different component by changing the component properties (**Category**, **Type**, **Description**, or **View**) on the **Properties** palette.

Figure 18–2

Figure 18–3

Hands-On

Creating a Wall Detail Using Detail Components

1. Start a new drawing using the AEC Model (Imperial - Stb) template.
2. Change to the **Top View**.
3. Click on the **03-Concrete** tool in the **Basic** tool palette of the **DETAILING** tool palettes.
4. Move your cursor over the **Properties** palette to open it, and set the settings shown in Figure 18-4.

Figure 18–4

5. In the **Description** field of the **Properties** palette, select the **6" SLAB WITH HAUNCH** option, and return to the Drawing Editor.
6. In the Drawing Editor, click and drag to the right, and then click again to establish the end of the slab.
7. Press **Enter** to complete the command (see Figure 18-5).
8. Click on the **04-Masonry** tool in the **Basic** tool palette of the **DETAILING** tool palettes.

Figure 18–5

> **Tip**
>
> ## Alternative Selection Method
>
> a. Select the **Detail Component Manager** from the **Navigation** toolbar to bring up the Detail Component Manager.
> b. In the Detail Component Manager, select **Division 03-Concrete > 03310-Structural Concrete > Slabs with Optional haunch**.
> c. Press the **Insert Component** button to return to the Drawing Editor and begin to place the component.
> d. Before placing the component, move your cursor over the **Properties** palette to open it allowing you to modify all the options of your component (see Figure 18–6).

Figure 18–6

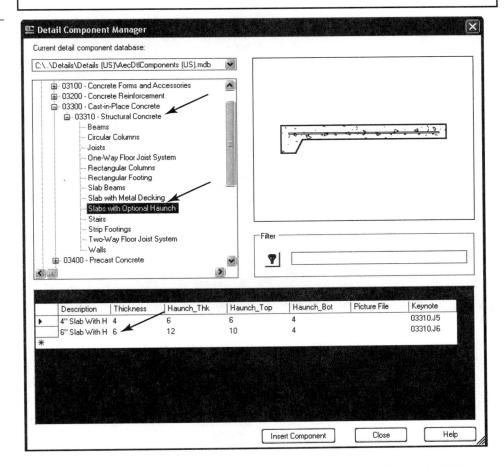

9. Move your cursor over the **Properties** palette to open it, and set the settings shown in Figure 18-7.

10. Click at the left edge of the slab you just placed, drag vertically, enter **2'** in the **Command line** and press **Enter**. This will make a 2'-high masonry wall.

11. Select the **Detail Component Manager** from the **Navigation** toolbar to bring up the **Detail Component Manager**.

12. Select **Division 09110 - Non-Load Bearing Wall framing > Interior Metal Studs**.

Figure 18–7

13. Select **3-5/8" Metal Stud**, and press the **Insert Component** button to return to the Drawing Editor.

14. In the **Properties** palette, set the **View** to **Elevation**.

15. Enter **L** (Left) in the **Command line** and press **Enter**.

16. With **Osnap** set to **Endpoint**, enter **fro** in the **Command line** and press **Enter**.

17. Enter **1"** in the **Command line** for the airspace, drag to the right, click again, drag vertically, enter **22-1/2"**, and press **Enter** to complete the command (see Figure 18-8).

18. In the **Detail Component Manager**, again select **Division 09110 - Non-Load Bearing Wall framing > Interior Metal Runner Channels**, and rotate and place runners at the top and base of the steel stud.

19. Click on the **06-Woods & Plastics** tool in the **Basic** tool palette of the **DETAILING** tool palettes.

20. Move your cursor over the **Properties** palette to open it, set the **Description** drop-down list to **2 × 4**, and **View** to **Section**.

21. Enter **R** (Rotate) in the **Command line** and press **Enter**.

22. Enter **90** in the **Command line** and press **Enter**.

23. Place the bottom right edge of the 2 × 4 with the top right edge of metal stud and runner you placed previously.

24. Select the **Detail Component Manager** from the **Navigation** toolbar to bring up the **Detail Component Manager**.

25. Select **Division 08410 - Metal-Framed Storefronts > Front Double Glazed**.

Figure 18–8

26. Select **Storefront sill at Finish,** and press the **Insert Component** button to return to the Drawing Editor.

27. Enter **B** (Base point) in the **Command line** and press **Enter**.

28. With **Osnap** set to **Endpoint,** click on the lower right corner of the storefront component.

29. Click on the top right of the 2 × 4 you previously placed (see Figure 18-9).

Figure 18–9

30. Click on the **09-Finishes** tool in the **Basic** tool palette of the **DETAILING** tool palettes.

31. Move your cursor over the **Properties** palette to open it, and select **1/2″ Gypsum Wallboard** from the **Description** field

32. Enter **L** (Left) in the **Command line** and press **Enter**.

33. Click at the bottom right of the metal stud, and drag upwards to the midpoint of the right side of the storefront sill component.

34. Select the gypsum board you already placed, **RMB,** and select **Add Selected** from the contextual menu that appears.

35. Place a copy of 1/2" gypsum wallboard on the left side of the metal stud.

You now need to cap the gypsum wallboard at the storefront component.

36. Select the **Detail Component Manager** from the **Navigation** toolbar to bring up the **Detail Component Manager**.

37. Select **Division 09270 - Gypsum Wall Board Accessories**.

38. Select **1/2" J Casing Bead**, and press the **Insert Component** button to return to the Drawing Editor.

39. Enter **B** (Base point) in the **Command line** and press **Enter**.

40. With the **Endpoint Osnap** on, relocate the base point.

41. Enter **R** (Rotate) in the **Command line** and press **Enter**.

42. Enter **270** in the **Command line** and press **Enter**.

43. Place the casing bead as shown in Figure 18-10.

Figure 18–10

44. Click on the **07-Thermal & Moisture Protection** tool in the **Basic** tool palette of the **DETAILING** tool palettes.

45. Move your cursor over the **Properties** palette to open it. Select **Batt Insulation** from the **Type** field, **3-1/2" R-11 Fiberglass Batt Insulation** from the **Description** field, **Section** from the **View** field, and **Normal** from the **Density** field.

46. Click at the bottom center of the metal stud, drag upwards, and click again to place the insulation (see Figure 18-11).

Chamfer the Brick Sill

47. Select the brick directly below the storefront, **RMB**, and select **AEC Modify Tools > Trim** from the contextual menu that appears.

48. Select two points for a trim plane and then select the side to trim (see Figure 18-12).

Create Sill Flashing

49. Select the **Polyline** icon from the **Draw** toolbar, and create the flashing shown in Figure 18-13.

50. Select the **Detail Component Manager** from the **Navigation** toolbar to bring up the **Detail Component Manager**.

Figure 18–11

Figure 18–12

51. Select **Division 07620 - Sheet Metal Flashing**.

52. Select **Aluminum Flashing** from the list, and press the **Insert Component** button.

53. Select the polyline you just created and press **Enter** twice to complete the command. You have now applied aluminum flashing component information to the polyline that will control the keynote.

Figure 18–13

Hands-On

Keynoting

Keynoting is Architectural Desktop 2005's automated system for labeling detail components.

First you need to set your text style. This author prefers the Stylus BT text style because it looks like hand printing.

1. Select **Format > Text Style** from the **Main** menu to bring up the **Text Style** dialog box.

2. Select **Arch-Dim** from the **Style Name** drop-down list.

3. Select **Stylus BT** from the **Font Name** drop-down list, and close the **Text Style** dialog box.

4. Set the **Scale** drop-down list below the Drawing Editor to **1″ = 1′-0″**.

5. Change to the **Document** tool palettes.

6. Select the **Reference Keynote** tool from the **Annotation** palette, **RMB**, and select **Properties** from the contextual menu that appears to bring up the **Tool Properties** dialog box.

7. Set the settings shown in Figure 18-14 and press the **OK** button.

8. Click on the storefront, select a point to start the keynote arrow, and then click a second point to place the keynote. The correct keynote for that particular detail component will appear on the drawing.

9. After placing the first keynote, press the space bar on your computer to repeat the keynote command for the next component.

10. Place all the keynotes (see Figure 18-15).

NOTE: By changing the **Default** text to **?REFNOTE**, only the name of the material will be placed and not its CSI number.

NOTE: By setting the **Mask** background to **NO**, you will not see a grey background behind the keynote text.

Figure 18–14

Figure 18–15

19

Property Set Definitions and Property Sets

When you finish this section, you should understand the following:

- ✔ How to create a property set definition.
- ✔ How to create and use an automatic property.
- ✔ How to create and use a manual property.
- ✔ How to create and use a formula property definition.
- ✔ How to create and use the property data format.

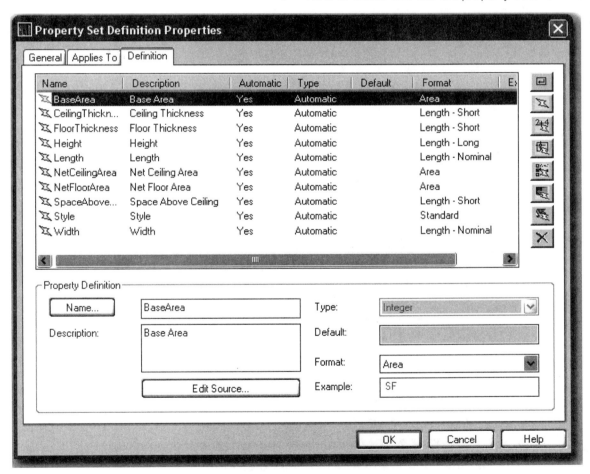

Autodesk Architectural Desktop 2005 uses property set definitions and property sets as means of codifying information concerning objects in the virtual building model.

Property Set Definition

A properties set definition specifies the characteristics of a group of properties that can be tracked with an object. Each property has a name, description, data type, data format, and default value.

Property Sets and Property Data

A property set is an object created from a property set definition. It contains a user-definable group of related object properties. When you attach a property set to an object or style, the property set becomes the container for the property data associated with the object.

Automatic Properties

Automatic properties are built into objects and styles when they are created. Examples are width, length, height, etc.

Manual Properties

Manual properties are properties that are entered manually such as manufacturer, price, etc.

Hands-On

Adding the Automatic Properties

1. Start a new drawing using the AEC Model (Imperial - Stb) template.
2. Select **Format > Style Manager** from the **Main** menu to bring up the **Style Manager**.
3. Expand the **Documentation Objects** folder.
4. **RMB** on **Property Set Definition**, to create a **New Style Property Set Definition**.
5. Name the new style **TESTPROPERTYSETDEFINITION** (see Figure 19-1).
6. Double-click on **TESTPROPERTYSETDEFINITION** to bring up the **Property Set Definition Properties** dialog box.
7. Select the **Applies To** tab.
8. Select the **Objects** radio button and press the **Select All** button.
9. Change to the **Definition** tab.
10. Select the **Add Automatic Property Definition** icon (see Figure 19-2).

Because you have selected all the objects in the **Applies To** tab, you will get a warning message telling you that it will take some time to compile the list of data sources. Press the **Yes** button to proceed.

11. When the **Automatic Property Source** dialog appears, scroll through it to see all the properties available for all the objects (see Figure 19-3).

Figure 19-1

Figure 19-2

12. Press **Cancel** to return to the **Property Set Definition Properties** dialog box.

13. Change back to the **Applies To** tab.

14. Press the **Clear All** button, and then check the **Wall** check box.

15. Return to the **Definition** tab and press the **Add Automatic Property Definition** icon to bring up the **Automatic Property Source** dialog box.

16. Check the **Height** check box, and press **OK** to return to the **Property Set Definition Properties** dialog box.

17. Select **Length-Nominal** from the **Format** drop-down list. This will format the height in feet and inches (see Figure 19-4).

Figure 19-3

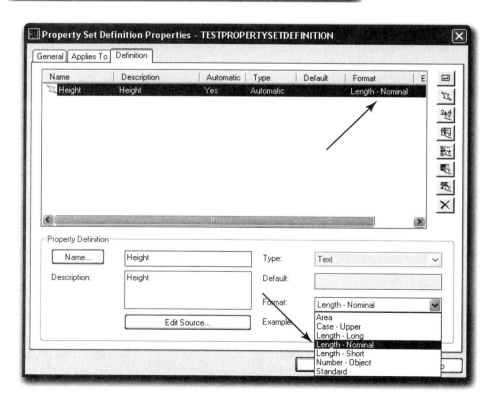

Figure 19-4

18. Repeat Steps 15 through 17, but this time hold down the **Shift** key and select **Length**, **Area-Left Gross**, **Area-Left Net**, **Height**, **Length**, and **Object Type**.

19. In the **Property Set Definition Properties** dialog box, select **Area** from the **Format** drop-down list for **Area-Left Gross** and **Area-Left Net**. This will format the areas in square feet.

20. In the same dialog box, select **Length-Nominal** from the **Format** drop-down list for **Length** This will format the length in feet and inches.

21. In the Drawing Editor place a 15'-long wall (the style doesn't matter).

22. Double-click the wall you placed to open the **Properties** palette.

23. Change to the **Extended Data** tab.

24. Select the **Add Property Sets** icon to bring up the **Add Property Sets** dialog box (see Figure 19-5).

Figure 19-5

25. Press the **Select All** button.

26. Double-click the wall again to open the **Properties** palette again.

27. Again change to the **Extended Data** tab and notice that the height, length, and gross and net areas as well as object type are shown.

You will now be able to read any changes in the length, height, and gross and net areas of that wall in the **Extended Data** tab of the **Properties** palette (see Figure 19-6).

Figure 19-6

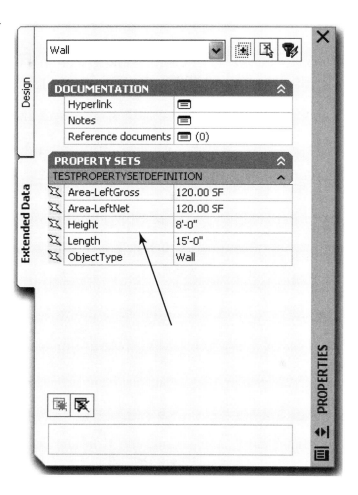

You can add as many automatic properties as you wish, and they will all appear in the **Properties** palette. Later you will be able to pull this data into a schedule object.

28. Select the wall, **RMB**, and insert a door in the wall.

29. Double-click on the wall to open the **Properties** palette. Notice that the **Area-Left Net** field shows how much area has been subtracted by the door (see Figure 19-7).

Figure 19-7

<hr>

Hands-On

Using the Manual Properties

1. Using the previous exercise, select **Format > Style Manager** from the **Main** menu to bring up the **Style Manager**.

2. Expand the **Documentation Objects** folder, and double-click on **TESTPROPERTYSETDEFINITION** to bring up the **Property Set Definition Properties** dialog box.

3. Select the **Add Manual Property Definition** icon to bring up the **New Property** dialog box (see Figure 19-8).

Figure 19-8

4. Enter **PRICEPERSQ** in the **Name** field, and press **OK** to return to the **Property Set Definition** properties dialog box.

5. Set PRICEPERSQ's **Type** to Text.

6. Double-click the wall you placed in the previous exercise to open the Properties palette.

7. Change to the **Extended Data** tab.

8. You will now see a field called **PRICEPERSQ**; enter **2.5** in the field (see Figure 19-9).

Figure 19-9

Hands-On

Using the Formula Property Definitions

1. Using the previous exercise, select **Format > Style Manager** from the **Main** menu to bring up the **Style Manager**.

2. Expand the **Documentation Objects** folder, and double-click on **TESTPROPERTYSETDEFINITION** to again bring up the **Property Set Definition Properties** dialog box.

3. Select the **Add Formula Property Definition** icon to bring up the **Formula Property Definition** dialog box (see Figure 19-10).

4. Enter **WALLCOST** in the **Name** field.

5. Select **Area-Left Gross** under **Property Definitions**, then the **x** (times) above **Property Definitions**, and then **PRICEPERSQ** under **Property Definitions**.

Figure 19-10

You have now created a formula that multiplies the area of the wall by the entered price per square foot (see Figure 19-11).

6. Press **OK** to close the dialog box.

7. Double-click on the wall in the Drawing Editor to open the **Properties** palette, and notice that **WALLCOST** has been calculated, but it is not in dollars (see Figure 19-12).

To format **WALLCOST** in dollars, you will need a new property data format.

8. In the **Style Manager**, expand the **Documentation Objects** folder, **RMB** on **Property Data Formats**, and select **New** from the contextual menu that appears.

9. Name the new style **DOLLARS**.

10. Double-click on **DOLLARS** to bring up the **Property Data Format Properties** dialog box.

11. Change to the **Formatting** tab.

Figure 19-11

Figure 19-12

12. Enter **$** in the **Prefix** field, **Decimal** in **Unit Format**, and **0.00** in **Precision** (see Figure 19-13).

13. Press **OK** to return to the **Style Manager**.

Figure 19-13

14. Open up **TESTPROPERTYSETDEFINITION** again, and select **DOLLARS** (that will now be available) from the **Format** drop-down list for **WALL-COST**.

15. Now press the **OK** buttons to close all the dialog boxes and return to the Drawing Editor.

16. Again double-click on the wall to open the **Properties** palette.

17. Again change to the **Extended Data** tab.

WALLCOST will now read **$300.00**. If you change the value in **PRICEPERSQ**, **WALLCOST** will change. If you change the length or height of the wall, **WALLCOST** will also reflect that change.

The best way to learn is to practice. Add different properties, and see their results in the **Properties** palette.

Save this drawing file to use with the schedule and schedule tags exercies in the following section

Section

20

Schedules and Schedule Tags

Door Schedule

Window Schedule

Space Inventory Schedule

Room Finish Schedule

When you finish this section, you should understand the following:

- ✔ How to create schedule tags and a **Schedules** tool palette.
- ✔ How to create a schedule.
- ✔ How to test a schedule.
- ✔ How to modify a schedule.
- ✔ How to schedule across drawings.
- ✔ How to place door and window tags.
- ✔ How to place schedules.
- ✔ How to use schedules to locate objects.
- ✔ How to create and use custom schedules.

Hands-On

Making a New Schedule Tag and Schedules Tool Palette

1. Create a new tool palette and name it **Schedules**.
2. Select the **Content Browser** icon from the **Main** tool bar to launch the **Content Browser**.
3. In the **Documentation Tool Catalog – Imperial**, locate the **Schedule Tables** folder.
4. Drag the **Door** and **Window** schedules into the new tool palette you created.

5. In the **Autodesk Architectural Desktop Documentation Tool Catalog – Imperial**, locate the **Schedule Tags** folders.

6. Drag the **Door Tag** and **Window Tag** tags into the new tool palette you created.

7. Click and hold on the tab of your new tool palette and drag a copy to **My Tool Catalog** in the Content Browser.

Schedules work in concert with property set definitions, property data formats, and schedule tags.

Hands-On

Creating a Schedule

1. Open the file you saved with the property set definitions from the property set definitions exercises.

2. Select **Format > Style Manager** from the **Main** menu to bring up the **Style Manager**.

3. Expand the **Documentation Objects** folder.

4. **RMB** on **Schedule Table Styles** to create a new style schedule table style.

5. Name the new style **TESTSCHEDULE**.

6. Double-click on **TESTSCHEDULE** to bring up the **Schedule Table Style Properties** dialog box.

7. Change to the **Applies To** tab.

8. Press the **Clear All** button, and then check the **Wall** check box (see Figure 20-1).

Figure 20-1

9. Change to the **Columns** tab.

10. Press the **Add Column** button to bring up the **Add Column** dialog box.

11. Change to the **Categorized** tab, and notice that it contains the properties that you set in the exercise on property set definitions in the previous section.

12. Select **WALLCOST**, enter **Cost of Walls** in the **Heading** field, select **DOLLARS** from the **Data Format** drop-down list, check the **Total** check box, and press **OK** (see Figure 20-2).

Figure 20-2

13. You will now return to the **Columns** tab of the **Schedule Table Style Properties** dialog box.

14. Check the **Include Quantity Column** check box to add a **Quantity** column (see Figure 20-3).

15. Press **OK**, and close all the dialog boxes to return to the Drawing Editor. Save this file.

Figure 20-3

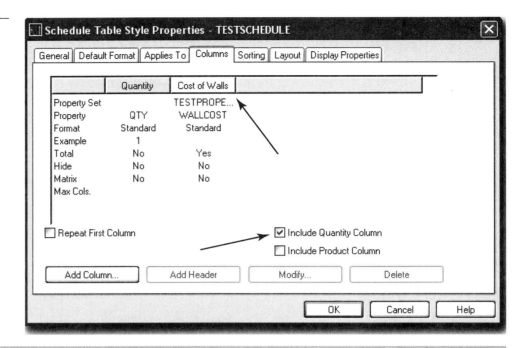

![Hands-On]

Testing the New Schedule

1. Using the drawing from the previous exercise, select the **Brick-4 Brick-4 wall** from the **Walls** tool palette, and place a 15'-long wall 10' high in the Drawing Editor.

2. Double-click on the wall to open the **Properties** palette.

3. Change to the **Extended Data** tab.

4. Press the **Add Property Sets** icon, attach the **TESTPROPERTYSETDE-FINITION** property set (see Section 19 for directions on doing this operation), and press **OK**.

The property set information will now appear in the **Extended Data** tab.

5. In the **Extended Data** tab, enter **2.5** ($2.50) in the **PRICEPERSQ** field, and the **WALLCOST** will read **$375**.

6. Open the **Schedules** tool palette you created in the first exercise, and set **Auto-hide** to keep the palette open.

7. Select **Format > Style Manager** from the **Main** menu to bring up the **Style Manager**.

8. Expand the **Documentation Objects** folder.

9. Drag **TESTSCHEDULE** from the **Style Manager** into the **Schedules** tool palette (see Figure 20-4).

10. Select **TESTSCHEDULE** you just placed in the tool palette, select the brick-4 brick-4 wall you placed previously in the Drawing Editor, and press the **Enter** key on your keyboard.

11. In the **Top View**, click a placement point below the wall, and then press **Enter** again to place the schedule (see Figure 20-5).

Figure 20-4

Figure 20-5

Schedule Table	
Quantity	Cost of Walls
1	$375
	$375

Notice the size of the type in the schedule in relation to the size of the wall. This is because the default scale of the model layout is 1/8" = 1'-0".

12. Change the **Scale** at the bottom of the Drawing Editor to **1/4" = 1'-0"**, and insert **TESTSCHEDULE** again.

Notice the size of the type in the schedule in relation to the size of the wall. This is because the scale of the model layout is now 1/4" = 1'-0" (see Figure 20-6).

Figure 20-6

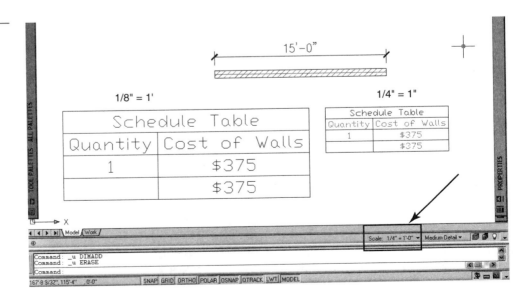

13. Erase the first schedule you placed, leaving only the 1/4" scale schedule.

14. Double-click the schedule to open the **Properties** palette.

15. In the **Design** tab, under **Update automatically**, select **Yes**. Under **Add new objects automatically**, also select **Yes** (see Figure 20-7).

Figure 20-7

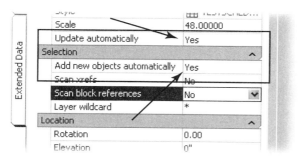

The schedule will now reflect automatically any additional walls having the same property set definition.

16. Press the **Esc** key to clear any selections.

17. Select the wall, **RMB**, and select **Add Selected** from the contextual menu that appears.

Add more walls; the schedule automatically updates (see Figure 20-8). Save this file.

Figure 20-8

Schedule Table	
Quantity	Cost of Walls
1	$375
1	$99.36
1	$69.29
1	$134.19
4	$677.84

Hands-On

Modifying the Schedule

1. Using the previous file, select **Format > Text Style** from the **Main** menu to bring up the **Text Style** dialog box.

2. Press the **New** button, and name the style **TESTTEXT**.

3. Select **Arial** from the **Font Name** drop-down list and **Bold** from the **Font Style** drop-down list.

4. Select **Standard** from the **Style Name** drop-down list, select **Arial** from the **Font Name** drop-down list, select **Regular** from the **Font Style** drop-down list, press the **Apply** button, and then press the **Close** button.

5. Select the schedule, **RMB**, and select **Edit Schedule Table Style** from the contextual menu that appears to bring up the **Schedule Table Style Properties** dialog box.

6. Select the **Layout** tab.

7. Enter **WALL Schedule** in the **Table Title** field, and press the **Title Override Cell Format** button to bring up the **Cell Format Override** dialog box.

8. Select **TESTTEXT** from the **Style** drop-down list (see Figure 20-9).

Figure 20-9

9. Press the **Column Headers Override Cell Format** button, select **TESTTEXT** from the **Style** drop-down list, and press the **OK** buttons to close all the dialog boxes and return to the Drawing Editor (see Figure 20-10).

Figure 20-10

10. **RMB** on the Wall schedule in the Drawing Editor and select **Edit Schedule Table Style** from the contextual menu that appears to bring up the **Schedule Table Style Properties** dialog box.

11. Change to the **Applies To** tab.

12. Press the **Add Column** button to bring up the **Add Column** dialog box.

13. Select **Wall Type** for **Type,** enter **WALL CODE** in the **Heading** field, press the **Insert Before** radio button, select **QTY** from the **Column** drop-down list, and press the **OK** buttons to return to the Drawing Editor (see Figure 20-11).

Figure 20-11

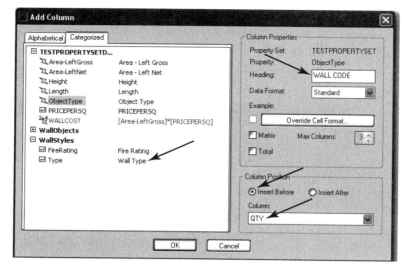

14. The WALL Schedule will now include a WALL CODE column, but it will not have codes. This is because the wall types have not been labeled (see Figure 20-12).

Figure 20-12

To label a wall, do the following (using CMU-8 as an example):

a. **RMB** on the **CMU-8** wall in the **Walls** tool palette and select **Re-import CMU-8 Wall Style** from the contextual menu that appears.

b. Again **RMB** on the **CMU-8** wall in the **Walls** tool palette and this time select **Wall Styles** from the contextual menu to bring up the **Style Manager**.

c. Double-click the **CMU-8** wall to bring up the **Wall Style Properties** dialog box.

d. Change to the **General** tab.

e. Select the **Property Sets** button to bring up the **Edit Property Set Data** dialog box.

f. Enter **A** in the **Type** field, and press the **OK** buttons to return to the Drawing Editor (see Figure 20-13).

g. Repeat Steps a through f for some of the other walls types.

Figure 20-13

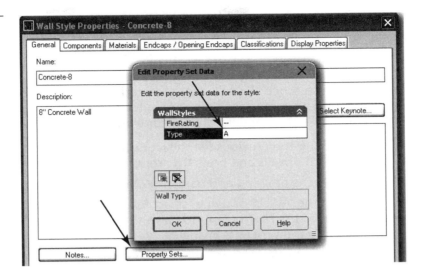

Once you have labeled walls, place the walls.

15. After placing some walls, select all the walls and double-click on one to open the **Properties** palette.

16. With all the walls still selected, select the **Extended Data** tab in the **Properties** palette.

17. Press the **Add property sets** icon and attach the **TESTPROPERTYSET-DEFINITION** property set.

18. Enter **2.5** in the **PRICEPERSQ** field. Press the **Esc** key to clear the grips.

Your wall schedule is now complete (see Figure 20-14). Save this file as SCHEDULE.

Figure 20-14

Hands-On

Scheduling across Drawings

Because schedules are not necessarily placed on the same page as the objects they are scheduling, Architectural Desktop's scheduling object has an option to schedule "across" drawings.

1. Using the previous file, select **Edit > Cut** from the **Main** menu. Select all the walls and press **OK**. Your schedule should clear.

2. Start a drawing and name it **WALLS**.

3. In the WALLS drawing, select **Edit > Paste to Original Coordinates** from the **Main** menu to paste the walls from the SCHEDULE drawing into the WALLS drawing.

4. Save the WALLS drawing. *This is essential*.

5. Double-click the schedule object in the SCHEDULE drawing to open the **Properties** palette.

6. Select **Yes** from the **Schedule** external drawing field in the **Advanced** section. This will then show an **External** drawing field.

7. Select **Browse** and locate the WALLS drawing (see Figure 20-15).

Figure 20-15

8. The schedule object in the SCHEDULE drawing will show a line across its surface telling you to update the schedule.

9. **RMB** on the schedule object and select **Update Schedule Table** from the contextual menu that appears. The schedule will now reflect the information from the WALLS drawing.

Note: If you change any wall in the WALLS drawing and save that drawing, the SCHEDULE drawing will be able to show those changes upon updating. In Architectural Desktop 2005, updating can be done automatically through the sheet set (see Figure 20-16).

Figure 20-16

Schedule Tags

In order to compile data into a schedule, objects must be tagged. Autodesk Architectural Desktop 2005 contains tags for the following objects:

- Doors
- Windows
- Room numbers
- Room finishes
- Spaces
- Beams, braces, and columns
- Equipment
- Furniture
- Walls

Hands-On

Placing Door and Window Tags

1. Using the previous drawing, select the **Wall** icon in the **Design** tool palette, and create a 30'-0" × 20'-0"-wide enclosure. Make the walls Standard 6" wide, 8' high.

2. Select a wall, **RMB**, and select **Insert > Door** from the contextual menu.

3. Place a 3'-0" wide Standard door in each wall.

4. Repeat Steps 2 and 3 placing 3' × 5' windows along side the doors (see Figure 20-17).

5. Select the **Door Tag** icon from the **Schedules** tool palette you created, select the bottommost door, and place the tag in the middle of the door opening.

The **Edit Property Set Data** dialog box will now appear. You can now change data such as **Fire Rating** (see Figure 20-18).

Figure 20-17

Door Tags

Window Tags

Figure 20-18

6. When you are finished, press **OK** in the dialog box to place the schedule tag.

If you do not want to see this dialog box every time you place a tag, do the following:

a. Select **Format > Options** to bring up the **Options** dialog box.

b. Select the **AEC Content** tab.

c. Uncheck the **Display Edit Property Data Dialog During Insertion** check box (see Figure 20-19).

Figure 20-19

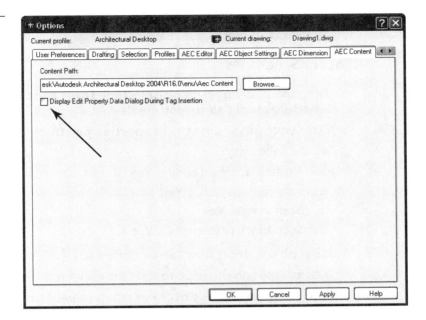

7. Repeat for the other doors.

8. Zoom close to the doors.

Notice that they are numbered incrementally automatically. To change the settings of the tag, do the following:

9. Select **Format > Style Manager** from the **Main** toolbar to bring up the **Style Manager** dialog box.

10. Select **Documentation Objects > Property Set Definitions > Door Objects**.

Property set definitions are groups of properties for particular objects that you want to manage in schedules. They can be automatic, deriving their values from the properties of objects, or user-defined.

11. Select **Door Objects, RMB**, and select **Edit** from the contextual menu to bring up the **Property Set Definitions** dialog box.

12. Select the **Definition** tab.

If you want to increment the objects number system automatically, select **Auto Increment** and set the start number as **Default**. The tags can also be created or modified to display the information defined in the property definition.

13. Place window tags for the windows. If the tags don't increment automatically, change their setting in the property definition set for window objects. Save this exercise.

Hands-On

Placing Schedules

1. Using the previous exercise, select the **Door Schedule** icon from the **Schedules** tool palette you created.

2. Move your cursor over the **Properties** palette to open it.

3. Set the following:

   a.   Update automatically = **Yes**

   b.   Add new objects = **Yes**

   c.   Scan xrefs = **Yes**

   d.   Scan block references = **Yes**

4. Select all the doors (this can be done with a selection window).

5. Click in a spot on the page to start the upper left corner of the schedule.

6. Press the space bar or **Enter** key when requested for the lower right corner.

Pressing **Enter** (Architectural Desktop calls it **Return** in the command line) causes the schedule to be scaled automatically at the size set by the drawing scale you set earlier.

7. Select all the doors and their tags, and press **Enter**.

8. Repeat Steps 1–5 for the window schedule (see Figure 20-20).

DOOR AND FRAME SCHEDULE

MARK	DOOR							FRAME					FIRE RATING LABEL	HARDWARE		NOTES
	SIZE			MATL	GLAZING	LOUVER		MATL	EL	DETAIL				SET NO	KEYSIDE RM NO	
	WD	HGT	THK			WD	HGT			HEAD	JAMB	SILL				
1	3'-0"	6'-8"	2"	--	--	0"	0"	--	--	--	--	--	--	--	--	--
2	3'-0"	6'-8"	2"	--	--	0"	0"	--	--	--	--	--	--	--	--	--
3	3'-0"	6'-8"	2"	--	--	0"	0"	--	--	--	--	--	--	--	--	--
4	3'-0"	6'-8"	2"	--	--	0"	0"	--	--	--	--	--	--	--	--	--

WINDOW SCHEDULE

MARK	SIZE		TYPE	MATERIAL	NOTES
	WIDTH	HEIGHT			
1	3'-0"	5'-0"	--	--	--
2	3'-0"	5'-0"	--	--	--
3	3'-0"	5'-0"	--	--	--
4	3'-0"	5'-0"	--	--	--
5	3'-0"	5'-0"	--	--	--
6	3'-0"	5'-0"	--	--	--
7	3'-0"	5'-0"	--	--	--
8	3'-0"	5'-0"	--	--	--

Figure 20-20

Hands-On

Updating Schedules

1. Remove two of the doors.

Notice that the schedule has a line going across it.

2. Select the door schedule, **RMB**, and select **Update Schedule Table** from the contextual menu.

The schedule will update, removing or changing object data.

3. Add more windows and window tags.

The schedule does not indicate the additions.

4. Select the window schedule, **RMB**, and select **Selection > Add** from the contextual menu.

5. Select all the windows and tags.

The window schedule updates, showing the new windows.

Hands-On

Using Schedules to Locate Objects

If you need to quickly locate an object listed in the schedule, do the following:

1. Select the door schedule, **RMB**, and select **Selection > Show** from the contextual menu.

2. Hold down the **Ctrl** key on the keyboard, and pick any number in a field.

The screen will zoom to the object in that field.

Hands-On

Exporting Schedules to Databases

If you have Microsoft Excel, or a text editor such as Microsoft Word or even Windows Notepad software, you can export your schedules to these formats.

1. Select the door schedule, **RMB**, and select **Export** the contextual menu to bring up the **Export Schedule Table** dialog box.

2. Select **Microsoft [Tab delimited] [*.xls]** from the **Output - Save As Type** drop-down list.

3. Browse to a convenient folder, and press **OK**.

You will be able to open the file in Microsoft Excel 95 and later.

4. If you set the **Output - Save As Type to Text [Tab delimited] [*.txt]**, you will be able to open the file in any text editor (see Figures 20-21 and 20-22).

Figure 20-21

Figure 20-22

Hands-On

Creating and Using Custom Schedules

The Drawing

1. Erase everything from the previous exercise
2. Place three circles in the drawing with radii of 2', 4', and 6'.

You are going to create a schedule that records information about the circles in your drawing. In order to make a schedule you will need to create a property set definition.

The Property Set Definition

3. Select **Format > Style Manager** from the **Main** toolbar to bring up the **Style Manager** dialog box from the main toolbar.

4. Select **Documentation Objects > Property Set Definitions**, **RMB**, and select **New** from the contextual menu to create a new property set definition.

5. Rename the new property set definition **CIRCLE SCHEDULE**.

6. Double-click on **CIRCLE SCHEDULE** to bring up the **Property Set Definition Properties** dialog box.

7. Select the **Applies To** tab.

8. Select the **Objects** radio button, and then select the **Clear All** button at the lower left of the dialog box. Check the **Circle** check box (see Figure 20-23).

9. In the same dialog box, select the **Definition** tab.

10. Press the **Add Manual Property Definition** icon button at the top right side of the dialog box, to bring up the **New Property** dialog box.

Figure 20-23

Property Set Definition Properties - CIRCLE SCHEDULE

General | Applies To | Definition

Applies To: ⦿ Objects
               ○ Styles and Definitions

Classifications: None available

Circle

☐ 2D Section/Elevation   ☐ Clip Volume
☐ 3D Face   ☐ Clip Volume Result
☐ AEC Dimension   ☐ Column Grid
☐ AEC Polygon   ☐ Curtain Wall
☐ Arc   ☐ Curtain Wall Unit
☐ Area   ☐ Dimension
☐ Area Group   ☐ Door
☐ Attribute Definition   ☐ Door/Window Assembly
☐ Bldg Elevation Line   ☐ Ellipse
☐ Bldg Section   ☐ Entity Reference
☐ Bldg Section Line   ☐ Hatch
☐ Block Reference   ☐ Image
☐ Camera   ☐ Layout Curve
☐ Ceiling Grid   ☐ Layout Grid 2D
☑ Circle   ☐ Layout Grid 3D

Select All   Clear All   Clear All

OK   Cancel   Help

11. Enter the word **NUMBER** in the **Name** section, and press **OK**.

This brings up the **Property Set Definition Properties** dialog box. In "Placing Door and Window Tags" you found that this dialog box is where you control the automatic increments. In this exercise you are creating a new property set definition, and you want the schedule to number each circle automatically (see Figure 20-24).

Figure 20-24

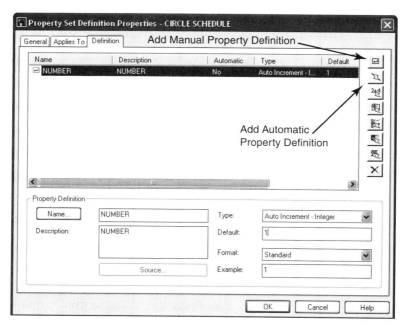

12. Set the **Type** to **Auto Increment - Integer** and **Default** to **1**, and **Format** to **Number - Object**.

13. Press the **Add Automatic Property Definition** icon button at the top right side of the dialog box to bring up the **Automatic Property Source** dialog box.

The **Automatic Property Source** dialog box shows all the properties of a circle (see Figure 20-25).

14. Check the **Area** check box, and press **OK** to return to the **Property Set Definition Properties** dialog box.

15. Add two more automatic property definitions called **radius** and **circumference**, and check their **Automatic Property Sources** check boxes for **radius** and **circumference**, respectively.

16. Press the **Apply** button to apply all this to the **CIRCLE SCHEDULE** property set definition.

You have now defined all the properties of circles that you wish to be recorded in a schedule (see Figure 20-26).

Creating the Table Style

17. Select **Format > Style Manager** from the **Main** menu to bring up the **Style Manager** dialog box.

18. Select **Document Objects > Schedule Table Styles**.

Figure 20-25

Figure 20-26

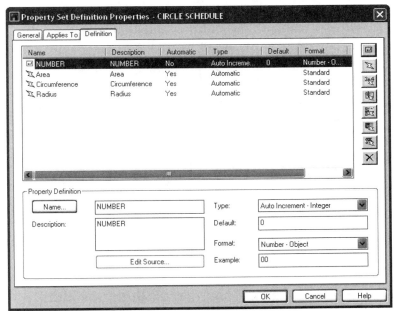

19. **RMB** on **Schedule Table Styles**, and select **New** from the contextual menu.

20. Name the new style **CIRCLE SCHEDULE**, and press the **Apply** and **OK** buttons.

21. Select **Format > Style Manager** from the **Main** menu to bring up the **Style Manager** dialog box again.

22. Select the **CIRCLE SCHEDULE** style you just created, **RMB**, and select **Edit** from the contextual menu to bring up the **Schedule Table Style Properties** dialog box.

23. Select the **Applies To** tab.

24. Press the **Select All** button to clear the list, and then check the **Circle** check box.

This tells the program that the schedule applies to circles and their properties (see Figure 20-27).

Figure 20-27

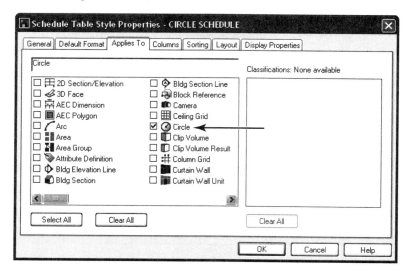

25. Change to the **Columns** tab and press the **Add Column** button at the lower left to bring up the **Add Column** dialog box.

You should now see the property definition set you created in Steps 3–25 (see Figure 20-28).

Figure 20-28

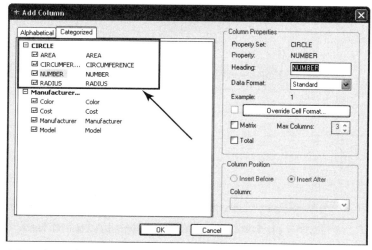

26. Select the **NUMBER** property and press **OK** to return to the **Schedule Table Style Properties** dialog box.

27. Again press the **Add Column** button.

28. Repeat the steps adding columns named **RADIUS**, **CIRCUMFERENCE**, and **AREA** (see Figure 20-29).

Figure 20-29

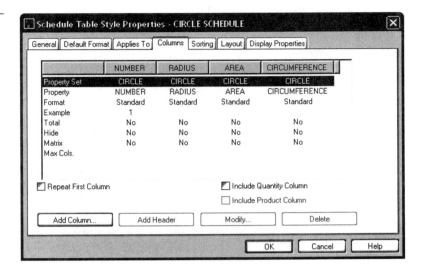

29. At the **Schedule Table Style Properties** dialog box, hold down the **Ctrl** key and select the **RADIUS** and **CIRCUMFERENCE** headers.

30. Press the **Add Header** button.

31. Enter a header name of **CIRCLE DATA** (see Figure 20-30).

Figure 20-30

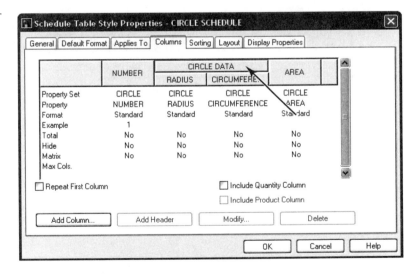

32. Change to the **Sorting** tab.

33. Press the **Add** button at the top left to bring up the **Select Property** dialog box.

34. Select **CIRCLE: NUMBER**, and press **OK** (see Figure 20-31).

35. Repeat for all the other properties.

36. Change to the **Layout** tab.

Figure 20-31

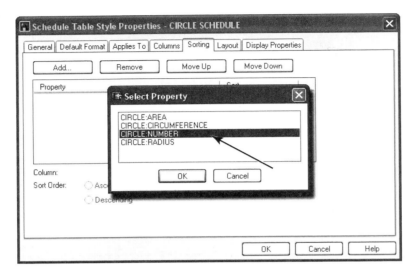

37. Enter a **Table Title** of **CIRCLE TABLE**, and press **OK** until you are out of all dialogs (see Figure 20-32).

The table style has now been created, and the columns and title have been named.

Figure 20-32

Using the Custom Schedule

38. Return to your drawing of the three circles (see Figure 20-33).

39. Select the **CIRCLE Schedule** icon from the **Schedule** tool palette you created.

40. Move your cursor over the **Properties** palette to open it.

41. Select the following:

Figure 20-33

   a. Style = **CIRCLE SCHEDULE**

   b. Add new objects automatically = **Yes**

   c. Scan xrefs = **Yes**

   d. Scan block references = **Yes**

42. Select all the circles in your drawing, and press **Enter**.

43. Place the upper left corner of the table, and press **Enter**.

!   **Note:** Remember, pressing **Enter** after placing the upper left corner of a schedule table automatically places the table according to your annotation scale settings (see Figure 20-34).

Figure 20-34

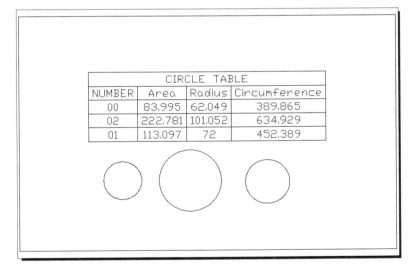

44. Select one of the circles, and use grips to change its size.

Note that the schedule automatically updates to reflect the change in circle size.

45. Add some more circles.

Note that they automatically show up in the table, but their sizes are represented by question marks.

46. Select the schedule, **RMB**, and select **Add All Property Sets** from the contextual menu.

47. The new circle is now listed in the schedule.

Sheet Sets

When you finish this section, you should understand the following:

✔ How to create a sheet set.

✔ How to modify a sheet set.

✔ How to test a new sheet set.

New Feature for Autodesk Architectural Desktop 2005

A sheet set is an ordered collection of sheets derived from several drawing files. You can manage, transmit, publish, and archive sheet sets as a unit.

Hands-On

Creating a New Sheet Set

1. Start a new drawing using the AEC Model (Imperial - Stb) template.

2. Type **sheetset** in the **Command line** to bring up the **Sheet Set Manager**.

3. Select the drop-down list shown in Figure 21-1, and select **New Sheet Set** to bring up the **Begin** dialog box.

4. Select the **An example sheet set** radio button, and then press the **Next** button to bring up the **Sheet Set Example** dialog box.

Figure 21-1

5. Select the **Select a sheet set to use as an example** radio button, select **Architectural Imperial Sheet Set,** and then press the **Next** button to go to the **Sheet Set Details** dialog box (see Figure 21-2).

Figure 21-2

6. Name the sheet set **TEST SHEET SET**.

7. Press the **Sheet Set Properties** button at the bottom of the dialog box to bring up the **Sheet Set Properties** dialog box. In this dialog box, you can control the location of a custom drawing template, sheet storage, client and project, etc. (see Figure 21-3).

8. Press the **Edit Custom Properties** button to open the **Custom Properties** dialog box. Here you can also edit information on the client, address, etc.

9. Press the **Add** button to bring up the **Add Custom Property** dialog box. Here you can add new places for information to be added automatically to the drawings (see Figure 21-4).

10. When you are finished, press the **OK** buttons to return to the Sheet **Set Details** dialog box. Press the **Next** button to go to the **Confirm** dialog box.

11. In the **Confirm** dialog box, if everything is **OK**, press the **Finish** button to create the sheet set. Save this file.

Figure 21-3

Figure 21-4

Hands-On

Testing the New Sheet Set

1. Type **sheetset** in the **Command line** to bring up the **Sheet Set Manager**.

2. Select **Open** from the the drop-down list.

3. Locate **TEST SHEET SET**.

4. Under **Sheets**, **RMB** on **Architectural**, and select **New Sheet** from the contextual menu that appears to bring up the **New Sheet** dialog box.

5. Enter **A-1** in the **Number** field, and **TEST ARCH SHEET** in the **Sheet title** field.

6. Press the **OK** button to return to the **Sheet Set Manager**.

7. Double-click on **A-1- TEST ARCH SHEET** to bring up the new drawing (see Figure 21-5).

Figure 21-5

8. Zoom in close to the title block. Notice that it automatically contains the various values you dictated in the set. Notice that it also places the date of drawing creation in the date field (see Figure 21-6).

Figure 21-6

Although the sheet set command is a new AutoCAD 2005 command, it has been seamlessly integrated in Architectural Desktop 2005 in the **Project Navigator**. Adding a sheet and double-clicking on it to bring it up in the Drawing Editor is performed in the identical manner in the **Project Navigator** as it was demonstrated in the Drawing Management section.

22

Mask Blocks

Mask Block

When you finish this section, you should understand the following:

✔ The purpose of mask blocks.

✔ How to create, modify, and use mask blocks.

Mask blocks are two-dimensional blocks that mask the graphic display of AEC Objects in Plan View.

Mask blocks are often combined with AutoCAD objects such as lay-in fluorescent fixtures to mask the AEC ceiling grid. With a thorough understanding of mask blocks, you will probably find a myriad of uses for these objects.

Hands-On

Creating a Custom Fluorescent Fixture Called New Fixture

1. Start a new drawing using the AEC Model (Imperial - ctb) template.

2. Change to the **Model Layout**.

3. Change to the **Top View**.

4. Using the standard AutoCAD drawing commands, draw the ceiling fixture shown in Figure 22-1.

5. Enter **Pedit** in the **Command line**, select the outline, and join the outline into a closed polyline.

Note: If you don't know how to convert and join a line into a polyline, consult the AutoCAD 2004 help for **Polyline Edit (Pedit)**.

6. **RMB** anywhere in the Drawing Editor and select **Basic Modify Tools > Offset** from the contextual menu that appears.

7. Enter **2"** in the **Command line**, and press **Enter** to create the 2" outline shown in Figure 22-1.

8. Select **Format > Style Manager** from the **Main** toolbar to bring up the **Style Manager** dialog box.

9. Open the **Multi-Purpose** folder and double-click on the **Mask Block Definitions** icon.

Figure 22-1

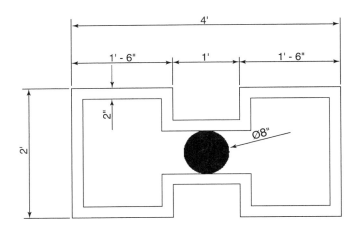

10. Select the **New Style** icon from the **Main Style Manager** toolbar.

11. Rename the new style to **NEW LIGHT FIXTURE**.

12. Select the **NEW LIGHT FIXTURE** icon, and select the **Set From** icon from the **Main Style Manager** toolbar.

13. Select the outline when asked to **"Select a close polyline"** at the **Command line**.

14. Accept **N** when asked to "**Add another ring?**" at the **Command line**.

15. Make the insertion point for the mask the center point of the outline.

16. Select everything except the outline when asked to **"Select additional graphics"** at the **Command line**.

17. In the **Style Manager** dialog box, press the **Apply** button, and then press **OK**.

The outline will become the mask block, and the interior objects of the drawing will become the fixture graphics.

Hands-On

Testing the New Light Fixture Mask Block

1. Erase everything.

2. Create a 30′ × 30′ standard wall enclosure 10′ high.

For this exercise you will need to add the **Mask Block** tool to your **Design** tool palette, so do the following:

a. Select the **Content Browser** icon from the **Main** toolbar to launch the Content Browser.

b. Locate the **Stock Tool Catalog**.

c. Locate the **Drafting Tools** folder.

d. From the **Drafting Tools** folder, drag the **Mask Block** tool into your **Design** tool palette.

3. Select the **Rectangle** icon from the **Draw** toolbar, and place a rectangle inside the 30′ × 30′ enclosure you created (see Figure 22-2).

Figure 22-2

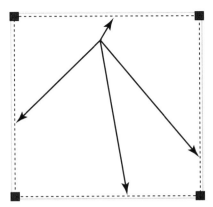

4. Change the **Display Configuration** to **Reflected**.

5. Select the **Ceiling Grid** icon from the **Design** tool palette, and enter **S** (Set boundary) in the **Command line**, and press **Enter**.

6. Select the rectangle you placed in Step 3 of this exercise.

7. Move your cursor over the **Properties** palette to open it.

8. Set the following:

    a. Specify on screen = **no**

    b. X-Width = **40'**

    c. Y-Depth = **40'**

    d. XAxis Layout type = **Repeat**

    e. XAxis Bay size = **2'-0"**

    f. YAxis Layout type = **Repeat**

    g. YAxis Bay size = **4'-0"**

9. Enter **SN** (Snap to center) in the **Command line**, press **Enter** twice, and then press the **Esc** key to complete the command.

You have now placed a centered ceiling grid, but it is located at elevation 0".

10. Select the ceiling grid again, and move your cursor over the **Properties** palette to open it.

11. Set the **Elevation** to **8'-0"** (see Figure 22-3).

Figure 22-3

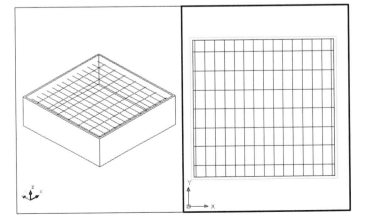

12. Select the **Mask Block** tool icon that you placed in the **Design** palette.

13. Move your cursor over the **Properties** palette to open it.

14. Enter **R** (Rotation) in the **Command line**, enter **90**, and press **Enter**.

15. Insert 12 copies of the mask block vertically.

16. Insert two more copies horizontally (see Figure 22-4).

Notice that the horizontal mask blocks cross over a grid (see Figure 22-5).

Figure 22-4

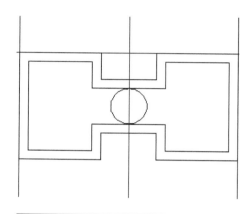

Figure 22-5

To correct this do the following:

17. Select the horizontal mass blocks you placed, **RMB**, and select **Attach Object** from the contextual menu that appears.

18. Select the ceiling grid to bring up the **Select Display Representation** dialog box.

19. Press **OK** to return to the Drawing Editor.

The grid is now masked by the NEW LIGHT FIXTURE mask block (see Figure 22-6). Save this file.

Figure 22-6

masked ceiling grid

Hands-On

Using Create AEC Content to Place the New Light Fixture in the DesignCenter

1. Erase everything but one NEW LIGHT FIXTURE in the **Top View**.

The icon that will be used in the **DesignCenter** will be taken from the current view.

2. Select the **Format > AEC Content Wizard** from the **Main** toolbar to bring up the **Create AEC Content Wizard** dialog box.

3. Select the **Masking Block** radio button, press the **Add** button to add the **NEW LIGHT FIXTURE** mask block to the **Content File**, and press the **Next** button (see Figure 22-7).

Figure 22-7

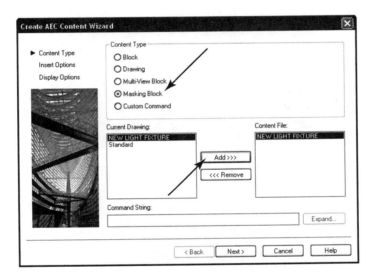

4. **Insert Options**, press the **Select Layer Key** button to bring up the **Select Layer Key** dialog box.

5. Select the **LIGHTCLG** under **Layer Key,** and press **OK** (see Figure 22-8).

Figure 22-8

Selecting the **LIGHTCLG** layer key assures you that when you insert the content it will be placed on that layer.

6. Select the **Next** button in the **Create AEC Content Wizard** dialog box.

7. In **Display Options** press the **Browse** button.

8. At the **Save Content File** dialog box, locate the **Program Files\Autodesk Architectural Desktop 2005\Sample\Design Center** folder, name the file **CEILING FIXTURES**, and press the **Save** button to return to the **Create AEC Content Wizard** dialog box.

9. Type in a description for the masking block in the **Detailed Description** space, and press the **Finish** button (see Figure 22-9).

Note that the current viewport drawing is shown as an icon.

Figure 22-9

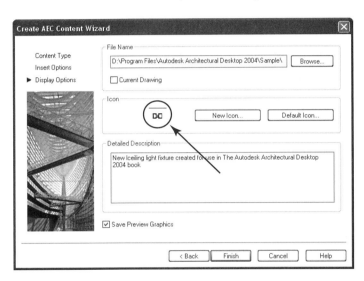

Hands-On

Testing the New Light Fixture Mask Block from the DesignCenter

1. Erase everything in the previous drawing.

2. Select the **DesignCenter** icon from the **Main** toolbar or press **CTRL + 2** to bring up the **DesignCenter** palette.

3. Click on the CEILING FIXTURES drawing that you saved.

4. Select and drag the **NEW LIGHT FIXTURE** icon into a new drawing, and zoom extents (see Figure 22-10).

The **Create AEC Content Wizard** will place blocks, drawings, masking blocks, and custom command strings in the **DesignCenter**. The process is essentially the same for all these different forms of content.

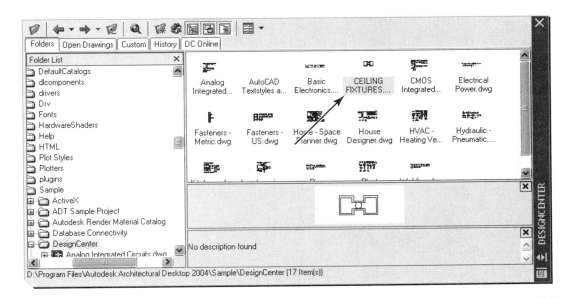

Figure 22-10

When you finish this section, you should be able to do the following:

✔ How to create the **Autodesk Website** icon
✔ How to go to the **chair at the Nsight** website
✔ How to create content from a 3D mesh
✔ How to create the multi-view block
✔ How to test the multi-view block

In combination with Autodesk Architectural Desktop's display system, the program uses a multi-view block system. This system allows you to place content in one view, and have the appropriate view appear in the other viewports. Although the program comes with a great deal of content, it includes controls that enable you to create your own custom content.

The following exercise illustrates the creation of a custom multi-view block.

The Chair

For this exercise you will need to use the Web to get content. You can go directly to the Web from inside Autodesk Architectural Desktop 2005 by activating the **Autodesk Website** icon from the **Main** toolbar.

Hands-On

Creating the Autodesk Website Icon

If you do not have this icon on any toolbar do the following:

1. **RMB** on any toolbar icon, and select **Customize** from the contextual menu that appears to bring up the **Customize** dialog box.
2. Change to the **Commands** tab.
3. Select **Tools** in the **Categories** list.
4. Drag the **Autodesk Website** icon to the Drawing Editor.

Hands-On

Going to the Chair at the 3D CAFE WEBSITE

1. Go to http://www.3dcafe.com/asp/househld.asp. Figures 23-1 and 23-2.

Figure 23-1

Figure 23-2

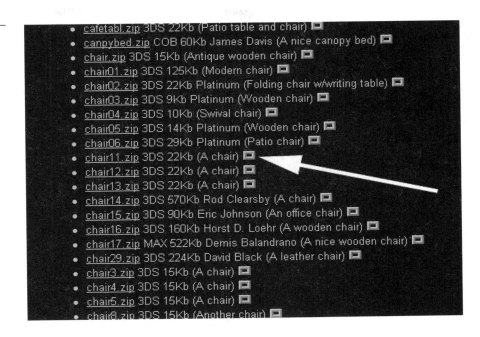

2. Download the **Chair 11,zip** file, unzip it, and place it in a folder on your computer.

Hands-On

Creating Content from a 3D Mesh

1. Start a new drawing using the AEC Model (Imperial - stb) template.

2. Change to the **Model Layout**.

3. Change to the **SW Isometric View**.

4. Select **Insert > 3D Studio** from the **Main** toolbar, and import the **Onsit3ds** file that was downloaded and unzipped from the Web.

5. At the **3D Studio File Import** dialog box select the Sofa1B mesh from the **Available Objects,** select the **Don't Assign a Material** radio button, press the **Add** button, and add it to the **Selected Objects** (see Figure 23-3). Press the **OK** button.

6. Change to the **Work Layout**.

7. Erase all the viewports.

8. Select **View > Viewports > 4** viewports from the the **Main** menu.

9. Change all the views in each viewport to **Top**, **Front**, **Left**, and **SW Isometric**, respectively, and Zoom Extents in all viewports.

You have now imported a 3D mesh model of a chair (see Figure 23-4).

Figure 23-3

Figure 23-4

10. Select the **Content Bowser** icon from the **Main** toolbar to open the Contact Browser.

11. Select the **Autodesk Architectural Desktop Stock Tool Catalog**.

12. Select the **Helper Tools** folder.

13. From the **Helper Tools** folder drag the **Hidden Line Projection** to the **Design** tool palette.

14. Select the **Hidden Line Projection** icon, select the chair, and press **Enter**.

15. Select any block insertion point, and type **Y** in the **Command line** to insert in **Plan View**.

16. Return to a **SW Isometric View** to see the chair and its new 2D hidden line projection.

You have now created a 2D hidden line projection of the left view of your model (see Figure 23-5).

Figure 23-5

17. Repeat this process for the **Top** and **Front Views** (see Figure 23-6).

18. Select an empty place in the viewport, **RMB**, and select **Basic Modify Tools > 3D Operations > 3D Rotate** from the contextual menu that appears. Rotate the front and side views, and place them as shown in Figure 23-7. Create insertion points that align all the views and the model.

19. Select **Format > Blocks > Block Definition**, and save each view as a block, naming them **CHAIR FRONT, CHAIR SIDE, CHAIR TOP,** and **CHAIR MODEL,** respectively, using the insertion points also shown in Figure 23-7.

Figure 23-6

Figure 23-7

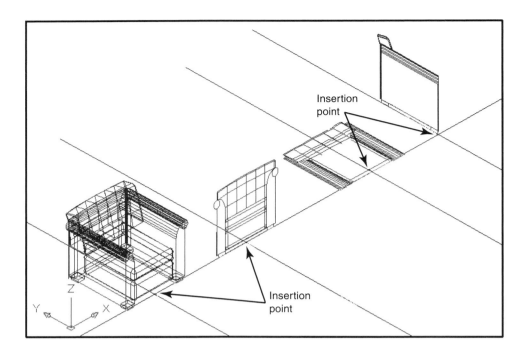

Insertion point

Insertion point

Hands-On

Creating the Multi-View Block

1. Select **Format > Multi-View Block > Multi-View Block Definitions** from the **Main** toolbar to bring up the **Style Manager** dialog box.

2. Select the **New Style** icon and create a new style; name it **CHAIR**.

3. Select **Chair Style, RMB**, and select **Edit** from the contextual menu that appears to bring up the **Multi-View Block Definition Properties** dialog box.

4. Select the **View Blocks** tab.

5. Select **General**, press the **Add** button, and select the **CHAIR FRONT** block.

6. After adding the **CHAIR FRONT** block, check the **Front** and **Back** check boxes under **View Directions** (see Figure 23-8).

7. Repeat this process for the **CHAIR SIDE**, and **CHAIR TOP** blocks selecting the check boxes as shown (see Figures 23-9 and 23-10).

8. Select **Model** from the **Display Representations**, add the **Model** block, and check the **Other** check box (see Figure 23-11).

You have now created the multi-view block.

Figure 23-8

Figure 23-9

Figure 23-10

Figure 23-11

Hands-On

Testing the Multi-View Block

1. Erase everything in the drawing.

2. Change to the **Work Layout**.

3. Activate the **Top View** viewport.

4. Select the **Content Browser** icon from the **Main** toolbar to open the Contact Browser.

5. Select the **Autodesk Architectural Desktop Stock Tool Catalog**.

6. Select the **Helper Tools** folder.

7. From the **Helper Tools** folder drag the **Multi-View Block Reference** icon to the **Design** tool palette.

8. Select **Multi-View Block Reference** icon from the **Design** tool palette.

9. Move your cursor over the **Properties** palette to open it.

10. Select **CHAIR** from the **Definition** drop-down list.

11. Click in the **Top** viewport, and press **Enter** to complete the command.

The correct view of the chair appears in all the different viewports. Zoom extents in each viewport (see Figure 23-12). Save this exercise.

There are many ways to make 3D content. You can use AutoCAD's 3D modeling capability, 3D Studio Viz, or search the Web for free content. With multi-view blocks, the sky is the limit.

Figure 23-12

The DesignCenter

When you finish this section, you should understand the following:

- ✔ How to use the **DesignCenter** to create a kitchen
- ✔ How to add appliances
- ✔ How to create the counter
- ✔ How to place the sink
- ✔ How to generate kitchen secton/elevation

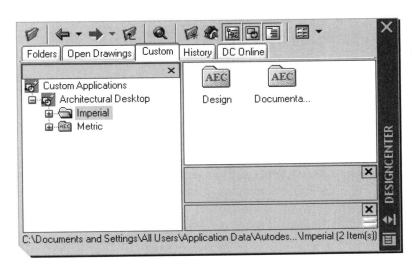

Note: Everything shown in this section can also be gotten from the Content Browser Catalogs; the DesignCenter is another method.

In order to understand architectural construction documents, designers include symbols of equipment such as bathroom fixtures, beds, chair, and kitchen cabinets. Autodesk Architectural Desktop 2005 includes a very comprehensive set of generic content symbols in both 2D and 3D. Much of the content is created utilizing Architectural Desktop's multi-view block representation system. (See Section 22, page XXX, "Using **Create AEC Content** to Place the New Light Fixture in the **DesignCenter**," and Section 23, "Multi-View Blocks," in this book). Multi-view blocks allow the Display System to place the representation of the object in the appropriate view (for example, 3D in Model View, plan representation in Plan View, etc.)

Content

All the symbols and as well as schedules, documentation symbols, and styles are contained in a folder called **Aec Content in C:\Documents and Settings\All Users\Application Data\Autodesk\Autodesk Architectural Desktop 2005\ R16\enu\Aec Content**. This content is placed in this location by default. Be sure you have sufficient space on your C drive regardless if you assign the Architectural Desktop 2005 program to a different drive than the C drive.

All content is held in standard AutoCAD drawings (DWG), and can be modified using standard AutoCAD commands.

Hands-on

Using the DesignCenter to Create a Kitchen

Creating the Kitchen

1. Start a new drawing using the AEC Model (Imperial - ctb) template.
2. Change to the **Model Layout**.
3. Change to the **Top View**.
4. Place a 15'-0" × 10'-0" rectangle.
5. Select the **Walls** icon from the **Design** tool palette, **RMB**, and select **Apply Tool Properties to > Linework** from the contextual menu that appears.
6. Select the rectangle.
7. Type **Y** (Yes) in the **Command line** to erase the geometry (rectangle), and press **Enter** to create walls.
8. With the walls still selected, move your cursor over the **Properties** palette to open it.
9. Set the following parameters:
    a. Wall width = **4"**
    b. Base height = **8'-0"**
    c. Justify = **Right**
10. Modify the walls to create the enclosure shown in Figure 24-1.

Adding the Appliances

11. Select the **DesignCenter** icon from the **Main** toolbar (or press **Ctrl + 2**) to bring up the DesignCenter.
12. Select the Custom tab. Select **Architectural Desktop > Imperial > Design > Equipment > Food Service > Refrigerator**.
13. Double-click the **Refrigerator** folder to open it.
14. Select the **Side-Side** refrigerator, and drag it into the Drawing Editor.

Figure 24-1

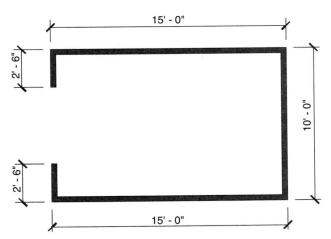

The refrigerator will come into the drawing with the insertion point at its rear center.

15. Type **R** in the command line and press Enter. Enter **270**, and press **Enter**, again.

16. Enter **B** (Base point) in the **Command line,** and press the space bar or **Enter.**

This will allow you to relocate the insertion point of the refrigerator. Select the upper left corner of the refrigerator in the plan.

17. With the **End point** Object Snap set, place the refrigerator as shown in Figure 24-2.

Figure 24-2

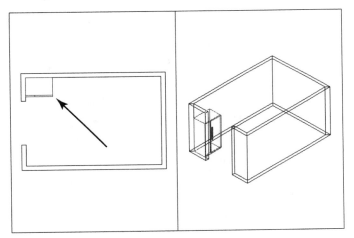

18. Return to the **DesignCenter** and select **Architectural Desktop > Imperial > Design > Furnishing > Casework.**

19. Double-click the **Base with Drawers** folder to open it.

20. Continue to place base cabinets, a stove, and a tall cabinet until you create a kitchen layout similar to the one in Figure 24-3. Save this drawing as **Kitchen.**

Figure 24-3

The Counter: The Splash Edge Style

1. Using the previous drawing.

2. Select the **Rectangle** icon from the **Draw** toolbar, and create a **1"× 4"-**high rectangle.

3. Select the rectangle, **RMB**, and select **Convert To > Profile Definition** from the contextual menu that appears.

4. Pick the lower right corner of the rectangle to bring up the **New Profile Definition** dialog box.

5. Enter **SPLASH PROFILE** in the **New Name** field, and press **OK** to create the profile.

6. Select **Format > Style Manager** to bring up the Style Manager.

7. Select **Architectural Objects > Slab Edge Styles**.

8. Select the **Slab Edge Styles** icon, **RMB**, and select **New** from the contextual menu that appears.

9. Rename the new slab edge style **SPLASH EDGE**.

10. Select **SPLASH EDGE**, **RMB**, and select **Edit** from the contextual menu to bring up the **Slab Edge Styles – SPLASH EDGE** dialog box.

11. Select the **Design Rules** tab.

12. Check the **Fascia** check box, and select **Splash Profile** from the drop-down list (see Figure 24-4).

13. Press **OK**, and close all the dialog boxes.

You have now created the splash edge style. You can keep this style for any future use.

Now it's time to place the counter.

1. In the **Top View**, place polylines where you want counters (make sure the polylines are on the 0 layer, and that it is the active layer).

2. Using the **Layer Manager**, turn off visibility for everything but the 0 layer (see Figure 24-5).

3. Select the **Slab** icon from the **Design** tool palette, **RMB**, and select **Apply Tool Properties to > Linework and Walls** from the contextual menu that appears.

Figure 24-4

Figure 24-5

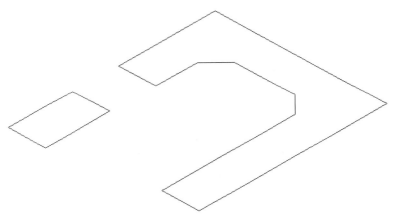

4. Select the two polylines you just created.

5. Enter **Y** (Yes) in the **Command line** and press **Enter**.

6. Enter **P** (Projected) in the **Command line** and press **Enter**.

7. Enter **36"** in the **Command line**, and press **Enter**.

8. Enter **T** (Top) in the **Command line** and press **Enter** to create the counter.

9. Turn the visibility of everything back on in the **Layer Manager**, and regenerate the drawing.

You have now created the counter over the base cabinets (see Figure 24-6).

10. Select a counter you created, and move your cursor over the **Properties** palette to open it.

11. Set the Thickness to **2"**, and press the **Edges** icon to bring up the **Slab Edges** dialog box.

12. Select all the edges, and then select **SPLASH EDGE** from the **Edge Style** drop-down list, and then press **OK**.

13. Repeat Steps 11 and 12 for the other counter.

Figure 24-6

You have now added a splash edge to all the edges of the counter. You need to remove the splash from the front edges. To do this, do the following:

a.   Select a counter, **RMB**, and select **Edit Slab Edges** from the contextual menu that appears.

b.   Select the slab edge you wish to remove, and press **Enter** to bring up the **Edit Slab Edges** dialog box.

c.   Select **Standard** from the **Edge Style** drop-down list and press **OK**.

d.   Repeat Steps b and c for the other counter.

You have now completed the counters (see Figure 24-7).

Figure 24-7

Placing the Sink

1. Change the **UCS** (User Coordinate System) to a **Z height** equal to the top of the counter.

This will allow the sink to be brought in at counter height.

2. Select the **Architectural Desktop > Imperial > Design > Mechanical > Plumbing Fixtures > Sink** from the **DesignCenter**.
3. Double-click the **Sink** folder to open it.
4. Select the **Kitchen-Double B** sink, **RMB**, and drag it into your drawing.
5. Place the sink in the center of the counter.

Turning on **Gouraud** shading shows that the counter cuts through the sink (see Figure 24-8).

Figure 24-8

Real counters need cutouts for sinks.

6. Select the **Rectangle** icon from the **Draw** menu and place a rectangle as shown in Figure 24-9.
7. Select the **Slab, RMB,** and select **Hole Add** icon from the contextual menu that appears.
8. Select the rectangle and press **Enter**.
9. Enter **Y** (Yes) in the **Command line** and press **Enter**.

Figure 24-9

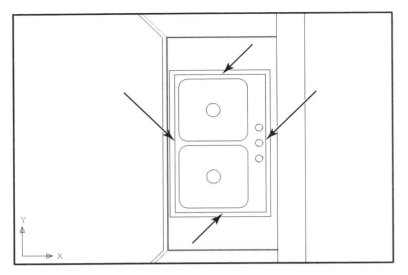

The sink and counter are shaded correctly (see Figure 24-10).

10. Place the upper cabinets, a window, and complete the kitchen (see Figure 24-11).

Figure 24-10

Figure 24-11

Kitchen Section/Elevation

11. Select the **Elevation Line** icon from the **Design** tool palette.
12. Place an elevation line through the kitchen as shown in Figure 24-12.

Figure 24-12

13. Select the elevation line, **RMB**, and select **Generate Elevation** from the contextual menu, and generate an elevation of your finished kitchen (see Figure 24-13).

Figure 24-13

VIZ Render

When you finish this section, you should understand the following:

- ✔ How best to learn to operate VIZ Render.
- ✔ Making a simple scene.
- ✔ Using VIZ Render.
- ✔ Separating surfaces.
- ✔ Applying materials.
- ✔ Creating and modifying materials.
- ✔ People and trees.
- ✔ Using ArchVIsion RPC content plug-in.
- ✔ Using the Bionatics EASYnat plug-in.

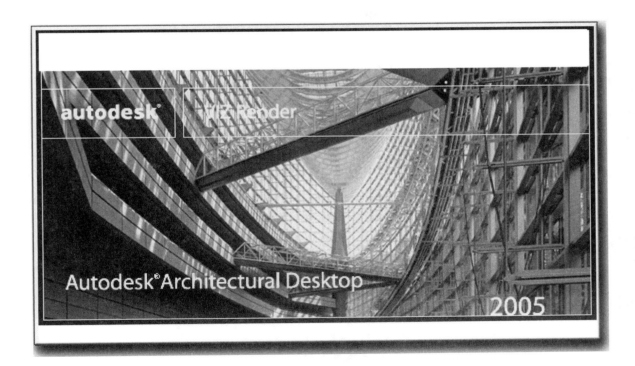

VIZ Render brings much of the power of Autodesk VIZ 4 to the program. Although the render engine is a separate module, it should be activated from within ADT directly. Selecting VIZ Render from within ADT links the two programs together. While the original ADT drawing has to be saved, once saved, any changes to the ADT drawing can be updated within VIZ Render.

Besides the ability to create and place materials, and to render (color wireframe models), VIZ Render brings radiosity and animation to ADT. Radiosity is a system that accurately and easily represents lighting. In this system, one places a sun, lightbulbs, light fixtures, and so on, and the render engine calculates the effects of these light sources on the scene. Rendered output can be a bitmap (JPG, TIF, TGA, GIF), a movie file (MOV, AVI, FLI), or other formats for the Web (PGN) and for $2^1/_2$ D programs such as Piranesi (RLA). Professional high-resolution movies can be made from numbered TGA, AVI, or MOV files, but can be played back best from the hard drive when used in conjunction with hardware compression devices such as Pinnacle's Pro-One video board. The movies can also be compressed as MP2 files and burned to CDs or DVDs giving excellent results.

Besides VIZ Render, ADT 2005 also comes with plug-ins from ArchVision and Bionatics. Using its RPC concept, ArchVision has become the de facto standard for architectural 3D digital content. Bionatics provides an excellent 3D vegetation solution, which can be modified by season. Its trees, flowers, bushes, and so on can be animated to show wind.

How Best to Learn to Operate VIZ Render

The best way to learn the VIZ Render techniques is to start out with a very simple structure. Once you have learned the techniques, you can easily apply those techniques to more complex structures. Keep your experimentation simple, make one change at a time, and observe the changes.

Hands-On

Making a Simple Scene

1. Start a new drawing using the AEC Model (Imperial - ctb) template.
2. Change to the **Model Layout**.
3. Change to the **Top View**.
4. Using Standard 6" × 8"-high walls, create a 20'-long by 10'-wide enclosure.
5. Place a roof on the structure with the following parameters:
   a. Thickness = **10"**
   b. Edge cut = **Plumb**
   c. Overhang = **1'-0"**
   d. Plate height = **8'-0"**
   e. Slope = **45.00**
6. Select the roof to activate its grips, and pull the center end grips to create gable ends (see Figure 25-1).

Figure 25-1

7. Enter **roofline** in the **Command line,** and press **Enter**.

8. Enter **A** (Auto project) in the **Command line**, and press **Enter**.

9. Select the two end walls, and press **Enter**.

10. Select the roof and press **Enter** twice to make the walls meet the roof peak, and finish the command (see Figure 25-2).

11. Add windows and doors as shown in Figure 25-3. The glass in the windows has been turned off; the doors have been opened to 90°.

Figure 25-2

Figure 25-3

12. Change to the **Front View**.

13. Place a rectangle as shown in Figure 25-4.

Figure 25-4

14. Select the rectangle, **RMB**, and select **Polyline Edit** from the contextual menu that appears.

15. Enter **E** (Edit vertex) in the **Command line** and press **Enter**.

16. Enter **I** (Insert) in the **Command line** and press **Enter**.

17. Repeat this process and place new vertices where shown in Figure 25-5.

Figure 25-5

18. Move the vertices until you achieve a result similar to that in Figure 25-6.

19. Enter **extrude** in the **Command line** and press **Enter**.

20. Select the modified rectangle that you just created and press **Enter**.

21. Enter **50'-0"** in the **Command line** and press **Enter** twice to finish the command. (I rotated the UCS 180° on the X axis before entering the extrude command. If you did not do this, just move the finished extrusion into position.) See Figure 25-7.

22. Create a new layer, and name it **BASE**.

23. Select the extrusion you created, and assign it the new layer **BASE**.

24. Save the file as **ADTVIZ RENDER PROJECT**.

You have now created a scene with a simple building and a base.

Figure 25-6

Figure 25-7

Hands-On

Using VIZ Render

1. Select the **Open drawing menu** icon as shown in Figure 25-8 to bring up its contextual menu.

After about 15 seconds, the VIZ Render interface and **File link Settings** dialog box will appear with your scene (see Figure 25-9).

2. Press **OK** to accept the defaults.

3. Select the VIZ **Minimize Viewport** icon to change the interface into four viewports (see Figure 25-10).

Link to Autodesk VIZ Render

Open drawing menu icon

Figure 25-8

Figure 25-9

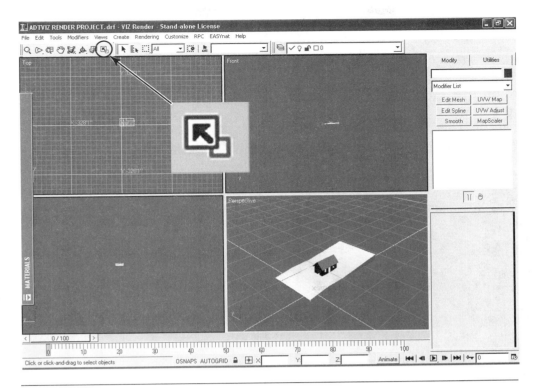

Figure 25-10

4. Select the **Zoom Extents All** icon to fill each viewport view (see Figure 25-11).

Figure 25-11

5. Select **Create > Daylight System** from the **Main** toolbar to bring up the **Daylight Object Creation** dialog box.

6. Press **Yes**.

7. Click in the Top viewport in the middle of the structure.

8. Move your cursor to the **Front View**, move the cursor vertically, and click again to place the daylight object (sun) (see Figure 25-12).

Figure 25-12

9. Select **Create > Cameras > Target Camera** from the **Main** toolbar.

10. Click to the left of the enclosure in the **Top** viewport, click again in the center of the enclosure, and move your cursor over the **Front** viewport; move the curosr vertically, and click again to set the camera (see Figure 25-13).

11. Click in the **Perspective** viewport, and press the letter **C** on the keyboard to change the **Perspective** viewport to a **Camera** viewport. (The **Camera** viewport shows what the camera sees.)

12. Change to the **Top** viewport, select the camera, **RMB**, and select **Move** from the contextual menu that appears.

13. Move the camera in the **Top** viewport while watching the camera viewport. You can adjust the height of the camera by moving it in the **Front View** (see Figure 25-14).

14. Select **Rendering > Render** from the **Main** menu to bring up the **Render Scene** dialog box.

15. Select the **Radiosity** tab.

Figure 25-13

Figure 25-14

16. Open the **Radiosity Processing Parameters** tree, and set the **Initial Quality** to **85%**.

17. In the **Radiosity** tab, open the **Rendering Parameters** tree, and press the **Render Direct Illumination** radio button.

18. Press the **Start** button at the top of the **Radiosity Processing Parameters** area.

The top bar above the process will indicate the progress in running the radiosity solution.

What Is the Radiosity Solution?

In order for the VIZ Render engine to create realistic lighting, a sadiosity solution is generated as a mesh throughout your scene. Each part of the mesh tells the render engine what shade of color and shadow to use for each area. If you move an object or change the number of light fixtures, you must reset the solution and start it again before rendering.

19. Open the **Common Parameters** tree.

20. Select the **Single** radio button, and press the **640x480** button for the **Output** size.

21. Select **Production with Radiosity** from the **Preset** drop-down list, **Camera** from the **Viewport** drop-down list, and press the **Render** button (see Figure 25-15).

Figure 25-15

The render engine will now create a 640×480 image with shading and shadows (see Figure 25-16).

22. Select **File > Save Copy As** from the VIZ Render **Main** menu, and save the file as **ADTVIZ RENDER PROJECT.drf**.

Figure 25-16

Hands-On

Separating Surfaces

1. Using the previous saved file.
2. Activate the **Camera** viewport, and press the letter **P** (Perspective) on the keyboard to change the viewport to the **Perspective View**.
3. Press the letter **W** on the keyboard to maximize the **Perspective** viewport. (This is an easier way to toggle viewports from minimize to maximize that was done with an icon in Step 3 of the previous exercise).
4. Select the roof of the building.
5. Select the **Edit Mesh** button in the **Modify** tab (a warning message will appear; read it, and then press **OK**) (see Figure 25-17).
6. The **Edit Mesh** tool controls will now appear.
7. Press the **Polygon** icon (it will select full faces of a mesh), and select the right roof face. The roof face will turn red when selected (see Figure 25-18).
8. In the **Edit Mesh** tools, press the **Detach** button to bring up the **Detach** dialog box.
9. Enter **RIGHT ROOF SURFACE** in the **Detach as**: data field, and press **OK**. This will create the right roof surface as a separate element called **RIGHT ROOF SURFACE** (see Figure 25-19).
10. Select the **Arc Rotate** icon from the VIZ Render **Viewport Navigation Tools** toolbar, and rotate the view so that you can see the left side of the roof. Repeat Steps 5–9 of this exercise, and detach the left roof as **LEFT ROOF SURFACE** (see Figure 25-20).

Figure 25-17

Figure 25-18

Figure 25-19

Figure 25-20

Hands-On

Applying Materials

1. Open the **Materials** palette.

2. Select the **Tiling** tab.

3. Press **H** on the keyboard to bring up the **Select Objects** dialog box.

4. Highlight **LEFT ROOF SURFACE** and **RIGHT ROOF SURFACE**, and press the **Select** button to select these elements that you previously created (see Figure 25-21).

Figure 25-21

5. Press the **Start Content Browser** icon to bring up the Content Browser.

6. Select the **Render Material Catalog > Finishes > Tiling** folder.

7. Drag the **Tiling.Ceramic.Checker** material into the **Materials** tool palette.

8. Select **Tiling.Ceramic.Checker** material in the **Materials** tool palette, **RMB**, and select **Apply To Selected** from the contextual menu that appears.

Since you selected the roof surfaces in Step 4 of this exercise, the **Finishes.Tiling.Ceramic.Checker** map is applied to those surfaces.

Note: A map is a bitmap of a material (see Figure 25-22).

9. To easily adjust the roof surface map, select the surfaces, press the **MapScaler** button, and change the scale in the MapScaler parameters (see Figure 25-23).

Figure 25-22

Figure 25-23

10. Repeat the exercises "Creating and Using Materials" and "Applying Materials," and add materials to the walls of the enclosure.

If you don't separate the faces of the walls, and just apply a material directly to a wall, all the walls will become that material. You can also add a material to the roof edges by separating them.

11. Press **C** on the keyboard to change the view back to the **Camera View**, and select **Rendering > Render** from the **Main** menu to bring up the **Render Scene** dialog box.

12. Press the **Render** button to render the scene (see Figure 25-24).

Figure 25-24

Adding the Sky

13. Go to http://www.3dcafe.com/asp/texturesky1.asp or hunt for a site with sky texture maps on the Internet.

14. Download and save one of the sky maps as a JPG, TIF, or BMP and place it in a folder labeled **Maps** on your computer (see Figure 25-25).

Figure 25-25

15. Name the bitmap **SKY**.

16. Select **Rendering > Environment** from the **Main** menu to bring up the Environment tab in the **Render Scene** dialog box.

17. Select the **None** bar to bring up the **Browse Images for Input** dialog box and **Browse** to the folder where you downloaded your SKY bitmap.

18. If you do not see your bitmap listed in the folder, change the **Files of type** to **All Files** in the drop-down list.

19. Select the sky you downloaded, and press the **Open** button to return to the **Environment** tab.

20. Under **Exposure Control** press the **Render Preview** button to see a preview of your scene with the sky (see Figure 25-26).

21. Press the **Render** button to render the scene (see Figure 25-27).

Figure 25-26

Figure 25-27

Hands-On

Creating and Modifying Materials

VIZ Render comes with a series of preconfigured materials, but you can also make your own. Materials can be made from bitmaps or directly from color. The bitmaps can be scanned or photographed images or they can be created in software programs such as Adobe PhotoShop or Illustrator. These bitmaps and colored materials can then be modified to have various levels of opacity and shininess. By using "bump map" versions of the images, which utilize the gray scale, additional 3D characteristics can be incorporated. Bump maps are often used to enhance materials such as brick.

People often ask if the materials can look "real"; in fact, they can look more than real. In VIZ Render you can even make transparent steel.

1. Open the **Materials** palette, and select the **Scratch** tab.

2. Select the **Create New** icon, **RMB**, and select **User Defined** from the contextual menu that appears to create a new user-defined material (see Figure 25-28).

3. Select the new **User Defined** material, **RMB**, and select **Properties** from the contextual menu that appears to bring up the **Material Editor** dialog box (see Figure 25-29).

Figure 25-28

Figure 25-29

4. Select the **Diffuse Color area,** to bring up the **Color Selector**.

5. Set the following (see Figure 25-30):

   a.   Red = **210**

   b.   Green = **217**

   c.   Blue = **32**

6. Set **Shininess** to **87.0**.

Notice the small highlight that gets smaller as the shininess is increased (see Figure 25-31).

Figure 25-30

Figure 25-31

To see if a material is transparent, you need a background behind the sample globe.

7. Set **Transparency** to **75.0**, **RMB** on the globe sample, and select **Background** to place a checkered background behind the sample (see Figure 25-32).

8. Return to Architectural Desktop 2005.

9. Enter **isolines** in the **Command line** and press **Enter**.

10. Enter **16** in the **Command line** and press **Enter**.

11. Enter **sphere** in the **Command line** and press **Enter**.

12. Create a new layer and name it **SPHERE**.

13. Place a 3'-0" sphere in the scene near the enclosure, and assign it to the SPHERE layer (see Figure 25-33).

Figure 25-32

Figure 25-33

14. Return to VIZ Render.

15. Select the **File Link Manager** button under the **Utilities** tab to bring up the **File Link Manager** dialog box.

16. Press the **Reload** button to bring up the **File Link Settings** dialog box.

17. Press **OK.**

The VIZ Render scene will now be reloaded from ADT 2005, and it will include the sphere you created in ADT 2005.

18. Press **H** on the keyboard to bring up the **Selection Floater**.

19. Select **Layer: SPHERE.01**, press the **Select** button, and close the Selection Floater.

20. Open the **Materials** palette and select the **Scratch** tab.

21. **RMB** on the new transparent yellow material you created, and select **Apply to Selected** from the contextual menu that appears.

With a normal video card, the sphere in the scene should be filled with small dots indicating that a transparent material has been applied to that object.

22. Press the **Render** button in the **Render Scene** dialog to render the scene (see Figure 25-34).

Create Grass

23. Open the **Materials** palette, and again select the **Scratch** tab.

24. Select the **Create New** icon, **RMB**, and select **User Defined** from the

Figure 25-34

contextual menu that appears to create a new user defined material.

25. **RMB** on the new material and select **Properties** to bring up the **Material Editor**.

26. Type **GRASS** in the drop-down list as shown in Figure 25-35.

27. Select the **None** button to the right of the **Diffuse Map** data field to bring up the **Material/Map Browser** (see Figure 25-35).

Figure 25-35

28. Click on the **Noise** icon, and press **OK** to bring up the **Material Editor** for the new GRASS material with the **Noise** options.

29. Set the following:

> Noise Type = **Turbulence**
>
> Size = **0.1**

Color #1

  a. Red = **0**

  b. Green = **109**

  c. Blue = **13**

Color #2

  a. Red = **79**

  b. Green = **84**

  c. Blue = **80**

30. Return to the **Materials** palette and drag the **GRASS** icon to the base in your scene.

31. Render the scene (see Figure 25-36).

Figure 25-36

Hands-On

People and Trees

VIZ Render comes with content from two developers, ArchVision and Bionatics.

ArchVision is the developer of the RPC people, foliage, and automobiles that have become the industry standard and are available in most of the leading visualization and CAAD packages. A sample demo person is included with VIZ Render, and more libraries are available by download at http://www.archvision.com.

Bionatics's EASYnat software brings highly customizable trees and plants to VIZ Render. Three trees and a plant are included, and more libraries are available online at http://www.bionatics.com. EASYnat trees can be made to wave in the wind, and can be modified automatically according to season.

To load the Archvision RPC plug-in do the following:

1. Return to Architectural Desktop 2005.
2. Select the **Content Browser icon** in the **Main** menu to bring up the Content Browser.
3. Select the **Architectural Desktop/VIZ Render Plug-ins** catalog.
4. Double-click on the **Architectural Desktop/VIZ Render–Plug-ins** catalog to open it. Inside the catalog are two folders—one labeled **RPC** and the other labeled **EasyNat**.
5. Double-click the **RPC** folder and follow the directions to go to the RPC website and download the RPC plug-in and Tina, the sample person. (You can also browse the dozens of RPC content libraries that include people, trees, cars, and even furniture.)

RPC content is unusual in that it is absolutely photorealistic, but renders very quickly. This is because it uses a unique system of compiled photographs of actual objects that appear correctly in relation to camera position. Content is being upgraded and improved constantly. RPC's Moving People content creates the most realistic architectural visualization animations available.

Once installed, the RPC content will become available as a menu choice on the **Main** menu bar.

To use ArchVision RPC content do the following:

1. Return to VIZ Render.
2. In VIZ Render, press **W** on the keyboard to change to four viewports.
3. Activate the **Top** viewport and press **W** on the keyboard again to maximize the **Top** viewport.
4. Select **RPC > RPC** from the **Main** menu to bring up the RPC tools.

I have more content than you will have if you use only the demo content, but the process will be the same. The demo person (Tina) does not have the highest resolution available.

5. Select the name of the person (**Tina** if only demo content) in the **RPC Selection** tree (see Figure 25-37).

Figure 25-37

6. Push the **RPC Selection** tools upward to expose the **RPC Parameters** tools.

7. Set the following:

   a.   Height = **5.6666**

If this is preset in meters, select **Customize > Units Setup** from the **Main** menu, and set the units to **feet and inches**.

   b.   Check the **Cast Reflections** check box if you intend to reflect your RPC content in windows or mirrors.

   c.   Uncheck the **Jitter** check box. Jitter is used when animating; makes smoother animated content.

   d.   Uncheck the **Billboard** checkbox. Billboard is used when you want to concentrate several pieces of content into one quick rendering object, such as trees into a tree line.

   e.   Check the **Cast Shadows** check box.

   f.   Uncheck the **Apply Filter Effect** check box. This allows you to use Photoshop filter effects on the content. The effects must be loaded into the RPC directory.

8. Move your cursor into your scene.

9. Click and hold the left mouse button to place and rotate Tina into position (see Figure 25-38).

10. Press **W** on the keyboard to change to four viewports, and adjust Tina in relation to the base.

11. Add more people if you have them, or just add more copies of Tina.

12. Since you have placed new content, it is a good idea to reset and start a new radiosity solution.

13. After finishing the radiosity solution, render the **Camera View** (see Figure 25-39).

Figure 25-38

Figure 25-39

Note that several of the figures are "washed out." To fix this do the following:

14. Press the **Mass Edit** button in the **RPC Edit Tools** tree above the **RPC Parameters** that you set in Step 12 to bring up the **RPC Mass Edit** dialog box.

15. Select all the people you used to populate the scene, and set their Self **Illumination** to **100.0** (see Figure 25-40).

16. If you have more RPC content such as trees or cars, add it, adjust the **Self Illumination**, and render the scene (see Figure 25-41).

Figure 25-40

Figure 25-41

To load the Bionatics EASYnat plug-in do the following:

1. Return to Architectural Desktop 2005.
2. Select the **Content Browser** icon in the **Main** menu to bring up the Content Browser.
3. Select the **Architectural Desktop/VIZ Render Plug-ins** catalog.
4. Double-click on the **Architectural Desktop/VIZ Render Plug-ins** catalog to open it.
5. Double-click the **EASYnat** folder and follow the directions to go to the EASYnat website and download the plug-in.

EASYnat content is a high-quality plant modeling program featuring virtual plants that can be modified for age and season. Once installed, the EASYnat content will become available as a menu choice on the **Main** menu bar.

To use Bionatics EASYnat content do the following:

1. Return to VIZ Render.
2. Delete the Archvision content you placed in the previous exercise.
3. Select **EASYnat > Create** from the **Main** menu to bring up the **Create EASYnat Plant** dialog box (see Figure 25-42).

Figure 25-42

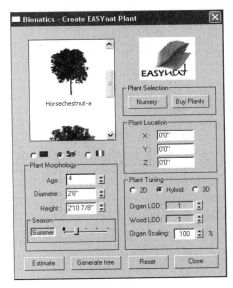

4. Select the tree desired from the main screen or press the **Nursery** button to open the **EASYnat Nursery** dialog box.
5. Double-click on **Horsechestnut**, and return to the **Create EASYnat Plant** dialog box.
6. Select the **Plant Tuning Hybrid** radio button, and set the **Age** of the tree to **12**.
7. Set the **Season** to **Summer**, and press the **Generate tree** button to generate the tree.

The **Tree Generation** timer will appear. After it closes, your tree will be in the scene.

8. Move your tree into position, and repeat the generation and place-ment of another tree, but set the **Age** to **9** for this tree.

9. Reset, start a new radiosity solution, and then render the scene (see Figure 25-43).

Figure 25-43

Select the different radio buttons for 2D and 3D trees, and then press the **Estimate** button to see the difference in triangles. The more triangles and the more they are realistic, the more time they take to render. The above scene with two hybrid trees took six minutes to render on a 2-GHz, 1/2-Gig RAM computer.

Putting It All Together

Tutorial Project

For the tutorial project, this author has chosen a small rehab building. The project progresses through the design process to the construction documentation stage.

The building is located in East Baltimore, was built in the 1920s, and has three floors.

Before starting the project, it will be necessary to create a customized plotting sheet that includes the company logo. Using Adobe Illustrator, Adobe Photoshop, Corel Draw, Paint Shop Pro, Macromedia FreeHand, Canvas, or even Windows Paint, create a JPG of your logo. My logo looks like Figure 26-1.

I started with an Adobe Illustrator file and exported it as an RGB JPG.

Note: the jpg must be in RGB mode; CMYK mode won't work in AutoCAD.

Figure 26-1

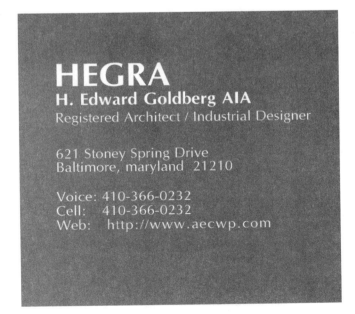

451

Hands-On

Placing the Logo in the Template File

1. Select **File > Open** from the **Main** menu to bring up the **Select File** dialog box.

2. In the **Look in** drop-down list, browse to the C drive.

3. Browse to **Documents and Settings > All Users > Application Data > Autodesk >ADT 2005 > Menu > Template**.

4. In the **File** dialog box, select **Drawing Template (*.dwt)** from the drop-down list.

The default template files will appear. This author suggests that novice users modify a predefined template file; seasoned AutoCAD users should be able to create template files from scratch and add blocks with attributes. Template files are ordinary AutoCAD files with a .dwt file extension.

5. Select the Aec Sheet (Imperial - stb).dwt template.

6. Change to the preset Arch D (24 × 36) Layout (see Figure 26-2).

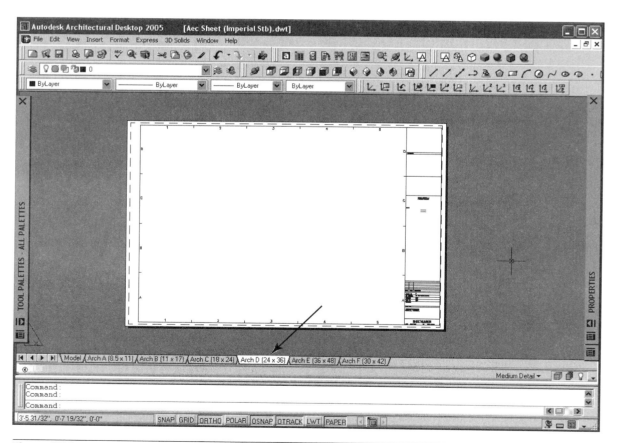

Figure 26-2

7. Select **Insert > Image** from the **Main** menu to bring up the **Select Image File** dialog box (see Figure 26-3).

Figure 26-3

8. Select the logo you created, and press **Open** to bring up the **Image** dialog box.

9. Check the **Insertion** and **Scale Specify on-screen** check boxes, and press **OK** to return to the Drawing Editor (see Figure 26-4).

Figure 26-4

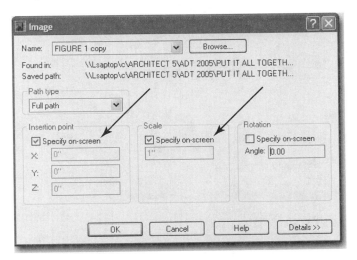

10. Place the logo JPG in the Aec sheet (Imperial - stb) template (see Figure 26-5).

11. Save the template drawing as **TEST PROJECT**, and be sure the **Files of type** drop-down list is set to **AutoCAD drawing Template (*.dwt)**. Press the **Save** button.

12. The **Template Description** dialog box will appear; enter a description of the template and press **OK** (see Figure 26-6).

You have now created a custom plotting sheet.

Figure 26-5

Figure 26-6

Setting Up the Project

1. Select the **My Computer** icon on your desktop or from the **Start** menu, select **All Programs > Accessories > Windows Explorer** to bring up the **My Computer** or **My Documents** dialog box.

2. Create a new folder and name it **TUTORIAL PROJECT**.

3. Select **File > Project Browser** from the **Main** menu to bring up the **Project Browser** dialog box.

4. Locate the **TUTORIAL PROJECT** folder, and press the **New Project** icon to bring up the **Add Project** dialog box (see Figure 26-7).

Figure 26-7

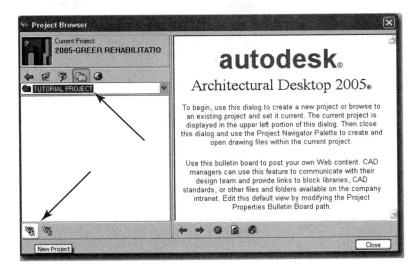

5. Enter the following:
    a. Number = **2005**
    b. Name = **GREER RENOVATION**
    c. Description = **3 Story Rehabilitation**
    d. Prefix Filenames with Project Number = **Yes**
    e. Leave all the templates as they appear (see Figure 26-8).

Figure 26-8

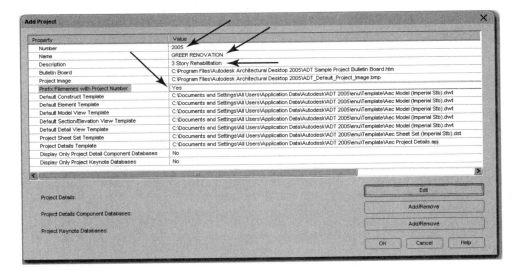

6. Press the **Edit** button to bring up the **Project Details** dialog box.
7. Enter **5217 YORK RD.** in the **Project Address** field. You can add any other information you wish in the remaining fields, or you can add fields. Press the **OK** buttons to return to the **Project Browser** (see Figure 26-9).
8. Press the **Close** button to close the **Project Browser** and bring up the **Project Navigator**.

Figure 26-9

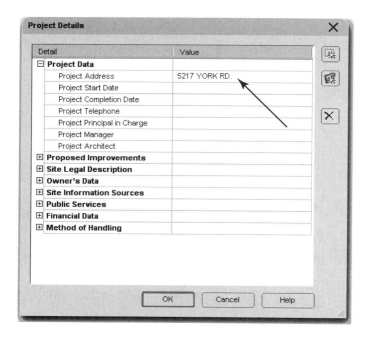

Assigning the Custom Sheet Template

1. Open the **Project Navigator**.
2. Change to the **Sheets** tab.
3. **RMB** on **Architectural** to bring up the **Subset Properties** dialog box.
4. Click on the **Sheet creation template for subset** browser to bring up the **Select Layout as Sheet Template** dialog box (see Figure 26-10).

Figure 26-10

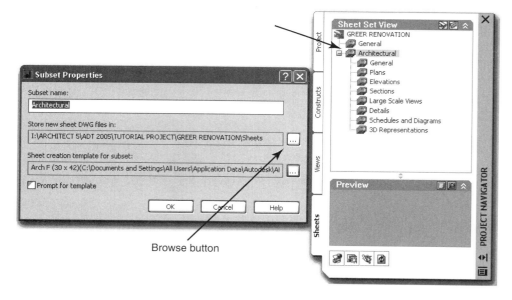

Browse button

5. Select the **Arch D (24 x 36)** layout from the **Select a layout to create new sheets** list, click the **Drawing template file name** browser, and select the **TEST PROJECT.dwt**, the template you created in the previous exercise (see Figure 26-11).

Figure 26-11

6. Press the **OK** buttons to close the dialog boxes and bring up the **Confirm Changes** dialog box (see Figure 26-12).

7. Press the **Yes** button to apply the changes you just made to all the nested subsets.

Figure 26-12

Testing and Modifying the Custom Sheet

1. In the **Sheets** tab of the **Project Navigator**, select **Plans**, and select the **Add Sheet** icon to bring up the **New Sheet** dialog box.

2. Enter **A-101** in the **Number** field, **SHEET TEST** in the **Sheet title** field, and press **OK** to return to the Drawing Editor.

3. In the **Sheets** tab of **Project Navigator**, double-click on **A-101 SHEET TEST** to bring that drawing up in the Drawing Editor.

4. Zoom in to examine the drawing, and notice that the title block contains the custom logo, owner's name, project number, CAD DWG file name, sheet title, and drawing number (see Figure 26-13).

5. **RMB** on **A-101 TEST SHEET** in the **Sheets** tab, and select **Properties** from the contextual menu that appears to bring up the **Sheet Properties** dialog box.

Figure 26-13

6. Put your in initials in the **Checked By** and **Drawn By** fields and then press **OK.**

7. **RMB** on the topmost icon in the **Sheets** tab (the project name) and select **Refresh Sheet Set** from the contextual menu that appears to update the set (see Figure 26-14).

Figure 26-14

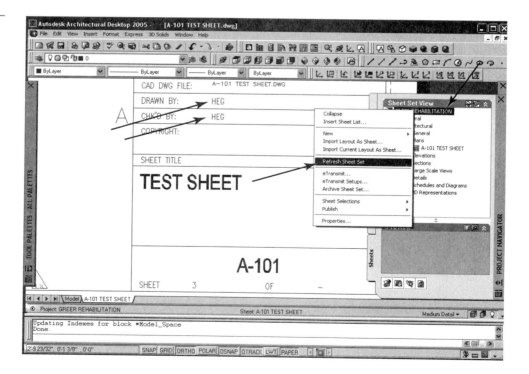

Making, Modifying, and Placing Sheet Lists

Autodesk Architectural Desktop 2005 features a sheet list option. This creates an automated table of all your drawings that can be added to a cover page.

1. Using the previous exercises, create several drawing files labeled **A-101** to **A-104**. Give each drawing a different name.

2. Select the **General** icon at the top of the **Sheets** tab, select the **Add Sheet** icon at the bottom of the tab, and name the sheet **TITLE SHEET**.

3. Double-click **TITLE SHEET** in the **Project Navigator** to bring it up in the Drawing Editor.

4. **RMB** the project name at the top of the **Sheets** tab, and select **Insert Sheet List** from the contextual menu that appears to bring up the **Insert Sheet list Table** dialog box (see Figure 26-15).

Figure 26-15

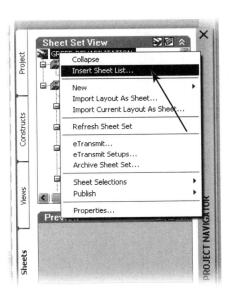

5. Select the **Standard Table Style**, and press **OK** to return to the Drawing Editor.

6. Place the sheet list in the TITLE SHEET (see Figure 26-16).

Figure 26-16

Sheet List Table	
Sheet Number	Sheet Title
--	TITLE SHEET
A-101	TEST SHEET
A-102	EVEVATIONS SHEET
A-103	SECTIONS SHEET
A-104	DETAILS SHEET

7. **RMB** the sheet list, and select **Edit Sheet List Table Settings** from the contextual menu that appears to bring up the **Edit Sheet List Settings** dialog box.

8. Press the **Add** button twice, select **Checked By** and **Drawn By** from the drop-down list shown in Figure 26-17, and press **OK** to return to the Drawing Editor.

The sheet list is now set for the project (see Figure 26-18).

Figure 26-17

Figure 26-18

Sheet List Table			
Sheet Number	Sheet Title	Checked By	Drawn By
--	TITLE SHEET	-	-
A-101	TEST SHEET	HEG	HEG
A-102	EVEVATIONS SHEET	-	-
A-103	SECTIONS SHEET	-	-
A-104	DETAILS SHEET	-	-

The Project

The building was photographed and field measured, a site plan was acquired from a tax record plat in the Baltimore planning department, and a planning meeting was set with the client. The client wanted to place a barber shop on the first floor; a beauty shop on the second floor; and a wash room, mechanical room, and small kitchen on the lower level. After reading the BOCA building code and consulting with the local permit department, it was agreed to meet the stricter requirements for an assembly use rather than a business use. This required the addition of a second floor rear fire escape.

Figure 26-19 shows a photograph of the building exterior.

After some meetings, a plan was conceived. Using @Last Software's SketchUp 3 software, a conceptual 3D model was presented to the client. Figure 26-20 shows the model.

Although it is not described in this book, there is an excellent SketchUp plug-in included with Autodesk Architectural Desktop 2005 that allows you to translate walls, slabs, and so on into ADT 2005 intelligent objects from a SketchUp model automatically. A full function eight-hour trial version of SketchUp and the free plug-in translator can also be downloaded from http://www.sketchup.com.

Figure 26-19

Figure 26-20

Creating the TITLE SHEET

1. Make sure that you have the GREER RENOVATION set as the current project in the **Project Browser**.

2. Close the **Project Browser** to bring up the GREER RENOVATION.

3. In the **Sheets** tab of the **Project Navigator**, create a sheet named **TITLE SHEET**.

4. In the TITLE SHEET, insert a sheet list as explained in the previous exercise.

5. Save and close the TITLE SHEET.

The Current Project Settings

1. Change to the **Project** tab.

2. Select the **Add Levels** icon to bring up the **Levels** dialog box.

3. Set the settings shown in Figure 26-21 and press **OK**.

Figure 26-21

Name	Floor Elevation	Floor to Floor Height	ID	Description
FLOOR 2	9'-6"	9'-0"	3	
FLOOR 1	6"	9'-0"	4	
GRADE	6"	0"	2	GROUND LEVEL
LOWER LEVEL	-8'-6"	9'-0"	1	

☑ Auto-Adjust Elevation

The SITE PLAN

1. Change to the **Constructs** tab.

2. Select the **Add Construct** icon and create a new construct called **SITE BOUNDARY**, check the **Grade Level** check box, and press **OK**.

3. Double-click on the **SITE BOUNDARY** icon to bring up the SITE BOUNDARY construct in the Drawing Editor.

4. Set the **Scale** to **3/16" = 1'-0"**.

5. In the SITE BOUNDARY construct, create the drawing shown in Figure 26-22.

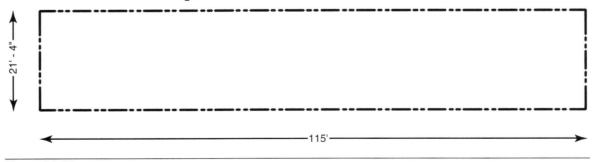

Figure 26-22

6. Add dimensions with the **AEC Dimension** option.

7. Press **Ctrl + S** on the keyboard to save the drawing.

8. Change to the **Views** tab.

9. Select the **Add View** icon to bring up the **Add View** dialog box.

10. Select the **General** view radio button and press **OK**.

11. Name the new view **SITE BOUNDARY VIEW** and press the **Next** button.

12. Check the **GROUND LEVEL** check box and press the **Next** button.

13. Press the **Finish** button to return to the Drawing Editor.

14. Change to the **Sheets** tab.

15. Select the **Add Sheet** icon to bring up the **New Sheet** dialog box.

16. Number the sheet **S-1**, title it **SITE PLAN**, and then press **OK**.

17. Double-click **SITE PLAN** in the **Project Navigator** to bring it up in the Drawing Editor.

18. Change to the **Views** tab, and drag the **SITE BOUNDARY VIEW** into the SITE PLAN.

19. Open the Content Browser (**Ctrl+4**), and open the **Document Tool Catalog -Imperial**.

20. Select the **Miscellaneous > North Arrows** folder, and drag **North Arrow A** into the **Annotation** tool palette.

21. Drag **North Arrow A** from the **Annotation** tool palette into your drawing.

22. Press **Ctrl + S** on the keyboard to save the drawing (see Figure 26-23).

Figure 26-23

The LOWER LEVEL EXTERIOR WALL Construct

1. Change to the **Constructs** tab.

2. Press the **Add Construct** icon and create a new construct called **LOWER LEVEL EXTERIOR WALLS**, check the **LOWER LEVEL** check box, and press **OK**.

3. Double-click on the **LOWER LEVEL EXTERIOR WALLS** icon to bring up the LOWER LEVEL EXTERIOR WALLS construct in the Drawing Editor.

4. Set the **Scale** to **1/4" = 1'-0"**.

5. From the **Constructs** tab, drag the **SITE BOUNDARY** into the LOWER LEVEL EXTERIOR WALLS construct.

6. Select the **Concrete-8 Concrete-16x8** footing wall from the **Walls** tool palette.

7. With the wall selected, move your cursor over the **Properties** palette to open it.

8. Set **Base height** to **9'-0"** and **Justify** to **Baseline**.

9. Place the exterior walls as shown in Figure 26-24.

Figure 26-24

10. Delete the SITE BOUNDARY from the LOWER LEVEL EXTERIOR WALLS construct.

11. Press **Ctrl + S** on the keyboard to save the construct (see Figure 26-25).

The FLOOR 1 EXTERIOR WALL Construct

1. Change to the **Constructs** tab.

2. Press the **Add** Construct icon and create a new construct called **FLOOR 1 EXTERIOR WALLS**, check the **FLOOR 1** check box, and press **OK**.

3. Double-click on the **FLOOR 1 EXTERIOR WALLS** icon to bring up the FLOOR 1 EXTERIOR WALLS construct in the Drawing Editor.

4. Set the **Scale** to **1/4" = 1'-0"**.

5. From the **Constructs** tab, drag the **LOWER LEVEL EXTERIOR WALLS** construct into the FLOOR 1 EXTERIOR WALLS construct.

Figure 26-25

6. Select the **Brick-4 Brick-4** wall from the **Walls** tool palette.

7. With the wall selected, move your cursor over the **Properties** palette to open it.

8. Set **Base height** to **9'-0"** and **Justify** to **Left**.

9. In the **Top View**, using the LOWER LEVEL EXTERIOR WALLS construct as a guide, snap the walls in place on top of the lower level exterior walls.

10. Delete the LOWER LEVEL EXTERIOR WALLS construct from the FLOOR 1 EXTERIOR WALLS construct.

11. Press **Ctrl + S** on the keyboard to save the construct.

The FLOOR 2 EXTERIOR WALL Construct

1. Change to the **Constructs** tab.

2. **RMB** on the **FLOOR 1 EXTERIOR WALLS** icon, and select **Copy Construct to Levels** from the contextual menu that appears to bring up the **Copy Construct** to Levels dialog box.

3. Check the **FLOOR 2** check box and press **OK**.

FLOOR 1 EXTERIOR WALLS (2) will now appear in the **Constructs** tab. To change the construct's name to FLOOR 2 EXTERIOR WALLS, do the following:

4. **RMB** on the **FLOOR 1 EXTERIOR WALLS (2)** icon to bring up the **Modify Construct** dialog box.

5. Change the **Name** to **FLOOR 2 EXTERIOR WALLS**, and press **OK** to return to the Drawing Editor.

6. Press **Ctrl + S** on the keyboard to save the construct.

The COMPOSITE PERSPECTIVE VIEW

1. Change to the **Views** tab.
2. Select the **Add View** icon to bring up the **Add View** dialog box.
3. Select the **General View** radio button and press **OK**.
4. Name the new view **COMPOSITE PERSPECTIVE VIEW**, and press the **Next** button.
5. Check all the check boxes, and press the **Next** button.
6. Press the **Finish** button to return to the Drawing Editor.
7. Change to the **SW Isometric View**.
8. Select the **3D Orbit** tool from the **Navigation** toolbar.
9. **RMB** in the Drawing Editor, and select **Projection > Perspective** from the contextual menu that appears.
10. Press the **Esc** key on your keyboard twice to end the command.
11. Enter **V** in the **Command line**, and press **Enter** to bring up the **View** dialog box.
12. Press the **New** button to bring up the **New View** dialog box.
13. Enter **PERSPECTIVE** in the **View name** field, select the **Define Window** radio button, and press **OK** to return to the Drawing Editor.
14. Select the view with a selection window, and press the **OK** buttons to close all the dialog boxes and return to the Drawing Editor.
15. Select the **Views** tab in the Project Navigator, and expand the **COMPOSITE PERSPECTIVE VIEW**. Notice that the COMPOSITE PERSPECTIVE VIEW drawing now contains the **PERSPECTIVE** view (see Figure 26-26).
16. Press **Ctrl + S** on the keyboard to save the sheet.

Figure 26-26

The ELEVATIONS

1. Double-click the **COMPOSITE EXTERIOR VIEW** in the **Views** tab to bring it up in the Drawing Editor.

2. Select **Exterior Elevation Mark A3** from the **Callouts** tab (see Figure 26-27).

Figure 26-27

3. In the COMPOSITE EXTERIOR VIEW drawing in the **Top View**, place a selection window around the building and click to bring up the **Place Callout** dialog box.

4. Check the **Generate Section/Elevation** check box, select **1/4″** from the **Scale** drop-down list, and select the **New View** drawing icon to bring up the **Add Section/Elevation View** dialog box.

5. Enter **ELEVATION VIEWS** in the **Name** field (this will appear as the drawing file name in the **Project Navigator**), and press the **Next** button to bring up the **Context** screen.

6. Check all the level check boxes except **GRADE**, and press the **Next** button to bring up the **Content** screen.

7. Make sure the **Constructs** check box is checked, and press the **Finish** button to return to the Drawing Editor.

8. Click to the right of the building (where you click doesn't matter because you are creating the elevations in the new drawing file).

9. Move your cursor down 10′ vertically (this will dictate the distance between the four elevations) and click your mouse button. The **Generate Elevation progress** dialog screen will appear telling you when the elevations have been created in a new file. You will also see four elevation symbols appear in the drawing.

10. Press **Ctrl + S** on the keyboard to save this drawing.

11. Select the four elevation symbols, and press **Ctrl + C** or select **Edit > Copy** from the **Main** menu.

12. Double-click **FLOOR 1 PLAN** in the **Views** tab to bring it up in the Drawing Editor.

13. Select **Edit > Paste to Original Coordinates** from the **Main** menu to paste the four elevation symbols in FLOOR PLAN 1.

14. Press **Ctrl + S** on the keyboard to save this drawing.

15. Change to the **Sheets** tab.

16. Select the **Elevations** icon.

17. Select the **Add Sheet** icon to bring up the **New Sheet** dialog box.

18. Number the sheet **A-102**, title it **ELEVATION PLANS**, and then press **OK**.

19. Double-click **A-102 ELEVATION PLANS** in the **Project Navigator** to bring the sheet up in the Drawing Editor.

20. Change to the **Views** tab.

21. Drag the **ELEVATION VIEWS** view into the A-101 ELEVATION PLANS sheet (they will appear one after the other into the plan) (see Figure 26-28).

Figure 26-28

22. Press **Ctrl + S** on the keyboard to save the sheet.

23. Select the **Add View** icon to bring up the **Add View** dialog box.

24. Select the **General View** radio button, and press **OK** to bring up the **Add General View** dialog box **General** screen.

25. Enter **LOWER LEVEL PLAN** in the **Name** field, and press the **Next** button to change to the **Context** screen.

26. Check the **LOWER LEVEL** check box, and press the **Next** button to change to the **Content** screen.

27. Press the Finish button to create the LOWER LEVEL PLAN.

28. Repeat Steps 1 through 6 of this exercise, creating a FLOOR 1 PLAN and FLOOR 2 PLAN with the FLOOR 1 EXTERIOR WALLS and FLOOR 2 EXTERIOR WALLS constructs, respectively.

29. Change to the **Sheets** tab.

30. Select the **Add Sheet** icon to bring up the **New Sheet** dialog box.

31. Number the sheet **A-101**, title it **FLOOR PLANS**, and then press **OK**.

32. Double-click **A-101 FLOOR PLANS** in the **Project Navigator** to bring it up in the Drawing Editor.

33. Change to the **Views** tab.

34. Drag the **LOWER LEVEL PLAN**, **FLOOR 1 PLAN**, and **FLOOR 2 PLAN** views into the A-101 FLOOR PLANS sheet.

The PLANS Sheet

1. Change to the **Views** tab.

2. Select the **Add View** icon to bring up the **Add View** dialog box.

3. Select the **General View** radio button, and press **OK** to bring up the **Add General View** dialog box **General** screen.

4. Enter **LOWER LEVEL** in the **Name** field, and press the **Next** button to change to the **Context** screen.

5. Check the **LOWER LEVEL** check box, and press the **Next** button to change to the **Content** screen.

6. Uncheck all check boxes. Press the **Finish** button to create the LOWER LEVEL view drawing.

7. Double-click **LOWER LEVEL** to bring it up in the Drawing Editor.

8. Change to the **Constructs** tab.

9. Drag the **LOWER LEVEL EXTERIOR WALLS** construct into the LOWER LEVEL view drawing in the Drawing Editor.

10. Press **V**, and press the **Enter** key on the keyboard to bring up the **View** dialog box.

11. Select the **New** button to bring up the **New View** dialog box.

12. Enter **LOWER LEVEL VIEW**, select the **Define Window** radio button, make a selection window around the floor plan, and press the **OK** buttons to complete the command.

You have now specified the view area for this view.

13. Repeat Steps 1 through 12 of this exercise, creating a FLOOR 1 VIEW and FLOOR 2 VIEW with the FLOOR 1 EXTERIOR WALLS and FLOOR 2 EXTERIOR WALLS constructs, respectively.

14. Change to the **Sheets** tab.

15. Select the **Add Sheet** icon to bring up the **New Sheet** dialog box.

16. Number the sheet **A-101**, title it **FLOOR PLANS**, and then press **OK**.

17. Double-click the **A-101 FLOOR PLANS** sheet in the **Project Navigator** to bring it up in the Drawing Editor.

18. Change to the **Views** tab.

19. Drag the **LOWER LEVEL PLAN**, **FLOOR 1 PLAN**, and **FLOOR 2 PLAN** views into the A-101 FLOOR PLANS sheet.

20. Press **Ctrl + S** on the keyboard to save the sheet.

Note: Before placing the three views, **RMB** to bring up a scale; here you can interactively set your view scale (see Figures 26-29 and 26-30).

Figure 26-29

Figure 26-30

The SECTIONS, DETAILS, and SCHEDULE Sheets

Using the methods shown in the previous exercises, create SECTIONS, DETAILS, and SCHEDULES sheets for later use. Label them **A-103**, **A-104**, and **A-105**, respectively.

The Sheet List Table Lists All the Sheets

In the **Sheets** tab of the **Project Navigator**, double-click on the **TITLE SHEET** to bring it up in the Drawing Editor. Notice that the Sheet List Table now records all the sheets that are in the sheet set (see Figure 26-31).

Figure 26-31

Modifying the Side Walls

1. Change to the **Constructs** tab.
2. Double-click on the **FLOOR 2 EXTERIOR WALLS** icon to bring up the FLOOR 2 EXTERIOR WALLS construct in the Drawing Editor.
3. Select the **Surface Hatch Toggle** icon to turn off the surface hatching, and drag the walls as shown in Figure 26-32.
4. Press **Ctrl + S** on the keyboard to save the drawing.

Creating the Vertical Metal Siding Wall

1. Select **Format > Style Manager** from the **Main** menu, and select **Walls Styles** from the **Architectural Objects** folder.
2. **RMB,** and copy and paste the **Brick-4 Brick-4 wall** style.
3. Rename the copy **VERTICAL METAL SIDING**.
4. Double-click the **VERTICAL METAL SIDING** wall style to bring up the **Wall Style Properties** dialog box.
5. Select the **Components** tab, and set the settings shown in Figure 26-33.
6. Select the **Materials** tab.
7. Select the **Add New Material** icon, and add a new material called **METAL SIDING**.

Figure 26-32

Surface Hatch Toggle

Figure 26-33

Add Component

8. Select **METAL SIDING**, and press the **Edit Material** icon to bring up the **Material Definition Properties** dialog box.

9. Select the **General Medium Detail Style Override** check box to bring up the **Display Properties** dialog box.

10. Change to the **Hatching** tab.

11. Set the settings shown in Figure 26-34, and press the **OK** buttons and return to the Drawing Editor.

Figure 26-34

12. Double-click the front wall, to bring up the **Properties** palette.

13. Select **VERTICAL METAL SIDING** from the **Style** drop-down list and set **Justify** to **Baseline**.

14. Toggle the **Surface Hatch Toggle** again to turn the surface hatch on (see Figure 26-35).

Figure 26-35

15. Press **Ctrl + S** on the keyboard to save the drawing.

16. In the **Constructs** tab of the **Project Navigator** double-click on the **FLOOR 2 EXTERIOR WALLS** construct to bring it up in the Drawing Editor.

17. Again, select **Format > Style Manager** from the **Main** menu, and select **Walls Styles** from the **Architectural Objects** folder.

18. Drag the **VERTICAL METAL SIDING** wall style into the **Walls** tool palette.

19. **RMB** on the **VERTICAL METAL SIDING** tool in the **Walls** tool palette, select **Apply tool Properties To > Wall** from the contextual menu that appears, and click on the front wall.

Note: If the brick veneer on the front wall shows through, edit the wall style, and set the **Material** for brick veneer and brick veneer (structural) to **Standard**.

20. Press **Ctrl + S** on the keyboard to save the drawing.

Creating the Front Wall Overhang

1. Bring up the FLOOR 2 EXTERIOR WALLS construct.

2. **RMB** on the front wall, select **Sweeps > Edit Profile in Place** from the contextual menu that appears, and select the front wall at the metal siding component.

3. When the blue profile appears, add an 18" x 8" rectangle as shown in Figure 26-36.

Figure 26-36

4. **RMB** on the blue **In-Place Edit** profile, and select **Add Ring** from the contextual menu that appears.

5. Select the rectangle you just created.

6. Enter **Y** (Yes) in the **Command line** and press **Enter**.

7. Enter **J** (Join) in the **Command line** and press **Enter**.

8. Press the **Save All Changes** icon on the **In-Place Edit** toolbar.

9. Press **Ctrl + S** on the keyboard to save the drawing (see Figure 26-37).

Figure 26-37

Adding the Second Floor Exterior Windows and Doors

1. With the FLOOR 2 EXTERIOR WALLS construct in the Drawing Editor, **RMB** the front wall, and insert three openings 6'-0" wide by 8'-0" high with a sill height of 1'-0".

2. Select the new **Isolate Objects/End Object** Isolation icon, and hide all the walls except the front wall (see Figure 26-38).

Figure 26-38

Isolate Objects

3. Change to the **Left View**.

4. Enter **bpoly** in the **Command line** and press **Enter**.

5. Select an internal point in one of the openings, and press **Enter** to create a polyline. Add a line also, as shown in Figure 26-39.

Figure 26-39

6. **RMB** on the **Curtain Wall** tool in the **Design** tool palette, and select **Apply Tool Properties to > Elevation Sketch** from the contextual menu that appears.

7. Select the polyline and the line and then press **Enter** twice.

8. Enter **Y** (Yes) in the **Command line**, and press **Enter** to create the curtain wall window (see Figure 26-40).

Figure 26-40

9. Change to the **SW Isometric View**, and move the window into place. Although it appeared in place in the **Left View**, the window was actually at a different location in space (see Figure 26-41).

Figure 26-41

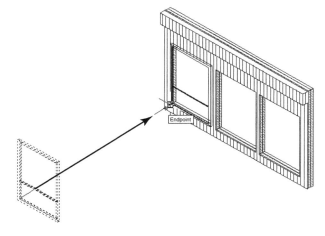

10. Select the curtain window you just created, **RMB**, and select **Frame/Mullion > Edit Profile In-Place**.

11. Select the horizontal mullion to bring up its blue **In-Place Edit** profile.

12. Stretch the profile and save the changes (see Figure 26-42).

Figure 26-42

13. Copy the curtain wall to the remaining openings, and unhide the other walls with the **Isolate Objects/End Object Isolation** icon (see Figure 26-43).

Figure 26-43

14. Change to the **Top View**, and place the rear exterior door and opening to the rear room.

15. Press **Ctrl + S** on the keyboard to save the drawing (see Figure 26-44).

Figure 26-44

Creating the Roofs

1. Bring up the FLOOR 2 EXTERIOR WALLS construct.
2. Change to the **Front View**.
3. Using the **polyline** command, draw the polyline shown in Figure 26-45.

4. **RMB** on the polyline, and select **Convert To > Mass Element** from the contextual menu.
5. Enter **Y** (Yes) in the **Command line** and press **Enter**.
6. Enter **21'-4"** in the **Command line** and press **Enter**.
7. Move the mass element into place.
8. **RMB** on the mass element, and select **Trim by Plane** from the contextual menu.
9. Enter **3** (3 points) in the **Command line** and press **Enter**.
10. Trim the mass element as shown in Figure 26-46.

Figure 26-46

11. Select the **Face UCS** icon from the **UCS** toolbar, and set the UCS parallel to the top surface of the sloping side walls.
12. Select the **Rectangle** icon from the **Draw** toolbar, and create a rectangle as shown in Figure 26-47.
13. **RMB** the **Roof Slab** tool in the **Design** tool palette, and select **Apply tool Properties to > Linework, Walls, and Roof**.

Figure 26-47

14. Select the rectangle and press **Enter**.

15. Enter **Y** (Yes) in the **Command line** and press **Enter**.

16. Enter **D** (Direct) in the **Command line** and press **Enter**.

17. Enter **T** (Top) in the **Command line** and press **Enter**.

18. Make sure the **Thickness** is set to **1'-0"** (check the **Properties** palette).

19. Reset the UCS to **World**.

20. Change to the **Top View**.

21. Using the **rectangle** command, create a polyline in the rear addition.

22. Select the **Roof Slab** tool again, and create another slab from the rear polyline.

23. Make the elevation of each slab 6" below the base height of the adjoining walls.

24. Press **Ctrl + S** on the keyboard to save the drawing.

Creating the Floors

1. Bring the **FLOOR 1 EXTERIOR WALLS** construct up in the Drawing Editor.

2. Change to the **Top View**.

3. Using a polyline, trace a closed polyline in the interior of the walls.

4. **RMB** on the **Slab** tool in the **Design** toolbar, and select **Apply tool Properties to > Linework and walls**.

5. Select the polyline and press **Enter**.

6. Enter **Y** (Yes) in the **Command line** and press **Enter**.

7. Enter **P** (Projected) in the **Command line** and press **Enter**.

8. Enter **8'-0"** (wall base height) in the **Command line** and press **Enter**.

9. Enter **B** (Bottom) in the **Command line** and press **Enter**.

10. Double-click the slab you just created to bring up the **Properties** palette, and set the **Thickness** to **12"**.

11. Press **Ctrl + S** on the keyboard to save the drawing.

12. Repeat Steps 1 through 10 for the LOWER LEVEL EXTERIOR WALLS construct to make the ceiling slab.

13. Using similar steps, create a 4" floor slab in the LOWER LEVEL EXTERIOR WALLS construct.

14. Press **Ctrl + S** on the keyboard to save the drawing (see Figure 26-48).

Figure 26-48

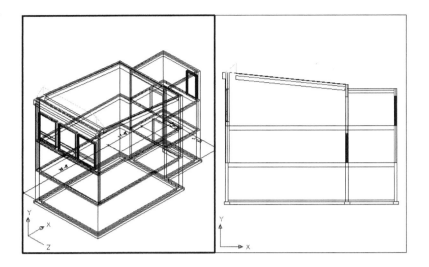

Creating the Inside Stairs

1. Bring the FLOOR 1 EXTERIOR WALLS construct up in the Drawing Editor.
2. Change to the **Top View**.
3. Place a 3'-0" wide Straight stair, 9'-0" high, with **Justify** set to **Left**, and **Terminated with** set to **Riser** (see Figure 26-49).

Figure 26-49

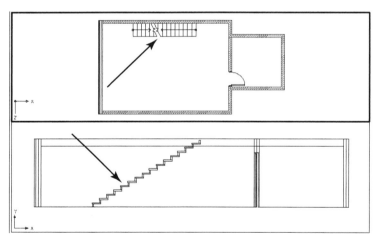

4. Copy the stair, and place the copy in the LOWER LEVEL EXTERIOR WALLS construct with **Edit >Paste to Original Coordinates**.
5. In the FLOOR 1 EXTERIOR WALLS construct, in the **Top View**, place a rectangle surrounding the stair.
6. Copy the rectangle, and place the copy in the FLOOR 2 EXTERIOR WALLS construct with **Edit >Paste to Original Coordinates**.
7. In the FLOOR 1 EXTERIOR WALLS construct, **RMB** on the ceiling slab, and select **Hole > Add** from the contextual menu.
8. Enter **Y** (Yes) in the **Command line** and press **Enter**.

9. Repeat Steps 7 and 8 for the LOWER LEVEL EXTERIOR WALLS construct (see Figure 26-50).

10. Press **Ctrl + S** on the keyboard to save the drawings.

Figure 26-50

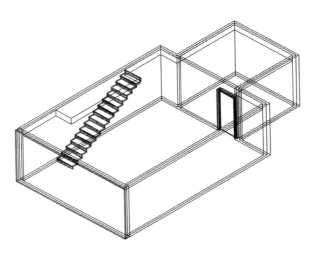

Creating the Bay Window

1. Bring the FLOOR 1 EXTERIOR WALLS construct up in the Drawing Editor.

2. Change to the **Top View**.

3. Draw a 2'6" x 10'-0" polyline similar to that shown in Figure 26-51.

Figure 26-51

4. Select the **Wall** tool from the **Design** tool palette, **RMB** and select **Apply tool Properties to > Linework**.

5. Select the polyline and press **Enter**.

6. Enter **Y** (Yes) in the **Command line** and press **Enter**.

7. While the new walls you just created are still selected, change the **Base height** to **18"**, **Justify** to **Left**, and **Elevation** to **6"**.

8. Select the **Curtain Wall** tool from the **Design** tool palette, and place curtain walls on top of the walls you just created. Make the curtain walls 6'-0" high.

9. Drag the back edge of the side curtain walls 1'-6" vertically (see Figure 26-52).

10. Select the new **Face UCS** icon from the **UCS** toolbar, and set the UCS parallel to the top surface of the sloping side curtain walls.

Figure 26-52

11. Place a rectangle and a line at the top of the curtain walls as shown in Figure 26-53.

12. **RMB** the **Curtain Wall** tool from the **Design** tool palette and select **Apply Tool Properties to > Elevation Sketch** from the contextual menu.

Figure 26-53

13. Select the rectangle and line you just created and press **Enter**.

14. Select the bottommost line of the rectangle as the **Baseline** and press **Enter**.

15. Enter **Y** (Yes) in the **Command line**, and press **Enter** to create the sloped roof of the bay window (see Figure 26-54).

Figure 26-54

16. **RMB** on the front wall, and insert directly behind the bay window a 6'-0" high x 9'-0" wide opening with a sill height of 18".

17. Press **Ctrl + S** on the keyboard to save the drawing.

Creating the Fire Stair

1. Change to the **Constructs** tab.

2. Press the **Add Construct** icon and create a new construct called **FIRE STAIRS**, check the **GRADE** check box, and press **OK**.

3. Double-click on the **FIRE STAIRS** icon to bring up the FIRE STAIRS construct in the Drawing Editor.

4. Change to the **Top View**.

5. Set the **Scale** to **1/4" = 1'-0"**.

6. Drag the **FLOOR 1 EXTERIOR WALLS** construct into the FIRE STAIRS construct in the Drawing Editor.

7. Select the **Stair** tool from the **Design** tool palette.

8. Place a stair with the settings shown in Figure 26-55.

9. Draw a 3'-6" rectangle for a landing, and using the **Slab** tool from the **Design** tool palette, Project a slab object 4" thick 8'-11" above grade elevation.

10. Select the **Guardrail – Pipe + Returns** railing from the **Design Tool Catalog** in the Content Browser and drag it into your **Design** tool palette.

11. **RMB** on the stair, and select **Add Railing** from the contextual menu that appears.

12. Enter **A** (Attach) in the **Command line** and press **Enter**.

Figure 26-55

13. Enter **F** (Flight) in the **Command line** and press **Enter**.

14. In the **Top View**, attach the railing to the stair flights (see Figure 26-56).

15. Again, select the **Guardrail – Pipe + Returns** railing from the **Design** tool palette.

16. Move your cursor over the **Properties** palette to open it, and select **Attached to > *NONE*** from the **Location** drop-down list.

17. Attach the rail to the stair landing as shown in Figure 26-57.

18. Select the railing you just placed, and change its **Elevation** to **4'-3"** in the **Properties** palette.

Figure 26-56

Figure 26-57

The railing is now on the landing, but the overhangs are not necessary. The overhangs are removed in the **Display Properties** (see Figure 26-58).

Figure 26-58

19. **RMB** on the railing, and select **Edit Object Display** from the contextual menu to bring up the **Object Display** dialog box.

20. Change to the **Display Properties** tab, and check the **Model - Object Override** check box to bring up the **Display Properties** dialog box.

21. Turn off the **Visible** icons (light bulbs), and press the **OK** buttons to close the dialog boxes.

22. Repeat this process where necessary. Remember to change the settings for the **Plan** direction also.

23. Place and the upper landing railings.

24. Press **Ctrl + S** on the keyboard to save the drawing. (see Figure 26-59).

Figure 26-59

Finishing the Building

1. Bring the FLOOR LOWER LEVEL EXTERIOR WALLS construct up in the Drawing Editor.

2. Change to the **Top View**.

3. Place a column in the center of the room (the author booleaned a mass element to the floor slab for a footing under the column and changed its display properties to show a hidden line).

4. Add walls and doors.

5. **RMB** the walls, and select **AEC Dimension** from the contextual menu to apply dimensions. (If you need to attach or detach objects and points from the dimension strings, **RMB** on the dimension strings and select the appropriate command.)

6. Press **Ctrl + S** on the keyboard to save the drawing (see Figure 26-60).

Figure 26-60

7. Bring the FLOOR 1 EXTERIOR WALLS construct up in the Drawing Editor.

8. Change to the **Top View**.

9. Add walls and doors.

10. **RMB** the walls, and select **AEC Dimension** from the contextual menu to apply dimensions.

11. Press **Ctrl + S** on the keyboard to save the drawing (see Figure 26-61).

12. Bring the FLOOR 2 EXTERIOR WALLS construct up in the Drawing Editor.

13. Change to the **Top View**.

14. Add walls and doors.

15. **RMB** the walls, and select **AEC Dimension** from the contextual menu to apply dimensions.

16. Press **Ctrl + S** on the keyboard to save the drawing (see Figure 26-62).

Figure 26-61

Figure 26-62

Placing the Furniture and Bath Fixtures

1. Bring the FLOOR 1 EXTERIOR WALLS and FLOOR 2 EXTERIOR WALLS constructs up in the Drawing Editor.

2. Change to the **Top View**.

3. Open the **Layer Manager**, and turn off the visibility of the **A-Anno-Dims** layer (Dimensions).

4. Create a **GREER** tool palette.

5. Drag chairs and desks from the **Design Tool Catalog** in the Content Browser into your **GREER** tool palette (see Figure 26-63).

6. Drag toilets, vanities, and so on from the **Design Tool Catalog** in the Content Browser into your FLOOR 1 EXTERIOR WALLS and FLOOR 2 EXTERIOR WALLS constructs.

7. Press **Ctrl + S** on the keyboard to save the drawings.

Adding the Sections and Details

1. Change to the **Views** tab in the **Project Navigator**.

2. Bring up the COMPOSITE EXTERIOR VIEW drawing in the Drawing Editor. (Make sure this view contains all your constructs.)

Figure 26-63

3. Change to the **Top View**.

4. Select the **Section Mark A2T** from the **Callouts** tool palette (see Figure 26-64).

Figure 26-64

5. Click and drag a cross section through the composite building.

6. Click again to bring up the **Place Callout** dialog box.

7. Enter **BUILDING SECTION** in the **Name** field, check the **Generate Section/Elevation** and **Place Titlemark** check boxes, set the **Scale** to **1/2"= 1'-0"**, and press the **Current Drawing** button.

8. Click a spot to the right of the building to place the section.

9. Press **Ctrl + S** on the keyboard to save the drawing (see Figure 26-65).

10. In the **Views** tab, double-click the **BUILDING SECTION** view you just created to bring it up in the Drawing Editor.

11. Select the **Detail Boundary B** callout from the **Callouts** tool palette, and place a selection window around the bay window in the BUILD-ING SECTION drawing (see Figure 26-66).

12. This will bring up the **Place Callout** dialog box.

13. Enter **BAY WINDOW DETAIL** in the **Name** field, check the **Generate Section/Elevation** and **Place Titlemark** check boxes, set the **Scale** to **1" = 1'-0"**, and press the **Current Drawing** button.

14. Click a spot to the right of the section to place the detail.

15. Press **Ctrl + S** on the keyboard to save the drawing (see Figure 26-67).

16. Change to the **Sheets** tab.

17. Double-click on the **A-103 SECTION** sheet drawing to bring it up in the Drawing Editor.

Figure 26-65

Figure 26-66

Figure 26-67

18. Change to the **Views** tab.

19. Drag the **BUILDING SECTION** view into the A-103 SECTION sheet.

20. Press **Ctrl + S** on the keyboard to save the drawing (see Figure 26-68).

Figure 26-68

21. Change back to the **Sheets** tab.

22. Double-click on the **A-104 DETAIL** sheet drawing to bring it up in the Drawing Editor.

23. Change to the **Views** tab.

24. Drag the **BAY WINDOW DETAIL** view into the A-104 DETAIL sheet.

25. Press **Ctrl + S** on the keyboard to save the drawing (see Figure 26-69).

Figure 26-69

There is still a lot of work left to complete this set of drawings, but you should have enough information to complete the project. Don't forget to set the property set definitions, and to create a **SCHEDULE** sheet.

After the drawings are finished, you can create a DWF set. DWFs are compressed Autodesk Architectural Desktop drawings that can be read by anyone that has the free DWF reader available from the Autodesk web site, http://www.autodesk.com. The new DWF Composer will allow clients and colleagues to redline the DWF files and return them for import.

This author always uses DWFs when having prints made by a service bureau.

To create a DWF set, do the following:

1. Open the project in the **Project Navigator**.
2. Change to the **Sheets** tab.
3. **RMB** on the project name in the **Sheets** tab and select **Publish > Publish to DWF** from the contextual menu that appears. The **Select DWF File** dialog box will appear.
4. Enter a name for the DWF file, and place it in a location on your computer.

The file will be created and placed on your computer.

Generating the Renderings

Clients always want a "pretty" picture of their building, and VIZ Render makes it so easy.

1. Open the project in the **Project Navigator**.
2. Change to the **Views** tab.
3. Create a new view called **TOTAL RENDERING**, and in the **Context** screen of **Add General View** dialog, check the **LOWER LEVEL**, **FLOOR 1**, and **FLOOR 2** check boxes.
4. Double-click the **TOTAL RENDERING** drawing you just created to bring it up in the Drawing Editor.
5. Change to the **Constructs** tab, and drag the all the constructs you want to appear into the TOTAL RENDERING drawing.
6. Select the **Polyline** icon from the **Draw** toolbar, and draw the rectangle shown in Figure 26-70.

The polyline will be used in VIZ Render to create a ground plane; this is why this author had you add vertices. You could model the ground in Architectural Desktop using mass elements or 3D solid modeling, but this method is the quickest.

7. Change to the **Front View**, and move the polyline to grade level.
8. Press **Ctrl + S** on the keyboard to save the drawing.
9. Click the **Open Drawing Menu** triangle icon at the bottom left of the Drawing Editor, and select **Link to VIZ Render** from the menu that appears (see Figure 26-71). VIZ Render loads automatically.
10. Select the **Minimize Viewport** icon to split the screen into four views (see Figure 26-72).

Figure 26-70

Figure 26-71

Figure 26-72

11. Press the **Zoom Extents All** icon (next icon left of the **Minimize Viewport** icon) (see Figure 26-73).

12. Select the ground plane you created as a polyline in ADT 2005, and press the **Edit Mesh** button in the **Modify** panel. You will get a warning message (don't worry); press **OK**. The polyline becomes a renderable mesh.

13. With the ground plane still selected, press the **Vertex** button that appeared when you pressed the **Edit Mesh** button (see Figure 26-74).

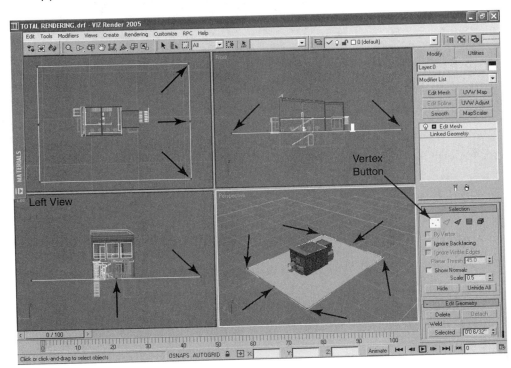

14. In the **Left View**, make a selection window around the rightmost vertices and drag them downwards (see Figure 26-75).

Figure 26-75

15. Select **Create > Cameras > Target Camera** from the **Main** menu. Place two cameras: one looking from the left front and another looking from the left rear (see Figure 26-76).

Figure 26-76

16. Select **Create > Daylight System** and add a daylight object.

> **Note:** This author usually checks the **Manual Override** check box under **Control Parameters**. This allows you to move the sun manually. If you uncheck this, the sun will be controlled by location, month, and time of day (see Figure 26-77).

17. Activate the **Perspective** viewport.

Figure 26-77

18. Press **C** on the keyboard to bring up the **Select Camera** dialog box. (If you only have one camera in a scene, this dialog box will not appear.)

19. Select the first camera and press **OK**.

20. The viewport will now be viewing through the first camera.

21. Activate the **Top** viewport.

22. Press **C** on the keyboard to bring up the **Select Camera** dialog box.

23. Select the second camera and press **OK**.

24. The viewport will now be viewing through the second camera.

25. Using the **Dolly Camera, Truck Mode** (pan), and **Orbit** tools from the **Viewport Navigation Tools** toolbar, adjust the camera views in each viewport.

26. Select **Rendering > Radiosity** from the **Main** menu to bring up the **Render Scene** dialog box.

27. Select the **Radiosity** tab.

28. Press the **Update & Start** button to create a radiosity solution.

29. When the solution has stopped, press the **Render** button at the bottom of the **Radiosity** tab.

30. Your rendering will now appear. Select the **Save Bitmap** icon at the top of the rendered image.

31. Place the image in a location on your computer.

Figures 26-78 through 26-81 are four views of the project.

Figure 26-78

Figure 26-79

Figure 26-80

Figure 26-81

Be patient. This tutorial was developed on a 2 GHz Pentium 4 computer with one gig of RAM. At the writing of this book, the programmers preferred a 3.4 GHz Pentium 4 computer with 1 to 2 gigs of RAM.

Good Luck.

Ed Goldberg AIA

Index